2/5/02

Dear Terry,

After all of our hard work and efforts, the book is finally out. Thank you so much for your ever-present help and (more importantly) your friendship and mentoring. This book simply would not be possible without you.

I hope you enjoy the book!

Your Student,

Jonathan

Inside Appellate Courts

Inside Appellate Courts

The Impact of Court Organization
on Judicial Decision Making in the
United States Courts of Appeals

Jonathan Matthew Cohen

Ann Arbor
THE UNIVERSITY OF MICHIGAN PRESS

2005   2004   2003   2002   4   3   2   1

A CIP catalog record for this book is available from the British Library.

Library of Congress Cataloging-in-Publication Data

Cohen, Jonathan Matthew
    Inside appellate courts : the impact of court organization on
judicial decision making in the United States Courts of Appeals /
Jonathan Matthew Cohen.
        p.   cm.
    Includes index.
    ISBN 0-472-11256-2 (cloth : acid-free paper)
    1. Judicial process—United States.   2. Judgments—United States.
3. United States. Court of Appeals.   4. Appellate courts—United
States.   I. Title.

KF8775 .C64   2001
347.73'24—dc21   2001004249

To my parents, Avrum and Susan Cohen, whose intellectual curiosity helped to inspire this book and whose constant love and support have inspired far more than they can know

Contents

Preface and Acknowledgments

The story of the U.S. Courts of Appeals in the late twentieth century is the story of an organization in flux. Traditionally, as Justice Benjamin Cardozo long-ago described,[1] judicial decision making has been viewed as an isolated, lonely occupation. In that view, a judge renders decisions only after pouring over legal tomes in a sagelike attempt to discover the law. However, under the burden of a perceived crisis caused by overwhelming caseload pressure and rapidly increasing organizational complexity and growth, this traditional role of the appellate judge faces a terrible challenge. How can a system constitutionally constructed to favor individual, solitary, and sagelike decision making continue to increase its productivity to accommodate more cases in less time?

How courts have answered that challenge has become one of the most significant and persistent questions regarding the administration of justice in the United States.[2] Yet the ways that the courts have responded to that challenge, as well as the success of those responses, remain veiled in ignorance and mystery. It is well established that the American judiciary now has more judges with larger staffs than at any time in history. And it is commonly accepted that changes in the size and scope of the judiciary have negatively affected the vitality and collegiality of the courts. With the caseload albatross hanging from their necks,

1. Benjamin Cardozo, The Nature of the Judicial Process (1921); *see also* Owen Fiss, *The Bureaucratization of the Judiciary*, 92 Yale L.J. 1442, 1442 (1983).

2. *See, e.g.,* William L. Reynolds & William M. Richman, *Justice and More Judges*, 15 J.L. & Pol. 559 (1999); Richard A. Posner, The Federal Courts: Challenge and Reform (1996); Martha Dragich, *Once a Century: Time for a Structural Overhaul of the Federal Courts*, 1996 Wisc. L. Rev. 11 (1996); Wolf Heydebrand & Carroll Seron, Rationalizing Justice: The Political Economy of Federal District Courts (1990); Thomas E. Baker, *A Compendium of Proposals to Reform the United States Courts of Appeals*, 37 U. Fla. L. Rev. 225 (1985) (summarizing proposals for changing the courts of appeals to accommodate an increased caseload); Richard A. Posner, The Federal Courts: Crisis and Reform (1985).

judges are now perceived as unable to live up to the image of Justice Cardozo's mythic lone judicial sage. In spite of these perceptions, however, there have been few empirical studies of courts and no comprehensive empirical studies of the U.S. Courts of Appeals. Accordingly, no one knows how the changing face of the judiciary has affected the ways that judges make their decisions and the quality of those decisions. Nevertheless, through this veil of ignorance, politicians, pundits, and scholars continue to suggest radical changes to the judicial system without fully understanding the potentially serious effects of such changes.

This book employs an organizational-behavior perspective to explain empirically how changes such as the increasing caseload burden, the increasing reliance of judges on their law clerks and other staff, and the courts' increasing organizational complexity have affected the ways that judges make decisions. As Professor Owen Fiss of Yale Law School has observed, "an account of the judiciary, such as Cardozo's, that focuses exclusively on the agony of a lonely, isolated judge seems somewhat dated. Today the judiciary must be seen as a large scale, complex organization."[3] This book seeks to show how the way that a court functions as an organization affects its ability to accommodate its increasing workload.

This book begins with the simple observation that judges on the courts of appeals make decisions in groups. That observation suggests that judges are affected by the same social factors that affect any group in decision making. That simple observation throws into doubt the purely rational, individualistic nature of the judicial process assumed by social scientists and legal philosophers alike. It throws into doubt the assumption that appellate judges ever could make their decisions in the solitary ivory tower of intellectualism assumed by Cardozo's myth.

Two important facts flavor this relatively simple starting point. First, social scientific studies of the courts are rare and relatively primitive. Only a single book approaches the courts as a complex organization, and it focuses exclusively on the U.S. District Courts, in which the dynamic of the decision-making process significantly differs because judges do not decide cases in groups.[4] There only are a small number of discussions of the internal functioning of the appellate courts, almost all of them written by single judges or former law clerks without the benefit of empirical research. Indeed, as J. Woodford Howard has claimed, "Circuit judges are surprisingly unaware of the practices of their fellows across the country."[5] I have found that circuit judges are surprisingly unaware of the practices of their brethren even within their circuits.

---

3. Fiss, *supra* note 1, at 1442.

4. *See* Heydebrand & Seron, *supra* note 2; *see also* Evan H. Caminker, *Sincere and Strategic Voting Norms in Multimember Courts*, 97 U. MICH. L. REV. 2297, 2298 (1999) (emphasizing effects of group decision making on judicial product).

5. J. Woodford Howard, *Decision-Making Procedures in U.S. Courts of Appeals for the 2d and 5th Circuits*, Research Report Number 1, Federal Judicial Center (1973).

Second, the interaction within a small group of judges is only the tip of the iceberg. In fact, appellate judges ordinarily make their decisions not only in panels consisting of groups of judges but also in groups within their chambers, including law clerks and other staff. Moreover, as has recently been the subject of some controversy,[6] a judge's law clerks interact with clerks from other chambers. That observation is little more than a rediscovery of Justice Lewis Powell's observation that an appellate court is akin to a group of "small independent law firms" in that each judge's chambers contains a judge who acts as a senior attorney and delegates tasks to law clerks who act as his associates.[7] But that is not all. Significant to the judicial organization are the central staff members, the court clerks, the circuit executive, and numerous other support staff members. The courts of appeals act far more like an organization than even Justice Powell had suggested.

Central to the organization of the appellate courts, therefore, is the balance between the autonomy of the individual judges and the high degree of interdependence that forces judges and their staffs to compromise and communicate in a manner unknown in the district courts. In that critical way, the courts' organizational structure resembles ordinary large multidivisional corporations, and that organizational structure is entirely foreign to Cardozo's concept of the lonely, isolated, solitary judge.

This book applies the analogy between courts of appeals and typical multidivisional organizations to explore the significance of the tension between the autonomy of the independent appellate judges and the task interdependence of judges on collegial appellate courts. That tension is complicated because, unlike large multidivisional corporations, the appellate courts lack any central administrative office to coordinate the interaction among the disparate chambers. Accordingly, the question at the heart of this book is how that balance is maintained in the absence of a central administrative office.

This book answers that question by observing that even as the unique organizational morphology of the court creates the critical tension between autonomy and interdependence, organizational features of the appellate courts serve

---

6. *See, e.g.,* Nadine J. Wichern, *A Court of Clerks, Not of Men: Serving Justice in the Media Age,* 49 DePaul L. Rev. 621 (1999); Edward Lazarus, Closed Chambers: The First Eyewitness Account of the Epic Struggles inside the Supreme Court (1998); *see also* Sally J. Kenney, *Puppeteers or Agents? What Lazarus's Closed Chambers Adds to our Understanding of Law Clerks at the U.S. Supreme Court,* 25 L. & Soc. Inquiry 185 (2000).

7. Lewis Powell, *What the Justices Are Saying . . . ,* 62 A.B.A. J. 1454, 1454 (1976) ("The Court does have strong institutional characteristics, but it is perhaps one of the last citadels of jealously preserved individualism. To be sure, we sit together for the arguments and during the long Friday conferences when votes are taken. But for the most part, perhaps as much as 90 per cent of our total time, we function as *nine small, independent law firms.* I emphasize the words *small* and *independent*" [first emphasis added, second and third emphases in original]).

to maintain an effective balance between those characteristics. This work posits that diverse elements, including formal, structural, and institutional aspects, have enabled the court to navigate the treacherous convergence of the court's discrepant organizational characteristics. The balance among these elements can serve as a natural safeguard against the malevolent effects of the court's changing environment and caseload. A radical change in the courts' organizational structure has the potential to disrupt this fine balance and cause more harm than good. Accordingly, this book concludes that the best defense against those malevolent effects is to preserve a balance by allowing the courts themselves to implement slow evolutionary changes.

This book would not have been completed without the support and assistance of many individuals, foremost among them the members of my family. My parents, to whom this work is dedicated, have provided moral, emotional, and financial support throughout the research and writing of this book. My wife, Jodi Birk Cohen, has been a stalwart source of support without which this book never could have been completed. I also would like to express my deep gratitude to my brother, Jordan Cohen, for the many fruitful conversations that clarified and refined my thinking.

During the course of my research, many people gave me guidance and assistance. In particular, I would like to thank Professor Terence C. Halliday, friend, scholar, and teacher, whose guidance and mentoring have been invaluable in the writing of this book. I also owe a deep debt of gratitude to Professor John Comaroff, Professor Fred Strodtbeck, Judge Richard Posner, and Judge Ferdinand Fernandez for their guidance, cogent criticisms, and helpful advice. Comments on issues raised in this book and on drafts of this book were provided by Edward Adams, David Becker, Elizabeth Cohen, Jeff Cohen, Bert Cohler, Malcolm Feeley, David Gemunder, Scott Gilbert, Krista Helferrich, Rachel Kronowitz, Scott Landy, Donald Levine, Bernardo Lopez, Chan-ung Park, Scott Parrott, Gerald Rosenberg, Martin Shapiro, Herwig Schlunk, Richard Shore, Denis Yen, and Tung Yin. Any errors, mistakes, or omissions are, of course, my own.

I am grateful for the financial assistance provided by the University of Chicago and by the Ogburn-Stouffer Center. I also would like to thank for their dedicated assistance the reference librarians at the University of Chicago; the Ninth Circuit Library in Pasadena, California; and the Georgetown University Law Library. I also would like to express my gratitude to Barbara Brody, Peggy King, Evelyn Pope, and Jackie Smith for secretarial assistance.

Finally, I would like to express appreciation to the many judges, clerks, secretaries, and court staff members who took time from their busy schedules to speak with me. Because I promised them anonymity, I cannot thank them by name, but their willingness to share their time and thoughts has made this book possible.

Tables

CHAPTER 1

The Bureaucratization of the
U.S. Courts of Appeals

A "bureaucratic spectre"[1] haunts the U.S. Courts of Appeals. Over the past forty years, the federal appellate courts have faced repeated barrages of criticism asserting that burgeoning caseloads have caused the court to become bureaucratized, crippling its ability to dispense justice. The threat of bureaucratization is that time pressure and organizational complexity will force judges to emphasize administration at the expense of adjudication and ultimately will cause a decline in the quality of the judicial product.[2] To combat this bureaucratization,[3] there have been numerous proposals to fundamentally change the appellate court system.[4]

Yet the discussion of bureaucratization has been conducted under a veil of

---

1. In 1982 Richard Hoffman asserted that a "bureaucratic spectre" of increasing bureaucratic complexity threatens to undermine the courts' adjudicative function, which he argued should be the gravamen of the judicial process. Richard Hoffman, *The Bureaucratic Spectre: The Next Challenge to the Courts*, 66 JUDICATURE 60, 60 (1982).

2. *See, e.g.*, Thomas E. Baker, *Some Preliminary Comments on the Final Report of the White Commission*, 15 J.L. & POL. 471 (1999); Richard J. Cardamone, *How an Expanding Caseload Impacts Federal Appellate Procedures*, 65 BROOKLYN L. REV. 281 (1999); WOLF HEYDEBRAND & CARROLL SERON, RATIONALIZING JUSTICE: THE POLITICAL ECONOMY OF FEDERAL DISTRICT COURTS (1990); John Kester, *The Law Clerks Explosion*, 9 LITIGATION 20 (1983); Hoffman, *supra* note 1, at 61–62; Alexander Bickel, *The Court: An Indictment Analyzed*, NEW YORK TIMES MAG., April 27, 1958, at 16, 64–69; William Rehnquist, *Another View: Who Writes the Opinions of the Supreme Court*, U.S. NEWS & WORLD REP., February 21, 1958, at 116; William Rehnquist, *Who Writes the Opinions of the Supreme Court*, U.S. NEWS & WORLD REP., December 13, 1957, at 74.

3. The term *bureaucratization* seems to have been first coined by Alvin Rubin. *See* Alvin B. Rubin, *Bureaucratization of the Federal Courts: The Tension between Justice and Efficiency*, 55 NOTRE DAME L. REV. 648, 648 (1980).

4. *See, e.g.*, J. Robert Brown, Jr. & Allison Herren Lee, *Neutral Assignment of Judges at the Court of Appeals*, 78 TEX. L. REV. 1037 (2000) (on the White Commission); Baker, 1999, *supra* note 2 (same); Charles E. Carpenter Jr., *Having Faced the Circuit-Splitting Conundrum—What About More Judges, Less Staff?* 15 J.L. & POL. 531 (1999) (same); Carl Tobias, *Suggestions for Studying the*

ignorance and misinformation. There are few empirically driven studies of the alleged bureaucratization, and the studies that exist have proven inadequate to provide an understanding of the court sufficient to assess potential problems. The bulk of books and articles have been written by court insiders, including judges, judicial clerks, and court personnel. These commentators rely on their personal backgrounds and view the ways of other judges through the filtered lenses of their own experiences. As Chief Justice William Rehnquist has said, "each [participant] is in a position to offer only a worm's-eye view of the [judicial process]."[5]

As a result, not enough is known about the way that the court operates to adequately understand the way that it might respond to increasing external pressures such as increased caseloads or increased staff availability. To put it simply, the nature of the court as a complex organization remains a black box with respect to claims about the effects of external pressure. How is it possible to evaluate an alleged bureaucratization of the court without understanding the court's organizational character?

Federal Appellate System, 49 FLA. L. REV. 189, 192 (1997) (discussing the work of the National Commission on Revision of the Federal Court Appellate System ["Hruska Commission"]); Thomas E. Baker, *A Compendium of Proposals to Reform the United States Courts of Appeals,* 37 U. FLA. L. REV. 225 (1985) (summarizing the proposals for changing the courts of appeals to accommodate an increased caseload); *see also* Martha Dragich, *Once a Century: Time for a Structural Overhaul of the Federal Courts,* 1996 WISC. L. REV. 11 (1996) (arguing that the only solution to the caseload crisis is the total overhaul of the federal judicial system); William Richman & William Reynolds, *Elitism, Expediency, and the New Certiorari: Requiem for the Learned Hand Tradition,* 81 CORNELL L. REV. 273 (1996) (assessing proposals to change the courts); Robert M. Parker & Leslie J. Hagin, *Federal Courts at the Crossroads: Adapt or Lose!* 14 MISS. C. L. REV. 211 (1994) (same); THOMAS E. BAKER, RATIONALIZING JUSTICE: THE PROBLEMS OF THE U.S. COURTS OF APPEALS (1994).

5. Rehnquist, 1958, *supra* note 2, at 74. Rehnquist made that observation shortly after clerking for U.S. Supreme Court Justice Jackson and long before becoming chief justice. His observation becomes all the more significant when one notes that Chief Justice Rehnquist changed his view regarding the uses and abuses of the law clerk when he wrote some thirty years later from his judicial perch. In his late 1950s articles, Rehnquist asserted that the clerks wield a great deal of influence on judicial decision making and could potentially bear at least partial responsibility for the courts' liberal bent. Writing as chief justice of the United States in 1987, Rehnquist commented,

I hope it is clear . . . that the law clerk is not simply turned loose on an important legal question to draft an opinion embodying the reasoning and the result favored by the law clerk. Quite the contrary is the case. . . . The law clerk is not off on a frolic of his own, but is instead engaged in a highly structured task which has been largely mapped out for him. (WILLIAM REHNQUIST, THE SUPREME COURT: HOW IT WAS, HOW IT IS 300 [1987])

Chief Justice Rehnquist repeats this statement in the second editon of his book, WILLIAM REHNQUIST, THE SUPREME COURT 262 (2001). This statement does not directly contradict Rehnquist's 1957 and 1958 statements about the potentially insidious influence of the law clerk but does go some distance to demonstrate how the perspectives of the law clerk and the judge are shaped by their relatively limited vantage points.

To fully understand how external pressures may affect the court and to evaluate potential changes in the judicial process, it is necessary first to understand how the court functions, what problems are inherent in the court's organizational structure, and what aspects of the court serve to ease these problems. And it is necessary to identify how the court's organizational features affect the ways that judges do their jobs. Only then is it possible to assess how external pressures and internal changes can affect judicial decision making and to assess proposals to alter the court system to accommodate increasing external pressures.

This book seeks to fill in the black box of the court's organizational character. By understanding the court as an organization, it becomes possible to better understand the threat of increasing external pressures and changes in the quality of the court's output and thus to better evaluate proposed changes in the court system designed to remedy those problems.

I.   The Concept of Judicial Bureaucratization

What do students of judicial administration mean when they speak of the "bureaucratization" of the judiciary? In the past forty years, federal appellate courts have undergone a "slow, but cumulative, process of change."[6] American courts have witnessed an increasing caseload almost overwhelming in its proportions.[7] The increased demand on federal appellate courts has been accompanied by the addition of many new organizational actors, including increased numbers of law clerks, staff attorneys, and court administrators.[8] Consequently, since at least 1960 there has been an increase in the demands placed on the federal courts, "coupled with a growing reliance on new forms of administration."[9] Critics have termed this increased administrative reliance *bureaucratization.*[10]

Numerous lawyers, judges, and academic commentators have condemned bureaucratization as harmful to the federal appellate judiciary. Judge Patrick E. Higginbotham, for example, has decried bureaucracy as the "carcinoma of the

---

6. Heydebrand & Seron, *supra* note 2, at 1.

7. *See* Baker, *supra* note 2, at 473–75; RICHARD POSNER, THE FEDERAL COURTS: CHALLENGE AND REFORM 61–64 (1996); RICHARD POSNER, THE FEDERAL COURTS: CRISIS AND REFORM 63–65 (1985).

8. *See id.; see also* FRANK COFFIN, ON APPEAL: COURTS, LAWYERING, AND JUDGING 200–212 (1994); Arthur Hellman, *Central Staff in Appellate Courts: The Experience of the Ninth Circuit,* 68 CAL. L. REV. 937 (1980); FRANK COFFIN, THE WAYS OF A JUDGE: REFLECTIONS FROM THE FEDERAL APPELLATE BENCH (1980).

9. Heydebrand & Seron, *supra* note 2, at 1.

10. *See, e.g.* Patricia Wald, *The Problem with the Courts: Black-Robed Bureaucracy, or Collegiality under Challenge?* 42 MD. L. REV. 766 (1983); Wade McCree, *Bureaucratic Justice: An Early Warning,* 129 U. PA. L. REV. 777 (1981); Joseph Vining, *Justice, Bureaucracy, and Legal Method,* 80 MICH. L. REV. 248 (1981).

federal judiciary."[11] Judge Robert S. Thompson has called the costs of bureaucratization "unacceptable."[12] Former Solicitor General Wade McCree has asserted that bureaucratization's costs to the quality of justice are "too high."[13]

Nevertheless, even as it is condemned as harmful, the concept of bureaucratization remains elusive.[14] Commentators generally do not mean *bureaucracy* in the technical organizational sense.[15] Rather, *bureaucracy* and *bureaucratization* refer to the lay concept of bureaucracy as demarking an impersonal, inefficient, delay-encumbered organization.

At the core of the concerns about bureaucratization rest certain assumptions about how courts should operate. Those assumptions regard courts as simple triadic structures in which a neutral third party resolves conflicts between antagonistic parties.[16] This triadic structure acts as a "prototype" of the court in which judges have a high degree of independence from external influences.[17] In that prototypical court, each judge makes decisions alone, in isolation from organizational and political influences.[18] Judicial actions "are defined in terms of the actions, judgment and explanations not of a committee, but of an individual."[19] In that idealized court, judges agonize in isolation in an attempt to "find" the right resolution to the conflicts before them—they do not "create" the law. This judicial independence enables judges to maintain the legitimacy necessary for the success of the judicial enterprise.[20]

When a court becomes *bureaucratized,* it moves away from the prototypical court in which decisions stem from the "agony of a lonely isolated judge."[21] Rather, decisions stem from a businesslike mass production. The threat of bureaucratization is that courts will undergo "an equivalent of the industrial revolution" in which they will become the "appellate counterpart of the assem-

---

11. Patrick E. Higginbotham, *Bureaucracy—The Carcinoma of the Federal Judiciary,* 31 ALA. L. REV. 261, 261 (1980).

12. Robert S. Thompson, *One Judge and No Judge Appellate Decisions,* 50 CAL. ST. B.J. 476, 476 (1975).

13. McCree, *supra* note 10, at 778.

14. *See* Robert Vaughn, *Normative Controversies Underlying Contemporary Debates about Civil Justice Reform: A Way of Talking about Bureaucracy and the Future of the Federal Courts,* 76 DENV. U. L. REV. 217, 219–22 (1998) (discussing the variation in how judges and commentators have used the term *bureaucracy*); Hoffman, *supra* note 1, at 61.

15. *See* Patricia Wald, *Bureaucracy and the Courts,* 92 YALE L.J. 1478, 1479 (1983) ("the federal judiciary does not function in the hierarchical fashion of a typical bureaucracy"); *cf.* Owen Fiss, *The Bureaucratization of the Judiciary,* 92 YALE L.J. 1442, 1444 (1983) (discussing judicial bureaucracy as the vertical elements of the courts, including the hierarchical elements of the appeals courts).

16. MARTIN SHAPIRO, COURTS: A COMPARATIVE AND POLITICAL ANALYSIS 18–19 (1981).

17. *Id.*

18. *Id.*

19. McCree, *supra* note 10, at 118

20. Shapiro, *supra* note 16, at 18–19.

21. Fiss, *supra* note 15, at 1442

bly line."[22] A bureaucratized court no longer functions as a collection of "professionally and collegially controlled, semifeudal domains of judges," but rather acts as a modern administrative agency concerned less with justice and more with speed, efficiency, productivity, simplification, and cost-effectiveness in the delivery of judicial services.[23]

Consequently, a bureaucratized court is depersonalized. Instead of providing the best quality of justice, the bureaucratized court must balance the quality of justice dispensed against the time and cost of each case.[24] As a result, bureaucratization brings about increased hierarchical structure, overspecialization, rigid rules and regulations, impersonality, resistance to change, and delegation of adjudicative duties to judicial staff.[25] In a bureaucratized court, judges' administrative responsibilities overwhelm their adjudicative ones, and the rationality of organizational efficiency overwhelms the goal of reasoned justice.[26]

II.   The Crisis of Volume as the Cause of Bureaucratization

Bureaucratization remains a salient concern because its perceived causes appear to be on the rise. Court observers commonly claim that increases in case volume, case complexity, and the nature of the caseload have forced the courts to become more administrative and more bureaucratic. As these causes continue to increase, judges must rely more heavily on their staff and on the court's bureaucratic safeguards to keep pace.

As Chief Justice Warren Burger observed, in modern courts, "the function of judges is to deliver the best quality of justice at the least cost in the shortest time."[27] For judges, the "overriding responsibility [is] to decide cases" and the overriding restraint is time.[28] As a result, judges must learn to employ time

---

22. Thompson, *supra* note 12, at 476.

23. Heydebrand & Seron, *supra* note 2, at 3.

24. *See* Warren Burger, *Report on the Problems of the Judiciary*, 93 S. Ct. Supp. 3, 3 (1972) (address to the American Bar Association annual meeting).

25. *See* Hoffman, *supra* note 1, at 61; *see also* Posner, 1996, *supra* note 7; Posner, 1985, *supra* note 7.

26. Although rationality is a valued goal of the judicial system, it is well accepted that some nonrational elements enter into a judge's consideration of the issues. *See* Paul Gewirth, *On "I Know It When I See It,"* 105 YALE L.J. 1023, 1039–40 (1996) (discussing the use in judicial opinions of policy and social consequences to justify results).

27. Burger, *supra* note 24, at 3; *see also* Eugene Wright, *Observations of an Appellate Judge: The Use of Law Clerks*, 26 VAND. L. REV. 1179, 1179 (1973).

28. Wright, *supra* note 27, at 1179.

"effectively and efficiently"[29] without sacrificing the personal attention that legitimizes the judge as a neutral decision maker.[30] Yet in recent years, a vastly increasing caseload has forced judges to increase the number of cases they decide without increasing the time in which to decide them.

Consequently, "[h]owever people may view other aspects of the federal judiciary, few deny that its appellate courts are in a 'crisis of volume' that has transformed them from the institutions they were even a generation ago."[31] Indeed, many legal scholars have decried the caseload stress as having the potential to damage the court system. Chief Justice Burger insisted in his 1971 State of the Federal Judiciary message that "we cannot keep up with the volume of work" for which the Court had become responsible.[32] Yet in the nearly thirty years since his statement, the caseload has continued to steadily increase. Thomas Davies calls the caseload stress "a fact of life in today's appellate courts."[33] Solicitor General McCree called the recent increase in federal litigation "staggering."[34] Judge Richard Posner asserts that the caseload increase constitutes a potentially devastating blow to the appellate judicial process.[35]

The common perception that the caseload has been increasing is far from illusory. Since at least 1960 there has been an "explosion"[36] in the quantity of cases coming to the federal courts. As Judge Posner explained, "The increase in cases filed in the district courts, however dramatic, was dwarfed by the increase in cases filed in the courts of appeals—from 3,765 in 1960 . . . to 29,580 in 1983—an increase of 686 percent."[37] This increase has continued steadily since Judge Posner first published these figures. In 1988 there were 37,524 appeals filed. By 1992 47,013 appeals were filed, and, by 1993 50,224 appeals were filed.

---

29. *Id.*

30. *See* Shapiro, *supra* note 16, at 22–24.

31. Report of the Federal Courts Study Committee 109 (April 2, 1990); *see also* Baker, 1994, *supra* note 4, at 32–43 (summarizing reports on the effects of caseload on appellate process prepared by the American Law Institute, the Hruska Commission, the Advisory Council on Appellate Justice, the American Bar Association Action Commission, the Department of Justice, the New York University Law Review Project, the American Bar Association's Standing Committee on Federal Judicial Improvements, and the Federal Courts Study Committee).

32. Warren Burger, *The State of the Judiciary—1971,* 57 A.B.A. J. 855, 859 (1971), quoted in Joseph Stewart & Edward Heck, *Caseloads and Controversies: A Different Perspective on the "Overburdened" Supreme Court,* 12 Just. Sys. J. 370, 371 (1987).

33. Thomas Davies, *Gresham's Law Revisited: Expedited Processing Techniques and the Allocation of Appellate Resources,* 6 Just. Sys. J. 372, 372 (1981).

34. McCree, *supra* note 10, at 777.

35. Posner, 1996, *supra* note 7; Posner, 1985, *supra* note 7.

36. Posner, 1985, *supra* note 7, at 63. Posner has noted that in the ten years following his 1985 book, the courts of appeals continued to see a rise in caseload. Posner, 1996, *supra* note 7, at 63.

37. Posner, 1996, *supra* note 7, at 59 (these figures exclude cases arising under local jurisdiction). Judge Posner first published these figures in 1985. Posner, 1985, *supra* note 7, at 63–65.

By 2000 filings in the U.S. Courts of Appeals attained a record high of 54,697 appeals.[38] (See table 1.)

As table 1 indicates, a greater number of cases has meant that although Congress steadily has increased the number of federal appellate judges, the caseload per judge and the caseload per panel have continued to grow. A mere increase in the number of cases a court must consider, however, does not necessarily indicate an increase in judicial workload. As Judge Posner has pointed out, "if an increase in case filings were associated with a decrease in the difficulty of the average case, the figures of caseload growth would exaggerate the actual increase in the workload of courts."[39] Thus, trends in case complexity may be more important than trends in case volume.

TABLE 1.   Appeals Commenced, Terminated, and Pending in the U.S. Courts of Appeals

Year	Authorized Judicial Positions	Appeals Filed	Appeals Filed per Panel	Appeals Terminated	Appeals Pending
2000	167	54,697	983	56,512	40,410
1999	167	54,693	983	54,088	42,271
1998	167	53,805	967	52,002	41,649
1997	167	52,319	940	51,194	39,899
1996	167	51,991	934	50,413	38,888
1995	167	50,072	899	49,805	37,536
1994	167	48,322	868	48,184	37,294
1993	167	50,224	902	47,790	38,233
1992	167	47,013	845	44,373	35,799
1991	167	43,027	773	41,640	33,428
1990	156	40,858	786	38,790	32,299
1989	156	39,900	767	37,509	30,614
1988	156	37,524	722	35,888	27,644
1987	156	35,176	676	34,444	26,008
1986	156	34,292	659	33,774	25,276
1985	156	33,360	642	31,387	24,758
1984	132	31,490	716	31,185	22,785
1983	132	29,630	673	28,660	22,480
1982	132	27,946	635	27,984	21,510
1981	132	26,362	599	25,066	21,548

Note: The data in this table are from the Annual Reports of the Director of the Administrative Office of the United States Courts, 1988, 1992, 1993, 1995, 1997, 1998, 2000.

---

38. Annual Report of the Director of the Administrative Office of the U.S. Courts, 1998.

39. Posner, 1985, *supra* note 7, at 66; *see also* Posner, 1996, *supra* note 7, at 65; Heyde'   d & Seron, *supra* note 2, at 45–46.

Although empirical measurement of the complexity of individual appeals is less direct than measurement of case volume, it is possible to identify three general underlying factors that indicate the level of case complexity: diversity of the cases on the docket, the complexity of the individual cases heard, and the uncertainty or unpredictability of the cases that might come before the court. As Judge Posner has shown, each of these three dimensions indicates that the courts of appeals face not only a larger caseload but also a more complex one.[40]

Recent developments in caseload composition suggest that this trend will continue. There have been substantial increases in some of the most complex types of cases, such as civil rights claims, personal injury/product liability claims, and prisoner petition appeals.[41] For example, the number of civil appeals has grown substantially, from 11,162 in 1978 to 35,426 in 1997, an increase of nearly 300 percent.[42]

In addition, there have been major changes in the substantive nature of the cases coming before the courts of appeals. For example, the number of appeals of criminal cases has grown from 4,487 in 1978 to 10,740 in 1997, an increase of almost 200 percent (although criminal appeals peaked in 1993 at 11,885). This increase reflects that only convictions could be appealed before 1987, while both convictions and sentences subsequently could be appealed.[43] Nevertheless, between 1988 and 1997 criminal appeals increased from 6,012 to 10,653, averaging an increase of approximately 5 percent each year (although a slight decrease in criminal appeals occurred between 1993 and 1997, with a decline of approximately 9.6 percent).[44]

With few exceptions, scholars accept that the caseload increase has caused the bureaucratization of the courts.[45] McCree asserts that "bureaucratic justice" exists as an accommodation of increasing caseloads.[46] Judge Harry Edwards sees it as "plain that judicial staffs have been enlarged in order to deal with the explosion in federal litigation."[47]

---

40. Posner, 1996, *supra* note 7, at 65–79; Posner, 1985, *supra* note 7, at 66–77; *cf.* W. RICHARD SCOTT, ORGANIZATIONS: RATIONAL, NATURAL, AND OPEN SYSTEMS 212–15 (2d ed. 1987) (discussing the relationship between organizational technology and complexity).

41. Posner, 1996, *supra* note 7, at 65–79; Posner, 1985, *supra* note 7, at 66–77.

42. *Id.*

43. *Id.*

44. *See Judicial Business of the United States Courts: Annual Report of the Director,* Administrative Office of the U.S. Courts for 1988 to 1993; *Federal Judicial Caseload: A Five-Year Retrospective,* Administrative Office of the U.S. Courts (1999) (available at www.uscourts.com).

45. *But see* Stewart & Heck, *supra* note 32, at 374–79 (suggesting that at least to some extent, the caseload increase has itself been caused by recent increases in judicial bureaucracy).

46. McCree, *supra* note 10, at 777.

47. Harry T. Edwards, *A Judge's View on Justice, Bureaucracy, and Legal Method,* 80 MICH. L. REV. 259, 262 (1981).

III.   The Perceived Consequences of Bureaucratization

Court observers define bureaucratization as harmful to the judicial process, depersonalizing the judiciary, causing judges to spend less time on adjudicative duties and to focus less attention on opinions, and provoking judges to work less collegially. While some judges and commentators claim that these harmful consequences already have come to pass, others warn that continuing bureaucratization potentially will have these effects. Either way, the vast increase in caseload already has produced concern among federal appellate judges. In a 1992 survey of 129 active circuit judges and 59 senior circuit judges conducted by the Federal Judicial Center, 33.5 percent of respondents stated that the volume of civil cases presented a large problem to the judiciary, 37.2 percent of these judges stated that the volume of criminal cases presented a large problem, and 34.6 percent considered the volume of criminal cases to be a grave problem.[48] The study further found that 62.3 percent of the judges considered the increasing complexity of the federal caseload to be problematic.[49] As a result of the caseload, 52.2 percent of the surveyed judges felt that delegation of judges' work to nonjudge personnel had become a problem, 70.8 percent felt that judges have insufficient time for judicial case preparation, and 57.4 percent felt that the impact of the workload on collegiality was problematic.[50] This section considers these perceived consequences of bureaucratization.

The Delegation Dilemma: Increased Reliance on Staff

Bureaucratization commonly is thought to have transformed the judicial process into an administrative process in which judges function as little more than staff managers and opinion editors.[51] The size of the judiciary has increased enormously in the past thirty years. In 1974, there were 97 authorized judgeships. That number jumped to 132 in 1979 and to 156 in 1985. In 1991 the number again increased to 167, where it has remained. Thus, in less than twenty years, the number of judges increased by 72 percent. In 1981 Congress created two new circuits, carving the new Eleventh Circuit out of what had previously been the Fifth Circuit and establishing the Court of Appeals for

---

48. Federal Judicial Center, *Planning for the Future: Results of a 1992 Federal Judicial Center Survey of United States Judges* 3 (1994).

49. *Id.*

50. *Id.* at 4.

51. *See* Nadine J. Wichern, *A Court of Clerks, Not of Men? Serving Justice in the Media Age,* 49 DePaul L. Rev. 621 (1999); Heydebrand & Seron, *supra* note 2; John Oakley & Robert Thompson, Law Clerks and the Judicial Process: Perceptions of the Qualities and Functions of Law Clerks in American Courts (1980); Kester, *supra* note 2, at 20.

the Federal Circuit, an appellate court of specialized jurisdiction. Congress currently is considering splitting the Ninth Circuit to create a new Twelfth Circuit. At the same time, the size of judges' personal staffs have increased from one secretary and two clerks to two secretaries and three clerks. Today, federal appellate judges may have as many as four clerks. These trends show no signs of slowing.

As judges use a greater number of staff members—in particular, law clerks—to keep up with the increasing caseload, commentators have expressed concern that the judges must spend more time supervising their clerks and consequently have less time to perform their proper judicial function. The result, some critics assert, is that judges begin to fall into a "judicial torpor" in which they delegate their decision-making power to clerks.[52] These critics aver that when this delegation occurs, judges may become increasingly intellectually lazy, relying on the clerks to rationalize any decisions the judges render. Such commentators argue that when judges rely on clerks for their reasoning, judicial decisions become increasingly arbitrary and opinions become decreasingly precise.

The view is that when judges do their own work, they must be concerned with how each point may be justified. With clerks to assist them, however, judges may act as arbitrarily as they please and then rely on clerks to prepare opinions that "really are just briefs to support a predetermined result."[53] This can hurt the quality of justice because it allows judges to make decisions without needing to consider justifications and thereby precludes an important opportunity for judges to be convinced of the error of their first positions.[54]

These criticisms manifest in the concern that judicial decisions will be more politically motivated and have fewer political checks. The concern is that law clerks will have too much political influence on the way that judges make decisions, leading to an increasingly politicized judiciary. The clerk is increasingly seen as a "legal Rasputin," whispering answers into judges' ears for judges to repeat as their own.[55]

Some observers have suggested that the substantial role of the clerks may allow them to carry significant influence into the judicial process. This potential influence has motivated concerns that clerks inject political and socioeconomic influence into judicial decisions. For example, in 1957, a young William Rehnquist, fresh from clerking for U.S. Supreme Court Justice Robert H. Jackson, asserted that because law clerks tended to be more liberal than the judiciary as a whole, their effect would be to liberalize the judiciary.[56] Therefore,

---

52. Kester, *supra* note 2, at 20.
53. *Id.* at 24.
54. *See* Posner, 1985, *supra* note 7, at 106–7.
55. *See* Rehnquist, 1958, *supra* note 2.
56. *See* Rehnquist, 1957, *supra* note 2.

because of a clerk's biases and because of significant clerk influence, the judiciary might become more politically motivated and less legally regulated.[57] This political concern still remains at the heart of the clerk debate.[58]

Overreliance on law clerks may have a "big impact" on the final judicial opinion.[59] First, as discussed earlier, this overdelegation enables judges to make decisions without carefully considering the logical or legal reasons for doing so. While judges traditionally have had to agonize over how a decision can be justified, now they merely can decide the case and ask their clerks to agonize over justifications. Second, delegating the initial opinion-drafting responsibility to clerks may seriously and adversely affect the opinions' clarity and style. Judge Posner, for example, perceives clerk-drafted opinions to be stylistically uniform, colorless, and longer, with superfluous arguments, citations, and quotations. As a consequence, Judge Posner worries that clerk-drafted opinions will be less clear and will lack the greatness that marked the opinions of the great jurists of the past.[60] Finally, Judge Posner worries that the perception that clerks draft opinions will threaten the credibility of judicial opinions.[61]

---

57. Clerks are not legally regulated as judges are. First, the "law clerk has no statutorily defined duties but rather performs a broad range of functions to assist his judge." *Fredonia Broadcasting Corp. v. RCA Corp.*, 569 F.2d 251, 255 (5th Cir. 1978). Second, unlike judges, clerks do not need to be nominated by the executive branch or confirmed by the legislative branch. Judges appoint clerks with virtually no regulation. *See* Trenton H. Norris, *The Judicial Clerkship Selection Process: An Applicant's Perspective on Bad Apples, Sour Grapes, and Fruitful Reform*, 81 CAL. L. REV. 765 (1993); *but see* Patricia Wald, *Selecting Law Clerks*, 89 MICH. L. REV. 152 (1990) (discussing attempts to regulate the law-clerk selection process); *cf.* Kevin Swan, *Protecting the Appearance of Judicial Impartiality in the Face of Law Clerk Employment Negotiations*, 62 WASH. L. REV. 813 (1987) (discussing the impact that the law clerk selection process has on the judicial process and on the appearance of judicial impartiality). The only real control over the institution of the law clerk is the legislative prerogative to budget for more or fewer clerks and legislative control over clerks' salaries, which, unlike judges' salaries, are not protected by Article III.

58. *See* Kester, *supra* note 2; Posner, 1985, *supra* note 7; Oakley & Thompson, *supra* note 51; Thompson, *supra* note 12; Paul Baier, *The Law Clerks: Profile of an Institution*, 26 VAND. L. REV. 1125 (1973).

59. Posner, 1985, *supra* note 7, at 107; *see also* Posner, 1996, *supra* note 7, at 140–41.

60. Posner, 1985, *supra* note 7, at 107. Posner, however, has more recently expressed some misgivings about his earlier conclusion that clerks are harmful to the greatness of appellate judicial decisions and undermine the emergence of great judges such as the Cardozos and Holmeses of earlier ages. Instead, Posner now concludes, "The outstanding judge of today is not overwhelmed . . . by law clerks. Law clerks, like the computer, are a resource." However, Posner reemphasizes that "only a minority of judges are outstanding" and reaffirms that law clerks pose a significant danger to the integrity of the opinions of a majority of judges. Posner, 1996, *supra* note 7, at 151. One scholar recently has taken Judge Posner's observation to task, undertaking to analyze the style of Judge Posner's own opinions. *See* Robert F. Blomquist, *Playing on Words: Judge Richard A. Posner's Appellate Opinions, 1981–1982, Ruminations on Sexy Judicial Style During an Extraordinary Rookie Season*, 68 U. CIN. L. REV. 651 (2000).

61. Posner, 1996, *supra* note 7, at 148–49.

The Collegiality Question: Relationships among Judges

A second concern is that bureaucratization will undermine the collegiality of appellate courts. Unlike trial courts, appellate courts make decisions in panels of three or more judges. Therefore, the ability of appellate judges to work collectively—to share ideas and work together to produce one decision of the court—becomes very important. Accordingly, appellate judges must adjust their behavior to the fact that they can only adjudicate cases collectively. Appellate judges deliberate together, join together in opinions, and make choices as a group.[62]

The term *collegiality* contains two separate but related significances. First, *collegiality* may refer to little more than civility. In that sense, a collegial court is one where its members speak to one another politely and maintain an air of civility in opinions. A second significance of the term *collegiality* is the more technical and more historically accurate[63] sense in which the court acts as a single unit. In that latter sense, the aim of a collegial court is "to produce performances that could in principle represent the unenhanced effort of a single person, but to bring that performance closer to the ideal."[64] A collegial court's trademarks are "collaboration and deliberation" resulting from a "shift in the agency of performance from the individual to the group."[65]

Thus, *collegiality* is not synonymous with multimember decision making. Instead, *collegiality* refers to the continuous, open, and intimate relationship judges share with one another.[66] A collegial court is marked by a lack of competition, pettiness, and enmity, and is measured by cohesiveness, friendliness,

---

62. *See* Lewis Kornhauser & Lawrence Sager, *The One and the Many: Adjudication in Collegial Courts*, 81 CAL. L. REV. 1, 7 (1993).

63. One judge interviewed for this study pointed out that the term *collegial* finds its etiology in the collective decision of the College of Cardinals to elevate a member to the papacy. He explained:

> I want to clarify the meaning of the word *collegiality*. It is often used in current discourse, at least on our court, to mean civility. And sometimes it's used to mean fraternal feelings. If you look it up in the dictionary, it doesn't really mean those things. So it may be acquiring a secondary meaning, that of civility or friendliness. The derivation of the word is from the Catholic Church, and what it means is making decisions as a group instead of individually, as when the College of Cardinals makes a decision. That is the sense in which I use the word *collegiality*. When I mean *civility*, I say *civility*, and when I say *collegiality*, I mean making decisions, at the court, acting as a group rather than as a faction or an individual.

In this sense, the term *collegiality* denotes more than simply a level of friendliness and politeness. Instead, the term denotes a "deliberately cultivated attitude among judges" that results in a "noncompetitive relationship" with one another in which pride of authorship is restrained and a commitment to the combined insight and experience of the judges on the court. *See* Coffin, 1994, *supra* note 8, at 215.

64. Kornhauser & Sager, *supra* note 62, at 3.

65. *Id.* at 3, 5.

66. Coffin, 1994, *supra* note 8, at 214.

and mutual respect.[67] Collegiality is important because it promotes judicial efficiency and a better judicial work product.[68] When a judicial opinion represents a unified and collegial court, it produces clearer and weightier precedent. If a court produces fragmented decisions marked by numerous separate opinions, the circuit's precedent becomes murky.[69]

A common criticism of the institution of law clerks is that they hurt collegiality by isolating judges. As judicial staffs grow, judges will become insulated from their colleagues, dealing with their staffs instead of with other judges, thereby "promot[ing] contentiousness"[70] in courts because "[y]oung, headstrong law clerks are less likely than their judges to be willing to compromise."[71] As a consequence, judges are less likely to be convinced of their colleagues' positions, and opinions become fragmented and unclear.

IV. The Organizational Black Box: Organizational Mediation of Judicial Decision Making

Ultimately, the concern over bureaucratization is that its effects will reduce the court's ability to determine the "right" answer and to explain that answer in a relatively clearly reasoned judicial opinion. As discussed previously, commentators generally believe that bureaucratization has caused, or soon will cause, a decline in the quality of the judicial product. Indeed, this conclusion has a certain logical appeal. It seems sensible that increasing the caseload burden while increasing the court's administrative aspects should result in a decrease in the amount of each judge's attention a case receives and ultimately in the quality of that judge's decision.

Nevertheless, it is not entirely clear that, even to the extent that there has been increasing bureaucratization, there has been any change in the quality of the judicial product. Measuring the quality of justice and the judicial product is an extremely difficult endeavor, and there have been almost no systematic empirical studies to establish whether this perceived effect of bureaucratization has come to pass.[72] A small number of authors, including Heydebrand and

---

67. Stephen Wasby, *Communication in the Ninth Circuit: A Concern for Collegiality*, 11 U. PUGET SOUND L. REV. 73, 76 (1987).

68. *See* Ruth Bader Ginsburg, *Remarks on Writing Separately*, 65 WASH. L. REV. 133 (1990).

69. *Id.*

70. Kester, *supra* note 2, at 23.

71. J. Daniel Mahoney, *Law Clerks: For Better or for Worse?* 54 BROOK. L. REV. 321, 338 n.70 (1988).

72. One notable exception is Judge Posner's study of the caseload crisis, which stands as the only attempt to assess changes in the quality of appellate justice as a result of bureaucratization. *See* Posner, 1996, *supra* note 7, at 124–89. Judge Posner compiled statistics regarding such variables as the number and length of judicial opinions, the number of footnotes per opinion (to indicate the

Seron in their groundbreaking study of the federal district courts, have attempted to draw conclusions from quantitative empirical trends in such areas as the delay between the filing of a case and that case's termination, the frequency and effects of plea bargaining, dismissals, and the use of juries. Yet there have been almost no attempts to demonstrate empirically whether the quality of appellate justice has suffered as a result of the caseload crisis.[73]

Because of the widely held perception of a decline in the quality of the appellate judicial product and regardless of whether such a change actually has taken place, politicians, pundits, and scholars have recommended revolutionary changes to the courts, ranging from dividing courts into smaller subunits to adding a new level to the federal judiciary to creating new courts with limited substantive jurisdiction. These palliatives are sold as being both necessary to avoid a caseload disaster and effective in doing so. Yet these recommendations cannot be evaluated without a firm understanding of how the appellate courts function as organizations.

It is known that the caseload has been increasing and has become more complex. It is known that the courts produce a greater number of decisions in the same amount of time, and some observers believe that this increase has resulted in a decline in the quality of justice. What is not known is precisely what happens between the inputs to the court (a case is filed) and the court's output (the court issues its decision). Without understanding how the court's organizational nature affects the way that judges make their decisions, it is impossible to understand how changes in the court's organizational nature will affect the judicial process and, ultimately, how such changes may affect the quality of justice. Indeed, it is not surprising that, without a more detailed account of how the court functions organizationally, the perception remains widely held that the departure from the ideal type of the solitary judicial sage has caused a decline in the quality of how courts function.

The organizational nature of the court can define an individual judge's ends and shape the means by which judges strive to accomplish those ends.[74] Thus, the organizational nature of the court serves as a significant source of mediation between the increasing caseload and its consequences. This should be no surprise, as it has long been understood that extrinsic factors such as the

---

effects of law clerks), and the time it takes the courts to decide appeals (to indicate efficiency). Even Judge Posner's study, though, relies primarily on his personal observations of the working of the Seventh Circuit and the "pure reason" of his economic theory.

73. An increasing number of scholars recently have called for empirical studies of the courts to aid in understanding the potential effects of the increasing judicial workload. *See, e.g.,* Frederick Schauer, *Incentives, Reputation, and the Inglorious Determinants of Judicial Behavior,* 68 U. Cin. L. Rev. 615, 636 (2000); Carpenter, *supra* note 4, at 556.

74. W. Richard Scott, *Unpacking Institutional Arguments* in The New Institutionalism in Organizational Analysis 164 (W. Powell & P. DiMaggio eds., 1991).

court's organizational structure act as an important mediator between the law and the way that cases are resolved.

By "organizational nature," I mean both the organization's formal and informal aspects that affect the decision-making process. By "formal aspects" I follow Lauren Edelman in referring to the "configuration of offices and positions and the formal linkages between them (the 'organizational chart') as well as to formal rules, programs, positions, and procedures."[75] "Informal aspects" refer to "the actual communication channels between offices and positions, the actual behavior of individuals who occupy them, and informal norms and practices."[76]

To fully understand the relationship between the inputs, such as the caseload explosion, and the outputs of the court, such as the collegiality or the clarity of the judicial opinion, it is necessary to understand the court's organizational nature and what problems are inherent in its structure. It is necessary to identify how the court's organizational features affect the ways judges do their jobs. Only then is it possible to assess how external pressures and internal changes can affect judicial decision making and to assess proposals to alter the court system to accommodate increasing external pressures.

This book aims to fill in the black box of the court's organizational character, providing a theoretical framework within which to understand the court as an organization. This framework will help to better understand the threat of increasing external pressure and to better evaluate proposed changes in the court system designed to remedy those problems.[77]

V. Methodology

Principal among the reasons that the court's organizational character remains a relatively unexplored feature of the appellate judicial process is that judges are highly protective of the inner workings of their chambers and their decision-

---

75. Lauren Edelman, *Legal Ambiguity and Symbolic Structures: Organizational Mediation of Civil Rights Law*, 97 Am. J. of Soc. 1531, 1542 (1992).

76. *Id.*

77. The book will serve as a first step toward understanding empirically how the way that a court is organized affects the ways that judges make their decisions and thus toward examining how court organization affects court quality (rather than the quality of the decisions made by the judges on that court). It is left for future studies to ascertain empirically whether and how changes in the quality of a court, indicated by independent variables such as changes in the courts' workloads, have affected the specific decisions that judges make and thus have affected the quality of justice. Such a next step may entail analyzing quantitatively such variables as the amount of "justice" that courts produce or the "quality" or "clarity" of judicial opinions. However, to understand how to operationalize such variables, it is first necessary to understand how the court's organizational character affects the decision-making process.

making processes.[78] As lawyers, judges are accustomed to the privilege that protects lawyers' work product and shades the behind-the-scenes work of legal professionals. Moreover, judges—particularly the justices of the U.S. Supreme Court—recently have been the subject of popularized "tell-all" accounts of the judicial process that often have been less than flattering, and judges naturally have become increasingly concerned that the purpose underlying a researcher's request for access may not be honorable.[79] Because judges have well-developed (and often well-justified) protective instincts regarding their decision-making processes, developing and effectuating a methodology to examine the inner workings of federal appellate courts requires special care and a sensitivity that judges, more than most social groups, will consider an outsider to be a potential threat that need not be endured.

In the face of this methodological difficulty, I gained unprecedented access to the inner workings of three U.S. Courts of Appeals. Data for this study were collected by two methods: open-ended interviews with judges, law clerks, and judges' secretaries in three circuits, and substantial firsthand observation during sustained periods within those circuits. This methodology allowed me access to virtually the entire appellate judicial process in diverse circuits. It also enabled me to confirm the results of interviews against a large body of observational data and vice versa. Moreover, by conducting research in multiple circuits, I was able to observe the variation among circuits and to investigate the plausibility of hypotheses across circuits.

Interviews were conducted with judges and law clerks in three courts of appeals: the U.S. Courts of Appeals for the District of Columbia Circuit, the Seventh Circuit, and the Ninth Circuit. I requested interviews with all of the active judges and many of the senior judges on each of these circuits, and I interviewed all of the judges who agreed to be interviewed. In the Seventh and Ninth Circuits, I interviewed the vast majority of the sitting judges.[80] In the D.C. Circuit, I interviewed approximately one-quarter of the active judges.[81] In

---

78. See Schauer, supra note 73, at 636 (noting difficulties of empirically studying judicial process).

79. See, e.g., EDWARD LAZARUS, CLOSED CHAMBERS: THE FIRST EYEWITNESS ACCOUNT OF THE EPIC STRUGGLES INSIDE THE SUPREME COURT (1998); BOB WOODWARD & SCOTT ARMSTRONG, THE BRETHREN: INSIDE THE SUPREME COURT (1979); see also David Garrow, "The Lowest Form of Animal Life"? Supreme Court Clerks and Supreme Court History, 84 CORNELL L. REV. 855, 855–56 (1999) (reviewing Lazarus, infra) (recounting the judicial and legal communities' criticism of the tell-all nature of Lazarus's work and of Woodward and Armstrong's insider accounts).

80. I interviewed eight of the eleven active judges on the Seventh Circuit and twenty-four of the thirty-nine active and senior judges on the Ninth Circuit.

81. Because some judges elected not to participate in interviews, there may be some threat that the results of the study will be subject to "insider bias"—the natural tendency of insiders of an organization to present an overly rosy picture of the organization in which they work. See Schauer, supra note 73, at 636 (noting potential inside bias of judges in their views toward judicial process).

addition, I conducted a supplementary interview with one of the six judges on the U.S. Court of Appeals for the First Circuit.[82]

The circuits were selected based on preliminary hypotheses regarding the diversity of numerical size and geographic dispersion. I hypothesized that dependent variables such as collegiality and frequency of communication varied with independent variables such as the geographic dispersion of a circuit and the number of judges and other staff on a circuit. The First Circuit has the fewest judges of the federal appellate courts, with six authorized judge positions, whereas the Ninth Circuit has the largest number of judges, with twenty-eight active authorized judge positions. The D.C. Circuit has the least geographic dispersion, with all of the judges keeping chambers in a single building in Washington, D.C., whereas the Ninth Circuit has the largest geographic dispersion, with judges maintaining home chambers in Alaska, Arizona, California, Hawaii, Idaho, Montana, Nevada, Oregon, and Washington. The Seventh Circuit sits in the middle on both of those axes, with eleven authorized judges and with more than half of its complement sitting in Chicago and the remaining judges sitting in Indiana and Wisconsin.

Interviews consisted of open-ended questions and discussions. Each interview included core topics and questions, including the process each judge uses to decide cases, the role of law clerks and other staff in the judicial process, the effects of circuit size and geographic spread on the decision-making process, the role of oral argument in judicial decision making and communication, the

---

There is no evidence, however, that judges who chose not to participate in the study did so because their decision-making processes differed systematically from those of judges who did participate or that the nonparticipating judges hesitated because they systematically had a different view of the causes or effects of bureaucratization. Rather, judges who declined to participate in interviews indicated numerous reasons for their decisions, including a desire to maintain confidentiality with respect to cases that they were reviewing, lack of time and interest in the study, and concern regarding the private nature of the appellate process. For example, one judge who declined to be interviewed indicated that the legitimacy of the judicial process hinged in no small part on the judges' abilities to change their minds during the consideration of cases and that allowing an outsider to view how this process works could threaten the public's confidence in the judicial process. Other judges who agreed to be interviewed felt that the public's perception of the judicial process would be helped by being allowed to see through empirical scholarship how the process is conducted. I discuss the issue of insider bias further in chapter 6.

82. Although I requested interviews from all six of the active judges on the First Circuit, only one judge agreed to be interviewed. One possible explanation for the fact that I received far more access in the Seventh and Ninth Circuits than I did in the D.C. and First Circuits is that I had strong sponsorship in the former circuits relative to the latter ones. In the Seventh Circuit, one judge allowed me to use his name to indicate to the other judges that I was conducting a legitimate social scientific study. In the Ninth Circuit, I was able to conduct interviews while serving as a law clerk (with the permission of the judge for whom I was clerking). Accordingly, judges may have viewed me as an insider and therefore as less threatening. I did not have such sponsorship in the D.C. or First Circuits.

timing and nature of communication in the judicial process, the effects of technology on the judicial process, the culture of the court, the impact of the caseload on the judicial process, the significance of visiting judges, and the role of publication of judicial opinions. These questions often raised other issues that provoked further discussion regarding how individual judges view their work and the ways that their work is affected by the court's organization. Interviews lasted from approximately thirty minutes to more than an hour.

I also formally (through interviews) or informally (through discussions during participant observations) spoke with at least forty law clerks in the three circuits. Some judges I interviewed permitted me to speak to their clerks, and I interviewed these clerks formally. Other judges did not allow me to interview their clerks. Interviews with law clerks focused on the same core issues and questions as did interviews with judges.

In addition, I conducted participant observations in three circuits (the Ninth Circuit, the Seventh Circuit, and the D.C. Circuit), observing firsthand the inner workings of three federal appellate judicial chambers. During three periods, I observed the judges, law clerks, and staff in these judges' chambers. During those periods, I spent a total of approximately two thousand hours observing and/or participating in virtually all of the chambers' work-related activities. For a six-week period I observed the law clerks for one judge on the Seventh Circuit. For approximately ten weeks I observed one judge's chambers in the D.C. Circuit. Finally, for twelve months I served as a law clerk for a judge on the Ninth Circuit and observed the judicial process as an insider. During participant observation, I observed the clerks discussing cases with one another, with clerks from other chambers, and with the judges; I had virtually unfettered access to the decision-making process. I observed the clerks researching cases and drafting memoranda on the cases. I went to lunch with the clerks and judges, socialized with the clerks and judges both inside and outside the chambers, and assisted the judges and clerks in their work. Furthermore, I attended conferences between the judges and their clerks and attended oral argument with the clerks. In short, during these periods of participant observation, I became a member of the chambers, and, as a law clerk, I became part of the judicial process itself.

Because many judges place a premium on protecting the secrecy of the judicial process, the issue of anonymity is a particularly significant and difficult one for any study of the federal judiciary. As discussed earlier, judges view their decision-making process as particularly confidential and sensitive and, therefore, often are extremely sensitive about participating in an empirical study of that process. To gain access to the inner workings of judicial chambers, it was necessary to provide the judges and judicial staff members participating in this study the promise of utmost confidentiality and anonymity. Although these assurances may sometimes hamper the ability to compare certain traits and patterns of the decision-making process, on balance, the access to the judicial process justifies any limitations that may result from the strict adherence to the assurances of anonymity.

Throughout this book, I have provided much—but not all—of the interview data in the form of raw quotes (although, to protect anonymity, quotes are not attributed to any particular judge). That way, the reader can acquire a flavor for how the judges approach the bureaucratization issue. This method of presentation also helps to resolve the problem of repeatability and perspective that sometimes can haunt qualitative analysis. To further protect the subjects' anonymity, I have not distinguished between statements made in formal interviews and those made during participant observation.

Moreover, to protect the judges who allowed me access to their chambers as an observer and as a law clerk, I have not discussed any specific case by name or provided facts regarding any case in which I was involved as a law clerk. In addition, I have not revealed any confidences or identified any facts specific to the chambers that I observed.

Finally, although the judiciary is mixed by gender and I interviewed judges of both genders, I have used the male pronoun *he* throughout in an effort to further safeguard the identity of the speaker. That is an uncomfortable solution, as gender may indeed play a role in how judges behave. Nevertheless, I believe this to be an evil necessary to safeguard the anonymity of the judges and staff members interviewed for this study.[83]

---

83. To further ensure anonymity, I have not identified the race, ethnicity, or other immutable characteristics of the interviewed judges, law clerks, and secretaries. Accordingly, this study does not speak to the potential effects of such characteristics.

CHAPTER 2

The Organizational Character
of the U.S. Courts of Appeals

A lmost twenty years ago, Herbert Jacob observed, "Many people express surprise when it is suggested that the courts are organizations."[1] Today, that belief is no longer surprising, nor is it surprising that there are strong empirical benefits to treating courts as organizations. Seminal research from such diverse scholars as Owen Fiss,[2] Wolf Heydebrand,[3] Carroll Seron,[4] and Judge Richard Posner[5] has demonstrated beyond question that courts have important organizational characteristics that play a central role in the judicial process. Because of the progress made by those theorists, the salient question for students of judicial administration no longer is whether courts technically are organizations but, rather, what kind of organizations courts are.[6] Students of the courts must go beyond the assumption that judicial decisions are the result of nothing more than a collection of individual decision makers to ask how the organizational context in which judges make decisions affects the way that those decisions are made.

---

1. Herbert Jacob, *Courts as Organizations* in EMPIRICAL THEORIES ABOUT COURTS 191, 191 (Keith O. Boyum & Lynn Mather eds., 1983).

2. *See* Owen Fiss, *The Bureaucratization of the Judiciary,* 92 YALE L.J. 1442 (1983).

3. WOLF HEYDEBRAND & CARROLL SERON, RATIONALIZING JUSTICE: THE POLITICAL ECONOMY OF FEDERAL DISTRICT COURTS (1990); *see also* Wolf Heydebrand, *The Context of Public Bureaucracies: An Organizational Analysis of Federal District Courts,* 11 L. & SOC'Y REV. 759 (1977); WOLF HEYDEBRAND, ADJUDICATION VERSUS ADMINISTRATION: ORGANIZATIONAL STRUCTURE AND PRODUCTIVITY IN FEDERAL DISTRICT COURTS: A RESEARCH PROPOSAL (1974).

4. *See* Carroll Seron, *Magistrates and the Work of the Federal Courts: A New Division of Labor,* 69 JUDICATURE 353 (1986).

5. *See* RICHARD POSNER, OVERCOMING LAW (1995); *see also* RICHARD POSNER, THE FEDERAL COURTS: CHALLENGE AND REFORM (1996); RICHARD POSNER, THE FEDERAL COURTS: CRISIS AND REFORM (1985).

6. *Cf.* Lawrence Mohr, *Organizations, Decisions, and Courts,* 10 L. & SOC'Y REV. 621, 624 (1975–76) ("the crucial question is not whether a court is technically an organization, but whether organization theory can productively be applied to the study of courts").

To construct the most comprehensive model of how the appellate courts function as organizations, this chapter draws on the extensive literature on judicial decision making to highlight three organizational dimensions of the appellate judicial process. First, at its most fundamental level, judicial decision making is the product of individual judges making choices in an effort to reach their individual policy, social, or legal goals. Second, because federal *appellate* judges cannot decide cases individually but, rather, make their decisions in panels, the interaction among judges affects the way that judges make their decisions. Third, the interaction among judges is affected by the fact that judges operate within potentially complex suborganizations (the chambers) consisting of the judge and his clerks and staff. Thus, the interaction among judges also consists of the interaction among these organizational subdivisions.

By focusing on these three dimensions of the court, this chapter identifies a critical tension at the center of the appellate judicial process: the tension between the autonomy of the individual judges' chambers and the interdependence of those chambers necessary to producing the appellate judicial product. The organizational structure that results from this tension is highly reminiscent of that of corporations organized in the multidivisional form, the most common organizational structure in corporate America. The multidivisional form is a decentralized management structure in which a firm is organized into highly autonomous subdivisions that must work interdependently to create the firm's products. Unlike typical multidivisional firms, however, the courts lack a central office to coordinate among the chambers and to ensure the balance between the chambers' autonomy and their interdependence. Accordingly, this chapter argues that the central organizational problem for the Courts of Appeals is to strike that balance. This chapter suggests that the impact of the threat of a changing environment (such as an increasing caseload and decreasing resources) is that it will tip the critical balance between autonomy and interdependence.

I.   The Court as an Aggregation of Individual Action

The starting point for any discussion of judicial decision making must be the judges themselves. At its most basic level, the appellate judicial process consists of individual judges considering legal arguments and making individual decisions. This very basic view of the court suggests a model of the judicial process that depicts the appellate courts as consisting of a collection of these individual decision makers involved in the occupation of the judicious mastication of cases. The individualist view derives from a weighty tradition in the social sciences and has attracted a great deal of attention from scholars of the judicial process.

Although an organization may be viewed as a single entity, it is made up of individuals who have their own goals, incentives, and motivations. An individualistic approach logically grows out of a focus on how individuals within an organization function rationally to achieve organizational and/or individual goals and, ultimately, a focus on how the rational action of individuals within an organization aggregates into collective action on the part of the organization.[7]

The individualistic approach has given rise to the traditional model of justice that Malcolm Feeley has called the "rational-goal" approach.[8] Underlying this approach is the assumption that actors within a bureaucratic organization act rationally to comply with the formal rules of the organization to accomplish the organization's goals. Thus, Feeley has observed that the rational-goal approach implies an elaborate process for the administration of justice that requires highly trained "experts" to perform ascribed, formally defined bureaucratic roles.[9] The consequence of this approach, Feeley states, is a focus on how the rules increase "'rationality' by minimizing discretion and arbitrary administration, through specifying with increasing precision the roles of the actors" and the organizational goals.[10] Rational-goal theorists, therefore, concern themselves with such topics as the internal consistency of rules[11] and the impact of those rules in altering the behavior of the bureaucratic actors.[12] In this sense, the individualistic model is closest to the legal tradition of the individual judge making case law that aggregates into the marketlike phenomenon of the common law.

A more sophisticated version of the rational-goal approach recognizes that judges are motivated by other factors as well and that those motivations may lead to judicial behavior potentially at odds with the organization's goals.[13] For example, in a relatively modest but highly probative study, Thomas Davies empirically confirmed a hypothesis regarding the use of expedited judicial techniques such as screening cases and issuing unpublished dispositions. Davies argues that resource dependency suggests "an appellate Gresham's

---

7. *See, e.g.,* James Coleman, Foundations of Social Theory (1990).

8. Malcolm Feeley, *Two Models of the Criminal Justice System: An Organizational Perspective,* 7 L. & Soc'y Rev. 407, 411 (1973).

9. *Id.* at 410.

10. *Id.*

11. *See, e.g.,* Abraham Goldstein, *The State and the Accused: Balance of Advantage in Criminal Procedure,* 69 Yale L.J. 1149, 1149–99 (1960).

12. *See, e.g.,* N. Lefstein et al., *In Search of Juvenile Justice,* 5 L. & Soc'y Rev. 491, 491–563 (1969).

13. *See, e.g.,* Tracey E. George, *Developing a Positive Theory of Decisionmaking on U.S. Courts of Appeals,* 58 Ohio St. L.J. 1635 (1998); Rafael Gely & Pablo T. Spiller, *A Rational Choice Theory of Supreme Court Statutory Decisions with Applications to the State Farm and Grove City Cases,* 6 J.L. Econ. & Org. 263 (1990).

Law" that "more attractive civil appeals will attract resources away from criminal appeals regardless of the incidence of "frivolous" criminal appeals.[14]

Other individualistic studies retain the assumption that judges act rationally to accomplish predetermined goals but reject the assumption that those goals are organizationally determined and approved. Instead, those theorists prefer to apply an economic–rational actor approach to judicial decision making. They assume that judges are rational decision makers who take advantage of doctrinal ambiguities to create new legal interpretations and, therefore, to apply political processes to create new law.[15] Because the economic approach to analyzing judicial decision making rejects the rule-based devotion to doctrinal certainty, economic theorists are left to ask, "What do judges maximize?"[16] The answer to that question has led to analyses of such elements as judges' political attitudes,[17] financial and professional incentives,[18] and other nonpecuniary incentives.[19]

The greatest strength of the individualistic approach is that its focus on individual utility maximization enables researchers to form readily testable hypotheses—a benefit that has been borne out in a small number of studies. For example, Mark Cohen has demonstrated empirically a relationship between variables such as "promotion potential"[20] and judicial ideology. Cohen also has presented empirical support for the hypothesis that discounts in sentencing for pleading guilty are related to the court's workload.[21]

However, the individualistic and economic approaches suffer from their focus on individual decision making exclusive of any significant focus on the organizational and institutional attributes that contextualize individual judges' utility functions.[22] Practitioners of the individualistic approach, for example,

---

14. Thomas Davies, *Gresham's Law Revisited: Expedited Processing Techniques and the Allocation of Appellate Resources*, 6 Just. Sys. J. 372, 401–3 (1981).

15. *See* Posner, 1995, *supra* note 5, at 109–44; Posner, 1985, *supra* note 5, at 4–5.

16. Posner, 1995, *supra* note 5, at 109–44; Richard Posner, Economic Analysis of Law 415 (2d ed. 1977); *see also* Frederick Schauer, *Incentives, Reputation, and the Inglorious Determinants of Judicial Behavior*, 68 U. Cin. L. Rev. 615 (2000) (revisiting Judge Posner's inquiry and noting that the question begs empirical examination).

17. *See, e.g.*, Lawrence Baum, The Puzzle of Judicial Behavior (1997).

18. *See, e.g.*, Posner, 1995, *supra* note 5, at 117–23.

19. *See id.*

20. "Promotion potential" was measured by looking at the age and party affiliation of judges.

21. *See* Mark Cohen, *The Motives of Judges: Empirical Evidence from Antitrust Sentencing*, 12 Int'l Rev. of L. & Econ. 13, 26–27 (1992); *see also* Mark Cohen, *Explaining Judicial Behavior, or What's "Unconstitutional" about the Sentencing Commission*, 7 J.L. Econ. & Org. 183 (1991).

22. That is not to say that Judge Posner and other practitioners of the economic approach have no place for institutional aspects of the judicial process. Judge Posner, for example, has suggested that judges on collegial courts feel constrained by institutional responsibility. Judge Posner views the need to produce signed opinions, as well as the importance attached to impartiality, as defining attributes of good judging. Posner, 1985, *supra* note 5, at 228–29. Judge Posner sees the

focus solely on the individual's preferences and strategies for accomplishing those goals. The rational-actor assumption underlying the economic approach allows the court to have no independent, institutional life of its own. Consequently, the economic approach underemphasizes the interaction among the judges. But that interaction provides the next step toward a comprehensive organizational theory of the appellate process.

II.   The Court as a Small Group

The most salient organizational characteristic that distinguishes the federal appellate courts from the federal district courts is that the judges on appellate courts make their decisions in groups of three or more, which suggests that the interaction among the members of those groups has some impact on the judicial process. Highly individualistic rational-actor approaches virtually ignore that key characteristic. Adding the study of the interaction among judges to the individualistic approach suggests a model of the court that views the appellate judicial process as the functioning of a small group of individual judges interacting with one another. Such an approach emphasizes the effect of judge-judge interaction on the individual judges and the nature of that interaction. Like the individualistic approach, the small group approach derives from an age-old and well-respected school of the social sciences that focuses on small group behavior. And, like the individualistic approach, the small group approach has manifested in research on the appellate judicial process.

Small group analysis focuses the researcher's attention on how the interaction among individuals affects not only each individual's decision-making process but also the decision to which each individual ultimately comes. As W. Chambliss and R. Seidman have argued, small group theory's emphasis on interaction has significant application in the study of appellate courts.[23] They thus argue that the court must itself be viewed as a small group "making decisions not merely on the basis of the merit of the problem to be solved, but also in terms of the personal relations between the judges themselves."[24] Small group analysis, they aver, is necessary to show how value preferences emerge and are introduced into the decision-making process.[25]

---

weakening of institutional responsibility as a serious problem endemic to the courts of appeals and to the Supreme Court. That problem, Judge Posner argues, has been a cause of lengthening opinions, increased dissenting and concurring opinions, and decreasing civility among judges on collegial courts. *Id.* at 234–35.

23. W. CHAMBLISS & R. SEIDMAN, LAW, ORDER, AND POWER 151 (1971); *see* CLIVE GRACE & PHILIP WILKINSON, SOCIOLOGICAL INQUIRY AND LEGAL PHENOMENA 102–5 (1978).

24. Chambliss & Seidman, *supra* note 23, at 151.

25. *See id.; see also* Grace & Wilkinson, *supra* note 23, at 104.

Similarly, the recognition that judges tend to vote in a manner that reflects their political attitudes (an individualistic concept) has spawned the study of the influence of relationships among judges on a collegial court—that is, the study of how the interaction among judges affects each judge's individual decisions.[26] That focus has manifested itself in studies of how ideological cliques affect group voting. Those small group studies differ from small group studies of juries because they focus on politically directed voting cliques rather than on the effects of interaction among a small and variable group of individuals. These studies observe the voting records of the Supreme Court to determine whether there are stable voting cliques and to determine on what basis those cliques form.[27] For example, Eloise Snyder reviewed voting blocs in the Supreme Court from 1921 to 1953 and concluded that the Court showed more agreement than disagreement. When there was disagreement, she found, the justices voted in the same groups or cliques over time, and these cliques could be classified into groups based on ideology. One stable group of justices voted consistently conservatively, while another stable group voted consistently liberally. She found that another stable group of justices did not vote consistently for one political ideology. That group, she concluded, held a decisive role because the votes of the conservative clique and those of the liberal clique canceled one another out. A more recent study by Melinda Hall confirmed Snyder's results.[28]

These studies go far toward empirically confirming the commonly held suspicion that extraindividualistic elements have some influence on judicial decision making. However, small group research into the judicial process has been limited because so much of the judicial process involves not only the deliberations among the judges but also the deliberations within and among the members of the chambers and the court. Therefore, even as the small group approach introduces a healthy emphasis on the interactive aspects of the appellate judicial process, it does not go far enough and overlooks the complex nature of the individuals who are interacting. A comprehensive organizational approach to the appellate process requires an appreciation of that complexity.

---

26. *See, e.g.,* Harold Spaeth & Michael Altfeld, *Influence Relationships within the Supreme Court: A Comparison of the Warren and Burger Courts,* 38 W. Pol. Q. 70 (1985).

27. Eloise Snyder, *The Supreme Court as a Small Group,* 36 Soc. Forces 232, 232–38 (1958) reprinted in The Courts: A Reader in the Judicial Process (Robert Scigliano ed., 1962).

28. Melinda Gann Hall, *Small Group Influences in the United States Supreme Court,* 12 Just. Sys. J. 359, 367–68 (1987); *see also* Spaeth & Altfeld, *supra* note 26, at 82 (empirically testing how justices influence one another by quantitatively establishing how often justices paired with one another in dissenting and concurring opinions); Burton Atkins, *Judicial Behavior and Tendencies toward Conformity in a Three Man Small Group: A Case Study of Dissent Behavior on the U.S. Courts of Appeals,* 54 Soc. Sci. Q. 41 (1973).

III.   The Court as a Group of "Small Independent Law Firms"

Justice Lewis Powell observed that appellate courts more closely resemble groups of "small independent law firms" than small groups of individual judges.[29] To put Justice Powell's observation into sociological terms, the courts are more than merely collections of individual judges interacting; rather, courts are collections of smaller suborganizations interacting. As Jeffrey Pfeffer and Gerald Salancik have explained, an organization may be defined as a "coalition of groups and interests, each attempting to obtain something from the collectivity by interacting with others, and each with its own preferences and objectives."[30] Accordingly, to understand how the court functions, one must focus not only on the interaction among the individual judges, but also on the interaction within the judicial chambers and the interaction among the various members of those judicial suborganizations. That suggests a model of the court as a small group of small groups analogous to a group of "small independent law firms."

A focus on the court's internal structure enables the researcher to draw conclusions about the interaction of the individuals within the social system.[31] Similarly, a focus on the court's internal structure enables researchers to identify the relationship between emergent organizational norms and their location in the structured systems of social relationships.[32] Finally, a focus on internal structure allows organizational analysts to question how the court's behavior will be shaped by the court's "technologies, communication channels, processing routines, norms, rules, vocabularies, socialization processes, and a variety of other organizational mechanisms."[33] Structural studies of appellate courts have consisted almost completely of studies on how judges on a collegial court communicate with one another[34] (an issue taken up in chapter 5) and the

---

29. Lewis Powell, *What the Justices Are Saying . . .* , 62 A.B.A. J. 1454, 1454 (1976).

30. Jeffrey Pfeffer & Gerald Salancik, The External Control of Organizations: A Resource Dependence Perspective 36 (1978).

31. *See* Barry Wellman, *Structural Analysis: From Method and Metaphor to Theory and Substance* in Social Structures: A Network Approach 19, 31–33 (B. Wellman & S. D. Berkowitz eds., 1988).

32. *Id.* at 33–35; *see also* John Meyer & Brian Rowan, *Institutionalized Organizations: Formal Structure as Myth and Ceremony* in The New Institutionalism in Organizational Analysis 41, 43–47 (W. Powell & P. DiMaggio eds., 1991).

33. Davies, *supra* note 14, at 377; *see also* James Eisenstein & Herbert Jacob, Felony Justice: An Organizational Analysis of Criminal Courts (1976); Feeley, *supra* note 8; George Cole, Politics and the Administration of Justice (1973); Jerome Skolnick, *Social Control in the Adversary System*, 11 Just. Sys. J. 247 (1967); Abraham Blumberg, Criminal Justice (1967).

34. *See, e.g.,* Stephen Wasby, *Communication in the Ninth Circuit: A Concern for Collegiality,* 11 U. Puget Sound L. Rev. 73 (1987); Stephen Wasby, *Communication within the Ninth Circuit Court of Appeals: The View from the Bench,* 8 Golden Gate U. L. Rev. 1 (1977).

potential doctrinal problems associated with decisions of a collegial court[35] (an issue taken up in chapter 6).

Viewing the court as a group of small independent groups suggests that interaction within a chamber may have a substantial impact on judges' decisions. Although it may be true that "beneath the formalities of the legal process . . . teems substantial variety [among judges within the U.S. Courts of Appeals] in business and behavior,"[36] social scientists have attempted to identify patterns among the work processes within judicial chambers. Studies of the inner workings of judicial chambers reflect the legal community's recent preoccupation with the role of the law clerk. As a result, two recent comprehensive empirical studies have examined law clerks' role in the judicial decision-making process.

In the first of these, John Oakley and Robert Thompson respond to the recent common criticism that law clerks have been playing a too significant role in the judicial process. Oakley and Thompson begin by laying out what they view as the traditional model of the relationship between a law clerk and a judge in which judges retain the responsibility for decision making and in which the clerk carries the adversary process into the chambers, forcing the judge to justify each step of the decision-making process.[37] They argue that the "traditional model of the relationship between law clerk and judge has acquired the status of an ideal"[38] and then set about evaluating how far adrift from that ideal judges have drifted in different levels of both the state and federal judiciaries.

Oakley and Thompson conclude that the way that judges use their clerks can be typified by court. At the appellate level, clerks typically are used to prepare bench memoranda. Oakley and Thompson state that the judges give careful review to the opinions of fellow panel members but use clerks to aid in that review. The authors report that appellate judges do not generally use their clerks to draft preargument memoranda in the form of draft opinions, but use law clerks to participate in conversations regarding difficult issues. Oakley and Thompson conclude that federal appellate judges use their clerks in a manner closer to their ideal than do judges at other levels of the federal and state judiciaries.[39]

---

35. *See, e.g.,* Lewis Kornhauser & Lawrence Sager, *The One and the Many: Adjudication in Collegial Courts,* 81 CAL. L. REV. 1 (1993); Ruth Bader Ginsburg, *Remarks on Writing Separately,* 65 WASH. L. REV. 133 (1990); Ruth Bader Ginsburg, *Reflections on the Independence, Good Behavior, and Workload of Federal Judges,* 55 COLO. L. REV. 1 (1983).

36. J. WOODFORD HOWARD, COURTS OF APPEALS IN THE FEDERAL JUDICIAL SYSTEM: A STUDY OF THE SECOND, FIFTH, AND DISTRICT OF COLUMBIA CIRCUITS 54 (1981).

37. JOHN OAKLEY & ROBERT THOMPSON, LAW CLERKS AND THE JUDICIAL PROCESS: PERCEPTION OF THE QUALITIES AND FUNCTIONS OF LAW CLERKS IN AMERICAN COURTS 37 (1980).

38. *Id.*

39. *Id.* at 93–97.

In a similar study, Charles Sheldon relied on questionnaire responses from 166 former law clerks who had served with justices from the Washington State Supreme Court.[40] Sheldon concluded that, while the relationship between justice and clerk is "highly personal," there are sufficient commonalities to allow for generalizations about the categories of clerk tasks. Accordingly, Sheldon observed four major roles that law clerks perform: preparatory, attendant, assistant, and extralegal. Sheldon typifies preparatory tasks as providing judges with the information "necessary for them to gain from and contribute to oral arguments and conference discussions."[41] Preparatory tasks include legal research and documentation. The attendant clerk aids his judge by accomplishing subsidiary or clerical tasks. Because judges have administrative tasks in addition to their adjudicatory ones, Sheldon observes that judges may become overburdened. Attendant support relieves some of that burden by providing the judge with additional secretarial or stenographic assistance. Sheldon contrasts the role of the attendant clerk with that of the assistant clerk, who aids the judge by providing legal research designed to hone an initial decision into a finished opinion. Accordingly, assistant tasks include drafting opinions, researching cases, editing style, and cite checking footnotes. Finally, extralegal clerkships are characterized by the clerk attending to a judge's personal needs, such as chauffeuring, performing clerical duties, making social arrangements, writing speeches, and working on a judge's academic articles.[42]

In addition, viewing the court as a group of small independent groups suggests that the interaction among nonjudicial staff can affect judges' ultimate decisions. Recent studies, for example, have suggested that law clerks have a communication network that judges occasionally use to aid in judge-judge communication[43] (an issue discussed in chapter 5). The "small independent law firms" approach also suggests that the court's central staff may be affected by internal organizational dynamics and that the judges' interaction with that central office may be significant.[44]

The "small independent law firms" approach offers the promise of further understanding the impact of court structure. Although the benefits are substantial, this approach lacks one important element: the limitations on the interaction within and among judicial chambers imposed by the environment

---

40. Charles Sheldon, *Law Clerking with a State Supreme Court: Views from the Perspective of the Personal Assistants to the Judges,* 6 Just. Sys. J. 346 (1981).

41. *Id.* at 353.

42. *Id.* at 354.

43. *See, e.g.,* Jonathan Cohen, *In the Shadow of the Law Clerk: Assessing the Role of Law Clerks in the Judicial Process,* 3 Long Term View 99, 104 (1995); Sean Donahue, *Behind the Pillars of Justice: Remarks on Law Clerks,* 3 Long Term View 77, 78 (1995).

44. *See, e.g.,* Posner, 1996, *supra* note 5; Posner, 1985, *supra* note 5; Arthur Hellman, *Central Staff in Appellate Courts: The Experience of the Ninth Circuit,* 68 Cal. L. Rev. 937 (1980).

and the organizational structure itself. Remedying that limitation is the last step in developing a comprehensive organizational model of the courts.

IV.   The Court as a Multidivisional Organization

The "small independent law firms" model emphasizes the role of the individual chambers as something akin to highly autonomous subdivisions. The chambers are autonomous in the sense that they retain "considerable responsibility for defining and implementing goals, for setting performance standards, and for seeing that standards are maintained."[45] The internal functioning of the judicial chambers, though, is influenced by the interaction necessary for the judges to take judicial action. That is, although the chambers retain a high level of autonomy, they still are embedded in a loosely coupled organization that must work as a unit to decide cases. In other words, the autonomy of individual chambers is limited because the chambers must function within the context of an umbrella-like organizational framework that requires the chambers to work together, interdependently, and thereby limits the manner by which those chambers function individually. In organizational terms, the chambers have a high degree of task interdependence, depending on "each other for assistance, information, compliance, or other coordinative acts in the performance of their respective tasks."[46]

A complete model of the appellate courts must account for the balance between the high degree of autonomy and independence that each chamber must maintain to effectively provide for a multijudge review of each issue and the interdependence required by the collegial nature of appellate decision making. That balance represents a critical tension fundamental to the organization of appellate courts; and, it is that balance that creates the difficulties inherent in the organization.[47] If the balance shifts so that individual chambers retain too

45. W. Richard Scott, Organizations: Rational, Natural, and Open Systems 236 (1987); W. Richard Scott, *Reactions to Supervision in Heteronomous Professional Organizations*, 10 Admin. Sci. Q. 65, 66 (1965). Some studies have considered the interdependence of judges on multijudge courts by applying a rational actor/strategic action approach to evaluate judicial action within multijudge panels. *See, e.g.,* Kornhauser & Sager, *supra* note 35, at 4–5; David Post & Steven C. Salop, *Rowing against the Tidewater: A Theory of Voting by Multijudge Panels,* 80 Geo. L.J. 743, 770–74 (1992); *see also* John M. Rogers, *Issue Voting by Multimember Appellate Courts: A Response to Some Radical Proposals,* 49 Vand. L. Rev. 997, 997–1040 (1996) (critiquing rational-choice scholarship on multijudge decision making).

46. Richard Walton & John Dutton, *The Management of Interdepartmental Conflict: A Model and Review,* 14 Admin. Sci. Q. 73, 73 (1969); *see also* E. J. Miller, *Technology, Territory, and Time,* 12 Hum. Rel. 243, 243–71 (1959).

47. The effects of loose coupling on the ability of professionals to do their jobs has been noted in other professional organizations, such as educational groups. For example, the amount of a

much autonomy at the expense of interdependence, the court suffers from a decline in collegiality that has the potential to weaken the court's moral and legal authority and to overemphasize each chamber's individual decision-making processes. In that case, the court no longer speaks with one voice. If, conversely, the balance shifts so that individual chambers rely too strongly on other chambers, resulting in a decline in autonomy in favor of interdependence, the court suffers from a decline in judicial independence that can undermine the court's legitimacy by reducing the multijudge nature of court decisions.

The court's morphology, together with its inherent tension between autonomy and interdependence, is highly reminiscent of the multidivisional organizational form. The multidivisional form is a decentralized management structure in which the firm is organized into subdivisions that each contain a unitary structure.[48] Each subdivision maintains responsibility for its own manufacturing, sales, and financial performance. In typical multidivisional organizations, the day-to-day decisions regarding production and marketing are assigned to executives within the relatively autonomous subdivisions.[49] Characteristically, multidivisional organizations have a central office responsible for long-range planning and financial allocations and coordinating among the disparate subdivisions.[50] The decentralization of profit centers enables the organization to efficiently coordinate production in large firms engaged in dispersed geographic and product markets.[51]

The pivotal problem in administering a multidivisional organization is the coordination of its highly autonomous and interdependent subdivisions. Neil Fligstein has described the internal dynamics of decision making in multidivisional organizations as an internal power struggle.[52] The struggle between the

---

teacher's autonomy over a student's education can affect not only the teacher's ability to educate the student but also the definition of which topics deserve the most attention. *See* Karl Weick, *Educational Organizations as Loosely Coupled Systems*, 21 ADMIN. SCI. Q. 1, 8 (1976); *see also* Adam Gamoran & Robert Dreeban, *Coupling and Control in Educational Organizations*, 31 ADMIN. SCI. Q. 612, 628 (1986).

48. Neil Fligstein, *The Spread of the Multidivisional Form among Large Firms*, 50 AM. J. OF SOC. 377, 378 (1985); *see also* ALFRED CHANDLER, STRATEGY AND STRUCTURE 15 (1962).

49. NEIL FLIGSTEIN, THE TRANSFORMATION OF CORPORATE CULTURE 17 (1990); *see also* Donald Palmer et al., *The Economics and Politics of Structure: The Multidivisional Form and the Large U.S. Corporation*, 32 ADMIN. SCI. Q. 25, 25 (1987).

50. *See* Fligstein, 1990, *supra* note 49, at 17; Palmer et al., *supra* note 49, at 25; Fligstein, 1985, *supra* note 48, at 378.

51. Robert Eccles & Harrison White, *Firm and Market Interfaces of Profit Center Control* in APPROACHES TO SOCIAL THEORY 203, 205–6, 219–20 (S. Lindenberg et al. eds., 1986); *see also* Palmer et al., *supra* note 49, at 25; OLIVER WILLIAMSON, MARKETS AND HIERARCHIES: ANALYSIS AND ANTITRUST IMPLICATIONS (1975); Chandler, *supra* note 48.

52. Fligstein, 1990, *supra* note 49, at 17.

autonomous subdivisions pushes the organization in certain directions through the subunits' power struggle. That power structure shapes the way that actors within the subunits think and ultimately determines the organization's strategies.[53] That multidivisional organizations are shaped by internal struggles is natural given the highly differentiated and independent nature of the subdivisions. As Paul R. Lawrence and Jay Lorsch have suggested, highly differentiated organizations breed internal discontent among the departments because they are highly likely to develop disagreements and conflicts.[54] Richard Walton has similarly noted that conflicts among departments commonly develop out of mutual task dependence, task-related asymmetries, conflicting performance criteria, dependence on common resources, communication obstacles, and ambiguity of goals[55]—all potential characteristics of an appellate court.

Thus, although loose coupling of organizational subdivisions may be highly adaptive for some organizations,[56] and may be the only organizational form open to an appellate court,[57] the decentralization analogous to the multidivisional form suggests that the courts suffer an integration dilemma caused by the tension between the autonomy of the loosely coupled judicial chambers and the interdependence required of them.

As Alfred Chandler suggested[58] and Fligstein emphasized,[59] the standard large multidivisional organization overcomes the tension between autonomy and interdependence by reliance on a central office that retains ultimate control over the subdivisions' resources and interaction. That is also true in loosely coupled professional organizations, such as school systems.[60] The appellate courts, though, lack strong centralized management. As Feeley has observed, the courts have "virtually no instruments to supervise practices and secure compliance to the formal goals of the organization."[61] The appellate courts lack a hierarchical managerial system and a common center of accountability with regard to a judge's handling of a case.[62] As Lawrence Mohr has said, "The crux

---

53. *Id.; see also* Fligstein, 1985, *supra* note 48, at 378–79.

54. Paul R. Lawrence & Jay Lorsch, Organization and Environment: Managing Differentiation and Integration 54–83 (1967); *see also* Scott, 1987, *supra* note 45, at 253.

55. Walton & Dutton, *supra* note 46; Richard Walton et al., *A Study of Conflict in the Process, Structure, and Attitudes of Lateral Relationships* in Some Theories of Organization 444, 444–65 (Chadwick Haberstroh & Albert H. Rubenstein eds., 1966).

56. *See, e.g.,* Weick, *supra* note 47, at 1–19.

57. That is because the multijudge structure is externally imposed on the court by congressional mandate.

58. Chandler, *supra* note 48.

59. Fligstein, 1990, *supra* note 49.

60. *See* Gamoran & Dreeban, *supra* note 47, at 628.

61. Feeley, *supra* note 8, at 422.

62. *See* Posner, 1985, *supra* note 5, at 227–28; Eisenstein & Jacob, *supra* note 33. There is some limited accountability in that dissatisfied litigants can petition the court for a rehearing en banc

of the problem is that courts do not have what organization theorists mean by a 'management.'"[63]

What central management the courts do have lacks any of the significant characteristics of a central managerial office in a typical multidivisional organization. Each circuit court has a chief judge who retains many administrative duties and stands as the court's figurehead to the world outside of the court.[64] The chief judge, however, lacks any authority—or even desire—to control the other chambers in any meaningful organizational sense. The chief judge lacks any control over the other judges on the court, except insofar as the chief judge enjoys the benefits of seniority in doling out responsibilities to the others. The chief judge has as his responsibility only administrative responsibilities, which, while significant in terms of regulating the flow of cases and perhaps the authority over the central staff, has little direct impact on other judges' decision making. Significantly, the chief judge has no extra influence in determining which judges are assigned to which panels, which cases are assigned to which panels, how judges do their work within their chambers, or how judges interact with one another. Moreover, the chief judge lacks the authority to hire or fire another judge or another judge's staff.

Similarly, the courts' central administrative offices, including the clerks of the courts, lack any managerial control over the judges or their staffs and have little direct influence on the ways that judges come to their decisions. The central staff has as its main function regulating the flow of cases within a court. Although the clerk therefore has the power to docket cases and to assign judicial panels, those tasks are done randomly, and the clerk's office carries no significant agenda-setting power. The clerk's office, therefore, serves the judges as an aid to the judicial process; it does not carry the centralized authority attributed with a central manager or executive office in a typical multidivisional organization.

Because the courts of appeals have no centralized executive office, the ten-

---

and can petition the Supreme Court for certiorari. As discussed in chapter 3, however, the Supreme Court hears so few cases that the hierarchical element of accountability is virtually nonexistent. Similarly, appellate courts rehear very few cases. In any event, the appellate court itself lacks a central office to which a litigant can complain about the way that a judge decided a case rather than the result that the judge reached.

63. Mohr, *supra* note 6, at 624.

64. Judge Posner has noted that the leadership structure in the Supreme Court better approximates the centralization typical of private sector organizations because the chief justice of the Supreme Court is appointed to the post and has the power to assign the majority opinion in the cases in which he is in the majority. Although the senior judge on appellate courts also ordinarily has this power, it is a more substantial power on the Supreme Court because the Supreme Court always sits en banc and the chief justice is always on the panel, with only rare exceptions for recusal. In contrast, appellate court chief judges sit on relatively few panels because panels ordinarily contain only three judges and the makeup of those panels shifts. Posner, 1985, *supra* note 5, at 227–28.

sion between autonomy and interdependence, already significant in centralized multidivisional organizations, becomes critical. Accordingly, the analogy to the multidivisional organizational form suggests a research question not yet explored in the organizational analysis of appellate courts: without a central managerial office, how do appellate courts achieve and maintain the required balance between the autonomy of individual judicial chambers and the interdependence inherent in the multijudge decision-making process of collegial appellate courts? In other words, the analogy to the multidivisional organizational form suggests that mechanisms independent of centralized management serve to enable a highly decentralized multidivisional organization to retain the integral balance between autonomy and interdependence.

The significance of the multidivisional organizational model is that it adds another dimension to the ideal type of the appellate court as a collection of solitary judges rendering decisions after a lonely independent analysis of the case law. Under the multidivisional organizational model, the ideal court is not one in which each judge functions as a solitary sagelike decision maker whose determinations stem from the "agony of a lonely isolated judge."[65] Rather, the quality of an appellate court should be measured by the court's balance between the judges' autonomy (that is, the judges' ability to function as independent lone decision makers) and their interdependence (that is, the judges' ability to function together to create a single, collegial court). The optimum court, therefore, is one in which there is an ideal balance between the judges' autonomy and their interdependence.

V. The Nature of the Threat of Bureaucratization

Understood in terms of the multidivisional organizational model of the appellate courts, the threat of the caseload crisis is that changes necessitated to keep up with increasing workload demands will undo the central balance between the judges' autonomy and their interdependence. There already is a modest literature on the effect on the judicial process of the interaction between a court and its environment. This literature suggests that the bureaucratization occurring in reaction to the increasing caseload demands already has challenged that critical balance. Heydebrand and Seron's study of the rationalization of the U.S. District Courts is the most comprehensive study of how the courts have been affected by the pincerlike threat of increasing caseload and decreasing organizational resources.[66]

---

65. Owen Fiss, *The Bureaucratization of the Judiciary*, 92 YALE L.J. 1442, 1442 (1983) (discussing traditional ideal type of the judge as a solitary decision maker).

66. *See* Heydebrand & Seron, *supra* note 3.

Heydebrand and Seron conceptualize the district courts as "public, heteronomous, professional service organizations that receive requests for decisions from individual and corporate actors residing in a jurisdictional and interorganizational environment with fixed boundaries but variable complexity, and that provide dispositions under conditions of labor-intensive service and relatively low levels of bureaucratic formalization and centralization."[67] Accordingly, Heydebrand and Seron understand the district court to be significantly affected by its environment because its jurisdiction and its workload are externally determined.

Viewing the organization's relationship to its environment as the critical dimension dictating the organization's behavior, Heydebrand and Seron hypothesize that the rationalization of the court significantly involves the interaction of the environment with the court's internal organizational structure. They advance a model in which the court's environment (including demographic, economic, and legal-governmental characteristics) functions as an independent variable and the court's output serves as a dependent variable measurable in terms of factors such as the volume, nature, and timeliness of the court's dispositions. Heydebrand and Seron also suggest that the complexity of the court's task structure and resources represent intervening variables measurable in terms of the court's caseload, the complexity and variability of the court's calendar, the court's geographic dispersion, and the court's financial and organizational resources.[68]

Heydebrand and Seron conclude that the district court must contend with a critical organizational paradox: while judges remain the professional core of judicial decision making, the courts' organizational structure affects the process and outcome of those decisions.[69] By measuring judicial productivity by the number of terminations per judge, they conclude that the district courts' productivity has risen but that it has done so thanks in large part to the rise of an elaborate organizational support structure.[70] For Heydebrand and Seron, the consequence of that change is that the extrajudicial personnel no longer can be thought of merely as organizational support; instead, the relationship between professional staff and organizational support must now be thought of as one of interdependence.[71] Heydebrand and Seron thus conclude that the district courts have experienced a shift from adjudication to administration in part as a

---

67. *Id.* at 23.
68. *Id.* at 10; *see also* Carroll Seron, *The Impact of Court Organization on Litigation*, 24 L. & Soc'y Rev. 451, 458–60 (1990).
69. Heydebrand & Seron, *supra* note 3, at 155.
70. *Id.* at 137–54.
71. *Id.* at 155–56.

result of environmental pressures (increasing caseload) and the external control of resources (resulting in a decrease in financial and other resources).[72]

Although Heydebrand and Seron demonstrate that change in a court's environment can create significant change in the quality and type of that court's output, they do not question what characteristics of a court's organizational form serve to safeguard against and mitigate the effects of those potential changes. This book argues that the court's umbrella-like organization has built-in organizational facets that maintain the balance between autonomy and interdependence and thus enable the court to retain its organizational resiliency in the face of otherwise potentially devastating environmental changes. Those facets are located both in the way that the organization interacts with its environment and in the way that the organization functions internally, both structurally and institutionally. In particular, this book hypothesizes that three broad categories of organizational facets serve to maintain the balance between autonomy and interdependence: formal features, structural features, and cultural/institutional features.

The Court's Formal Features

Like actors in any other organization, judges on courts of appeals are limited in the range of their behavior by formal rules defined both internally and externally to the organization. Key among those rules is the doctrine of stare decisis. Also important are procedural rules that control how judges and the participants in the judicial process must comport themselves and the rules for screening cases from the court's argument calendars. Those formal features of the court, together with the means by which those rules are enforced and the manner in which those rules are brought to the court's attention, set the field of possible behavioral options from which judges must choose. In so doing, the court's formal features define the degree of the judges' autonomy and demarcate the degree of interaction necessary to the appellate process.

The Court's Structural Features

How the court is structured both geographically and organizationally defines the way that judges and their staffs interact. The court's structural features include such diverse factors as the court's geographic spread, the number of judges on a court, the ways that judges communicate with one another, the technology that judges have at their disposal for communication, the interaction between judges and their staff, and the social distance that judges maintain with one another and with their staffs. In addition, how judges interact within

---

72. *Id.* at 188–90.

their chambers also may significantly affect the nature of the appellate judicial process. The structural aspect of the judicial process has an impact on judicial behavior whenever judges must coordinate their behavior and therefore involves significant problems of boundary spanning and gatekeeping. The court's structural features set both the basement and the ceiling for how much interchange judges may have during the decisional process and thereby establish the outer boundaries for the judges' autonomy and interdependence.

The Court's Cultural/Institutional Features

No less influential than the limitations set by formal rules and structural procedures are the court's informal normative rules. Whereas formal rules and structural difficulties may often be overcome by the actions of judges or legislatures, the informal norms of the court are derivative of the court's own culture and, therefore, can affect judicial behavior independent of the good intentions of legislative will or judicial sensibility. Normative rules not only establish how judges and their staffs interact within a judicial chamber, but also affect the frequency, timing, and nature of communication among chambers. Normative rules define how judges perceive the results of their interaction as well as the appropriate purposes behind judicial communication. Moreover, the court's culture can define how judges perceive their jobs and the state of the judicial enterprise and, in so doing, may limit or even eliminate the ability of structural or formal changes to ease the court's caseload.

VI. Conclusion

In this chapter, I constructed an organizational model of the appellate courts in which the courts are treated as analogous to multidivisional organizations. The appellate courts, like other typical multidivisional organizations, are divided into highly autonomous subdivisions (the judicial chambers) that must work interdependently to create the judicial product. And, like typical multidivisional organizations, the appellate courts have at their organizational core the tension between the autonomy and interdependence of the subdivisions. However, unlike typical multidivisional organizations, in which this critical balance is maintained through the services of a central office, the appellate courts lack such an office to coordinate among the chambers. To overcome this challenge, I suggested that the court's inherent organizational features serve to maintain the balance between autonomy and interdependence necessary for the court's continued functioning. The remainder of this book examines each of the organizational features with an eye toward understanding the significance of changes in the court's task environment.

CHAPTER 3

The Formal Features of the
U.S. Courts of Appeals

I t is far from extraordinary to observe that formal rules affect the way that appellate judges decide cases. Indeed, when thinking about what causes a panel of judges to decide an issue in a particular way, it would be an uncommon mistake to entirely overlook the weight that the judges give to the formal legal precedents and doctrines that they must apply to come to their decisions. However, in addition to these precedents and doctrines, judges also must act within the context of other formal organizational features that control how those doctrines can be applied.

The courts' formal features have a far wider influence than simply establishing the legal rules based on which judges must decide cases. These formal features establish which judges decide which cases, set the exoskeleton of the microprocesses of judicial decision making, and establish what resources are available. They also establish how and when judges are informed about the nature of the cases before them, how and when judges communicate with one another, and how much time judges have in deciding cases. Formal rules may derive externally to the organization or may be the product of internal rule making. In short, the court's formal features establish the playing field on which the judicial process is played out, determine who the players are and the resources at their disposal, and establish the rules of the judicial process.

This chapter considers how the formal features of the courts of appeals shape the ways that judges come to their decisions. It considers the variety of formal rules and procedures, how judges are made aware of those rules, the consequences for the organizational participants for the failure to follow the rules, and the importance of the rules in shaping how judges relate to one another.

I. Formal Rules in Organizational Theory

As Max Weber described, one aspect of a society's rationalization is the formalization of its rules and institutions.[1] For organizations, that means that an organization functions in an increasingly formalized environment and has increasingly formal structures and rules about how it acts. Organizations are formalized in the sense that "the rules governing behavior are precisely and explicitly formulated."[2] Formalization permits "stable expectations to be formed by each member of the group as to the behavior of the other members under specified conditions. Such stable expectations are an essential precondition to a rational consideration of the consequences of action in a social group."[3]

Formalization generally refers to the predictability and formal definition of an organization's structure and to the reification of the norms and rules that limit and shape the behavior of organizational actors. Thus, organizations rely on formal rules to secure consistent performance and consistently acceptable outcomes.[4]

Formal rules and processes have particular relevance in governmental organizations and public bureaucracies. Because the formal rules in such organizations can be defined externally, formal rules and processes act to ensure public control over potential loose cannons and mavericks whose actions may undermine the governmental organization's public purposes. In that way, externally dictated formal rules serve as a "basic source of legislative control over administration."[5]

Internally defined formal rules also enable the organization to control and influence organizational actors so that they behave in a way that furthers the organization's publicly defined goals.[6] Especially in professional organizations, however, internal rules may limit an organizational actor's behavior in unpredictable ways. Professional organizations often allow professionals to retain "considerable responsibility for defining and implementing the [organization's] goals, for setting performance standards, and for seeing to it that standards are maintained."[7] Thus, formal institutional rules that are defined internally can change organizational behavior in ways that are unpredictable and

1. Max Weber, *Rational and Irrational Administration of Justice* in MAX WEBER ON LAW IN ECONOMY AND SOCIETY 349 (Max Rheinstein ed., 1954).

2. W. RICHARD SCOTT, ORGANIZATIONS: RATIONAL, NATURAL, AND OPEN SYSTEMS 21 (1987).

3. HERBERT SIMON, ADMINISTRATIVE BEHAVIOR: A STUDY OF DECISION-MAKING PROCESSES IN ADMINISTRATIVE ORGANIZATION 100 (2d ed. 1957).

4. Scott, 1987, *supra* note 2, at 215.

5. Robert Peabody & Francis Rourke, *Public Bureaucracies* in THE HANDBOOK OF ORGANIZATIONS, 802, 820–21 (J. March ed., 1965).

6. *Id.* at 813.

7. W. Richard Scott, *Reactions to Supervision in a Heteronomous Professional Organization*, 10 ADMIN. SCI. Q. 65, 66 (1965).

sometimes contrary to the organization's interests.[8] Formal rules and procedures may be undermined because they create unpredictable incentives for
organizational actors.[9] Skilled professionals, though, often are able to work
within the organization's formal framework to make the organization work
effectively. How they do so is an issue of great organizational significance.[10]

II. The Doctrine of Stare Decisis

Judges are formally constrained to follow applicable formal legal precedents by
the doctrine of stare decisis. The doctrine is fundamental to the American system of justice and is embedded in fundamental notions of fairness and justice.
As Morris L. Cohen, Robert C. Berring, and Kent C. Olsen have explained,

> The doctrine embraces a basic concept of fairness, the sense that people
> similarly situated should be similarly dealt with, and that judgments
> should be consistent, rather than arbitrary, so that one may predict the
> consequences of contemplated conduct by reference to the treatment
> afforded similar conduct in the past.[11]

At its most fundamental level, the doctrine of stare decisis means nothing
more than the requirement that a court must follow its prior precedent and the
applicable legal precedents of higher courts. Much of the time, that means the
judges need only to find and follow a well-established legal precedent. As one
judge explained,

> In lots of cases the issues are pretty clear cut, and somebody can try to fash-
> ion a way to get around the controlling precedent, but that only succeeds
> either (a) because the judge determined that, by God, he is going to ignore
> the controlling precedent and get around it, or (b) because something else
> has intervened, some late-breaking case or some disclosure in oral argu
> ment that wasn't evidence before.

Or, in another judge's words, "I think that . . . 75 percent of the cases have a
right answer." Such cases are those in which the facts fall squarely within a formal rule of law and the factual particulars of the case do not distinguish it from
that rule.

---

8. *See* JAMES Q. WILSON, BUREAUCRACY: WHAT GOVERNMENT AGENCIES DO AND WHY
THEY DO IT 342–43 (1989).

9. *Id.* at 343–44.

10. *See, e.g.,* Michael Cohen et al., *A Garbage Can Model of Organizational Choice,* 17 ADMIN.
SCIENCE Q. 1, 2 (1972); Scott, 1987, *supra* note 2, at 279–80.

11. MORRIS L. COHEN ET AL., HOW TO FIND THE LAW 3 (9th ed. 1989).

Formal legal doctrinal rules thus limit a judge's officially sanctioned autonomy. As some judges described, the formal doctrinal rules may limit judges to deciding cases in very narrow and specific ways. Or, within the limits of the law, judges may find enormous latitude to bend results toward their views. Unless judges are willing to overstep their constitutional role, however, they cannot conclude cases in a manner that directly contradicts the formal rules. Nonetheless, because the rules are plentiful and complex, judges may err in their legal conclusions if they are not aware of the full range of applicable rules. Because the courts of appeals are the middle level of the judiciary pyramid, the hierarchical element is composed of both an up-looking and a horizontal aspect.

Up-Looking Aspects

For a court of appeals, the only higher court is the U.S. Supreme Court. Accordingly, court of appeals judges must respect the Supreme Court's interpretation of the formal legal rules and can be overturned by that Court for failure to do so.[12] Aside from the sense in which the legal rules can be set by a higher court, the judges on the courts of appeals, however, do not appear to be significantly affected by its position as an intermediate court.

One potential effect of stare decisis is that the judges on the courts of appeals could be motivated by a fear of being overturned. For the courts of appeals, though, being overturned is not a likely prospect and is becoming less so.[13] Although the number of appeals terminated by the courts of appeals increased by more than 100 percent from 1981 to 1999, the percentage of appeals for which Supreme Court review was sought remained almost constant, hovering at approximately 12–14 percent.[14] Moreover, the Supreme Court, which has discretion whether to review the appellate courts' decisions for which certiorari is sought, has declined to take certiorari in an increasing number of cases, resulting in a decline in the number of appeals that the Supreme Court decided to consider from approximately 7 percent in 1981 to approximately 1 percent in 1999. The number of cases that the Supreme Court reversed and vacated has remained virtually constant from 1981 to 1999. Indeed, the Supreme Court reversed a smaller percentage of cases in 1999 (39.5 percent) than it did in 1981 (41.7 percent). (See table 2.)

---

12. See Lewis Kornhauser, *Adjudication by a Resource-Constrained Team: Hierarchy and Precedent in a Judicial System*, 68 S. CAL. L. REV. 1605 (1995).

13. See STEPHEN WASBY, THE SUPREME COURT IN THE FEDERAL JUDICIAL SYSTEM 57 (3d ed. 1989); see also RICHARD POSNER, THE FEDERAL COURTS: CRISIS AND REFORM (1985).

14. Included in the number of petitions for certiorari filed are petitions seeking review of state supreme court decisions. *Harvard Law Review* statistics indicate that such petitions recently have constituted approximately 12 percent of the total U.S. Supreme Court docket.

TABLE 2. Appeals Terminated in the U.S. Courts of Appeals and Petitions for Certiorari Filed, Granted, and Decided in the U.S. Supreme Court

Year	Appeals Terminated by Courts of Appeals	Petitions for Certiorari Filed in Supreme Court	Terminated Appeals for Which Certiorari Was Sought[a]	Petitions for Certiorari Granted	Cases Decided on Certiorari		
					Reversed	Vacated	Affirmed
1999	54,088	7,339	13.57%	92 (1.25%)	47 (39.5%)	43 (36.1%)	29 (24.4%)
1998	52,002	7,002	13.46%	81 (1.16%)	44 (33.8%)	63 (48.5%)	23 (17.7%)
1997	51,194	6,717	13.12%	89 (1.32%)	41 (30.6%)	58 (43.3%)	35 (26.1%)
1996	50,413	6,685	13.25%	87 (1.30%)	52 (32.9%)	80 (50.6%)	26 (16.5%)
1995	49,805	6,608	13.27%	105 (1.59%)	47 (24.2%)	116 (59.8%)	31 (16.0%)
1994	48,184	7,130	14.81%	93 (1.30%)	53 (37.3%)	61 (43.0%)	28 (19.7%)
1993	47,790	6,675	13.95%	99 (1.48%)	40 (26.0%)	67 (43.5%)	47 (30.5%)
1992	44,373	6,335	14.27%	83 (1.31%)	56 (26.8%)	104 (49.8%)	49 (23.4%)
1991	41,640	5,824	13.99%	120 (2.06%)	67 (40.4%)	65 (39.1%)	34 (20.5%)
1990	38,790	5,409	13.94%	141 (2.61%)	79 (34.6%)	108 (47.4%)	41 (18.0%)
1989	37,509	4,906	13.07%	203 (4.14%)	77 (35.8%)	86 (40.4%)	52 (24.2%)
1988	35,888	4,804	13.39%	252 (5.25%)	63 (33.2%)	79 (42.2%)	48 (25.7%)
1987	34,444	4,396	12.75%	271 (6.16%)	55 (26.9%)	97 (47.6%)	52 (25.5%)
1986	33,774	4,338	12.84%	268 (6.18%)	69 (33.5%)	98 (47.6%)	39 (18.9%)
1985	31,387	4,287	13.66%	273 (6.37%)	70 (32.6%)	98 (45.6%)	47 (21.8%)
1984	31,185	4,261	13.66%	264 (6.20%)	94 (45.4%)	65 (31.4%)	48 (23.2%)
1983	28,660	4,155	14.50%	261 (6.28%)	91 (46.9%)	65 (33.5%)	38 (19.6%)
1982	27,984	4,185	14.95%	204 (4.78%)	75 (35.9%)	90 (43.1%)	44 (21.0%)
1981	25,066	4,450	17.75%	312 (7.01%)	96 (41.7%)	93 (40.4%)	41 (17.8%)

Note: The data in this table are from the Annual Reports of the Director of the Administrative Office of the United States Courts, 1988, 1992, 1993, 1995, 1997, 1998, 2000, and the annual November issues of the *Harvard Law Review.*

[a]The percentages in this column were determined using the total number of petitions for certiorari, which includes some petitions from state courts.

Because of the low frequency with which the Supreme Court overturns court of appeals decisions, the appellate judges are not motivated significantly by the prospect that their decisions will be overturned. One judge explained,

> I think last year we decided somewhere between two thousand and three thousand cases. The number that were certified [by] the Supreme Court was somewhere around ten. So, we can see that very, very few out of three thousand cases [were decided by the Supreme Court]. You do the best you can with each case, and you cannot really worry so much [about what the Supreme Court will do].

Moreover, as one judge said, even if a panel were to follow the Supreme Court's precedents as closely as possible, the Supreme Court might change its interpretation of the law, and the panel would be reversed.

Other judges reported that they were not motivated by a concern about being reversed, but rather were dedicated to achieving the right result within the context of the doctrine of stare decisis. One judge, for example, said that he does not think about whether the Supreme Court is likely to reverse "because it would not make any difference. I am just trying to do the right thing." Another judge responded to the question of whether his decisions are motivated by a concern about being overturned in the following way:

> Not independent of the question of whether I am deciding the case the correct way. That is, I want to decide the case in the same way that the justices who decide the case will as part of the Supreme Court. In part, because I want the case resolved in a way that gives the parties their entitlements which . . . resolves the questions the way the Supreme Court will resolve the case. And if I am out of step with them I am not delivering [the parties] their legal entitlements. So I want to be able to resolve the cases in a way that does things correctly for the parties.

Another potential consequence of the up-looking hierarchy is that appellate judges might be affected by the possibility of being appointed to the higher court. That also appears not to be a significant motivating factor to judges. Because the Supreme Court has only nine members, who are appointed for life, there are few vacancies on that Court. As a result, judges on the courts of appeals are very pessimistic about their chances for elevation and are, in turn, not significantly motivated by that prospect in their decision making. One judge explained,

> Becoming a federal judge in the first place is like being struck by lightning. It does not happen very often . . . . So, to start out, there are between 100

and 147 [circuit judges], and there are about 600 or 700 district judges. You could . . . just [say], "Well, you are going to select the next justice from the pool of court of appeals judges," which they have done [for] the last 3 [justices].[15] Then you are still talking about 1 out of 147, so the chances of it, even if you limited to that, are very, very slight. So, no, I do not spend a lot of time thinking about it.

In fact, in reaction to the recent string of harsh Senate confirmation proceedings, some judges report that they no longer even desire to be elevated to the Supreme Court. One judge related that he had a friend who would write a letter to the president every time there was an opening for a Supreme Court position. The judge reported that, after the Bork and Thomas hearings, he wrote a letter to his friend, saying, "Please, don't ever again suggest my name for the Supreme Court." Another judge said,

> It is impossible not to think about that because other people keep insisting that the president might or might not do something. But, if the question is, "Do I decide cases in particular ways because of it?" No. The causation runs the reverse. . . . People get mentioned as possibilities because their decisions—whether academic or judicial or any of the above—have been noted by the incumbent administration as being congenial or interesting or something of that sort, rather than the reverse. . . . Causation runs from "Here is what I am doing" and somebody else can like it or not. And besides, that is the only respectable way to do it. You do what you think is right, and other people can like it or not.

So, beyond the effect of the Supreme Court's role in interpreting cases and setting precedent, the up-looking hierarchical aspect of the judicial pyramid appears not to significantly affect appellate decision making.

Horizontal Aspects

In addition to the formal requirement that a court must follow the applicable precedents of higher courts, an appellate panel also must follow precedents set by earlier panels of the same court. As the Ninth Circuit has said, a "panel of this court cannot overrule a prior decision of this court."[16] The only way that a

---

15. In the 2000–2001 term, seven of the nine justices of the U.S. Supreme Court had been appointed from the ranks of the U.S. Courts of Appeals: Breyer (First Circuit); Ginsburg (D.C. Circuit); Souter (First Circuit); Thomas (D.C. Circuit); Kennedy (Ninth Circuit); Scalia (D.C. Circuit); and Stevens (Seventh Circuit). Only Chief Justice Rehnquist and Justice O'Connor were not appointed from the federal appellate courts.

16. *United States v. Camper*, 66 F.3d 229, 232 (9th Cir. 1995).

court of appeals can properly overturn an earlier decision is if the court sits en banc—that is, with "all judges present and participating"—rather than in the regular quorum of three judges.[17]

The en banc procedure serves two purposes. First, it enables the courts to speak as a unified and collegial body on new, important, or unusual areas of law. By speaking with a single voice, the court carries a degree of authority beyond that of a single panel. Moreover, by speaking as a single, collegial body, the court manifests its ultimate expression of interdependence in which each judge on the court must work with each other judge on the court to create a result. Second, the en banc procedure enables the court to resolve an intracircuit conflict that arises because the decision of a panel is in apparent conflict with the law of the circuit as determined by an earlier panel. That intracircuit enforcement role enables the court to function as a single collegial body because it enables the court as a whole to rope in maverick panels and judges and to maintain the order mandated by the doctrine of intracircuit stare decisis. In that way, the en banc procedure enables the court as a whole to patrol the outer boundaries of any individual judge's autonomy. The en banc process is considered in greater depth in chapters 5 and 6.

III. Standards of Review

As a legal institution, the U.S. Court of Appeals has as its function the review of decisions by lower courts and administrative agencies. However, its role in reviewing those decisions is limited. The lower courts and agencies have the responsibility of taking evidence, hearing testimony, and establishing the credibility of witnesses. Because the courts of appeals do not directly take evidence, there is a firmly rooted legal notion that the judges on these courts are less qualified to weigh the credibility of that evidence. Accordingly, the appellate court must defer to the lower courts' factual interpretations. In contrast, because the interpretation of the law is, at least ideally, an exercise in pure reason, the view is that judges on the courts of appeals are at least as capable of interpreting the laws. Moreover, because the appellate courts make decisions in three-judge panels rather than individually, the combined wisdom of three judges is thought to be superior to the wisdom of any single judge. Consequently, the panels of the courts of appeals are thought to be in a better position to interpret the laws than are the lower courts and agencies. That legal principle translates into the complex set of formal legal doctrines known as standards of review.

Standards of review represent the scope of the appellate court's discretion

---

17. BLACK'S LAW DICTIONARY 546 (7th ed. 1999).

in determining whether a lower court has erred. As W. Wendell Hall has explained, "standards of review define the parameters of a reviewing court's authority to determine whether a trial court has erred, and whether the error warrants reversal."[18] The standard of review thus dictates the power of an appellate court by demarcating how serious an error must be for an appellate court to overturn a lower court opinion.[19] Consequently, "the relevant standards of review are critical to the outcome" of numerous cases.[20]

The appellate court generally applies the de novo standard to issues that turn purely on the resolution of legal questions, reviewing "the case from the same position as the district court."[21] Under the de novo standard, the court gives no deference to the lower court's legal interpretation and considers the matter as though "no decision had been rendered below."[22] Conversely, when an appellate court reviews a lower court's purely factual determination, the court applies the "clearly erroneous" standard.[23] Review under the clearly erroneous standard is highly deferential and requires that the appellate court uphold the lower court unless the panel has "a definite and firm conviction that a mistake has been committed."[24] Under the clearly erroneous standard, "If the district court's account of the evidence is plausible in light of the record viewed in its entirety, the court of appeals may not reverse it even though convinced that had it been sitting as the trier of fact, it would have weighed the evidence differently."[25] Between those extreme standards rest other standards for review of determinations based on administrative decisions, application of lower court discretion, and other decisions intermediate between determinations based on fact and those based on law.

One major sociological consequence of the doctrines controlling the court's standards of review is that the record in appellate proceedings is limited to what went on before the fact-finding court, and the appellate court will not consider facts not before the lower court. The judges on the courts of appeals,

---

18. W. Wendall Hall, *Revisiting Standards of Review in Civil Appeals*, 24 St. Mary's L.J. 1045, 1048 (1993).

19. *See* Ronald R. Hofer, *Standards of Review—Looking beyond the Labels*, 74 Marq. L. Rev. 231, 232 (1991) (the standard of review applicable in a particular case serves as a "limiting mechanism which defines an appellate court's scope of review and hence its power" [internal quotation marks omitted]).

20. *Payne v. Borg*, 982 F.2d 335, 338 (9th Cir. 1992), *cert. denied*, 510 U.S. 843 (1993).

21. *Alaska Ctr. for the Environment v. United States Forest Serv.*, 189 F.3d 851, 857 (9th Cir. 1999).

22. *United States v. Silverman*, 861 F.2d 571, 576 (9th Cir. 1988).

23. *See* Fed. R. Civ. P. 52(a); *Exxon Co. v. Sofec, Inc.*, 54 F.3d 570, 576 (9th Cir 1995), *aff'd*, 517 U.S. 830 (1996).

24. *Concrete Pipe & Prod. v. Construction Laborers Pension Trust*, 508 U.S. 602, 623 (1993); *see also Sawyer v. Whitley*, 505 U.S. 333, 346 n.14 (1992).

25. *Anderson v. Bessemer City*, 470 U.S. 564, 573–74 (1985).

therefore, do not hear the evidence presented and must rely on a written record containing documents, exhibits, and court transcripts. Appellate judges must become familiar with a record that already is formed and factual determinations that already are made. Accordingly, a significant question arises as to how judges learn of the relevant documents from the record. This issue is discussed in the next section.

IV. Methods of Learning Legal Rules and the Factual Record

Because judges are constrained to follow applicable legal precedents by the doctrine of stare decisis and are allowed only to review certain factual issues by the applicable standards of review, judges must learn a relatively comprehensive set of applicable rules of law and the applicable facts of a case. Judges generally learn the law and the facts from at least five sources: (1) their own backgrounds and knowledge, (2) other judges, (3) lawyers, (4) judicial staff (particularly law clerks), and (5) the record from the lower court.

Judicial Backgrounds

Although they come from diverse professional backgrounds, judges on the courts of appeals uniformly come to the bench with substantial expertise. Judicial expertise takes two forms, legal and personal.[26]

Legal Expertise

Legal expertise is knowledge of the laws and regulations that control a substantive area of the law. To be nominated and confirmed to the courts of appeals, judges generally must have a high level of respectability within the legal profession. As one judge put it, "No one got here in a bingo game." That level of respectability rarely is achieved without gaining substantial legal expertise. Such expertise can be derived from a variety of backgrounds, including a judge's prior career in academia, private or government practice, or otherwise. Most federal appellate judges have practiced law in several settings, including both private and governmental practice, and many have sat on state courts and on federal district courts. But the common thread that runs through the members of the appellate judiciary is that the judges all have practiced law in some

26. For a discussion of the variety of the judges' professional backgrounds, see RICHARD POS-NER, THE FEDERAL COURTS: CHALLENGE AND REFORM 13–20 (1996).

form for many years. Consequently, judges almost always come to the bench with vast expertise in one or more legal fields.

Judges also develop legal expertise during their tenures on the bench. Because judges are required to learn the law for each case that they hear, judges gain knowledge of the legal rules each time that they hear a case. As one judge explained, "After you have been in the court a while, intuitively you know a certain kind of case may be more susceptible to being more routine than others. It is just because of the issues. We handle case after case under the same statute. You [learn] what to expect." Because federal appellate judges are appointed for life, the legal expertise that judges develop can become enormous even in relatively obscure areas of law. Conversely, federal judges are unable to specialize,[27] hearing whatever cases come before them. As one judge explained, "One of the disabilities that we have is that we are all generalists, and we never get a chance to do the same kind of [legal] problem over and over and over again. There is always that room for error." Some doctrinal areas, though, consistently present similar questions of law, and those areas lend themselves to the development of judicial expertise. One judge, for example, stated that he found that expertise could most easily be established in administrative areas, such as immigration law, social security law, and bankruptcy law.

The variation in the legal expertise a judge brings to the bench can affect not only the judge's perception of the formal rules but also a law clerk's influence on the judge. One clerk related,

> I would like to think we [had some influence on the judge]. When the judge came on the bench, he was a national expert [in several legal fields]. I would like to think that [when he was] taking a fresh look at areas that he did not know that much about, he would listen to what we had to say and was trying to learn the law in that area as well as we were. So there was a [more fruitful] kind of exchange

Several law clerks stated that they felt particularly able to convince their judges of points in more obscure areas of the law. For example, one clerk stated,

> Our ability to convince [the judge] was inversely proportional to his own sense of his expertise on the case in the area. We might have a fair chance to convince him of our way of thinking in a Federal Maritime Commission case. The odds of convincing him in [a case within his area of expertise]

---

27. The only U.S. Court of Appeals that has specialized subject-matter jurisdiction is the Federal Circuit. To a lesser extent, the judges on the D.C. Circuit are able to specialize because they hear a disproportionately large percentage of public and administrative law cases.

that his inclinations—as someone who taught [in that area] for twenty years—[were] wrong are slim.

Another clerk indicated that his influence was most profound in technical statutorily controlled areas, such as tax law, or particular administratively controlled areas, such as energy regulation.

Some judges and clerks reported that the judge's background plays a significant role only early in proceedings because, as several judges stated, by the time the decision needs to be made, the judge has studied the particular legal questions to the point where he is comfortable that he has achieved expertise sufficient to decide the case. One judge said that before he decides a case, "I would have to be persuaded that I understand the case well enough to make an informed judgment. [If the law remains unclear after conferring with the clerks,] you have to suspect that you don't have a firm enough handle on it." Another judge stated that, although clerks' influence should not depend on the judge's legal expertise, in cases where he lacked expertise, he relied more heavily on his clerks to inform him of the law:

> Suppose I have a [case in my area of specialty], I am not going to give them a research assignment [on that topic]. That [area] is my academic specialty. On the other hand, if I have a question under [an area of law in which I lack expertise], I am very likely to say, "Hey, what about if we try to track [this area's law] down." And I hope by the end of the case I still won't know anything about it, but . . . I will temporarily know enough to decide. But I do not seek to increase my long-term supply of knowledge by that subject.

Personal Expertise

In addition to a vast array of legal expertise, judges also bring to the decisional process personal experience that helps them to understand how formal legal rules apply to particular circumstances. Personal expertise consists of knowledge on the subject of a case regarding the situation or the actors involved in it. One judge highlighted the diversity of judges' personal backgrounds as follows:

> One of the interesting things [about] courts like this is [that its] members have diverse backgrounds: economically, socially, and so on. [Some judges are from families with] millions of dollars, and some people were born into poor families. There are members of this court that went to Ivy League schools, state universities, private schools, and urban-renewal schools.

Because judges on the courts of appeals come from diverse backgrounds, they have a great variety of life experiences that can come into play in determining how formal rules apply to a case.[28]

One judge, for example, described a case involving horse racing in which his personal expertise with horses enabled him to perceive singular aspects of the case that his brethren could not see: "I have always been a horse rancher. I have raised horses. I was in the horse cavalry for a while, captain of [a] polo team, and I don't think [the other judges on the panel] know anything about this, so they got the case turned around." The judge explained that he believed that the way the lower court had decided the case was incorrect because the logic in the argument failed to account for the horse's behavior. Based on his personal expertise, the judge was able to make a decision on a case that the other judges were unable to make.

Examples of the role of personal expertise are not commonly as apparent as in this situation, but personal expertise nevertheless often comes into play. Judges reported that they frequently observed that a legal argument simply made no sense. While that often may mean that the logic of the argument fails, it also sometimes indicates that the legal argument simply fails to resonate with how the judge perceives the world. One law clerk, for example, described a case in which a person had been denied disability benefits because he recreationally rode horses, and the agency had determined that if he could ride horses, his disability did not prevent him from working. The clerk reported that his judge, who had some expertise in horseback riding, felt that horsemanship did exemplify some physical ability and, therefore, was inclined to agree with the agency's application of the formal disability regulations.[29]

Contact with Other Judges

Judges learn of formal legal rules from other appellate judges whose legal or personal expertise assists in the understanding of legal intricacies and how the law applies to the case before the court. Because of the variety of judges' legal and personal expertise, the judges provide one another a potentially substantial resource for assistance in learning the rules that control the outcome of a case and for testing reasoning about how those rules should apply to the unique facts of each case. The ways that judges learn from one another are discussed in depth in chapter 5.

---

28. Many of the judges expressed the view that their courts are highly diversified. That diversity, however, may not reflect diversity relative to society more broadly.

29. While it may appear otherwise from these examples, judges do have personal expertise in areas other than horsemanship.

Appellate judges also learn from the lower court dispositions being reviewed. As one judge explained,

> The first thing I do is read all the briefs on a case. Then, after I do that, I usually pull out the excerpt [of the record]—sometimes after I read the briefs or while I am reading the briefs. And one of the very first things I look for is whatever it is the district court judge has said or done that is part of the controversy. I learned that from a district court judge. He said, "You guys always read these briefs, and one side is distorting it one way and another side is distorting it another. Why don't you start out by reading what I have said?" . . . So I try to get the findings of fact, conclusions of law, the opinions, the orders—whatever it is that we are really reviewing—take a hard look at that while or after I read the briefs.

Lower court opinions, however, may be of limited use because they may be incorrect (which may be why they are the subject of an appeal) and/or short and summary, lacking long elocution of precisely why the lower court or agency decided as it did. Consequently, judges must look to the lawyers to further clarify the issues and further indicate what cases and legal rules govern the case.

The Lawyers

The participants in the appellate process most familiar with the law and facts of any particular case generally are the attorneys representing the litigants. The lawyers play an enormous role in instructing the judges as to the law and convincing the judges to adopt particular interpretations of the law. Lawyers generally have two opportunities to instruct the court: briefs and oral argument.

Briefs

The briefs are the lawyers' best opportunity to present what they view as the relevant case law and how they believe that the law ought to apply to the facts. As Judge Frank Coffin has written, the brief is the "heavy artillery of appellate practice"[30] because it often provides the judge's and clerk's first and most significant introduction to the legal and factual arguments of a case. Moreover, both judges and law clerks rely on the briefs to define the issues on appeal. In fact, the formal procedural rules of the courts demand that if a party fails to raise an issue in a brief or if the brief does not discuss the issue sufficiently, the

---

30. FRANK COFFIN, ON APPEAL: COURTS, LAWYERING, AND JUDGING 107 (1994).

issue will be outside of the scope of the appeal and therefore will be considered to be waived.[31]

Briefs are generally anything but brief, ranging in length from five to fifty or more pages. Each brief, however, must compete for the court's attention not only with the other briefs in a case but also briefs of all of the other cases that the panel must consider. Judges uniformly reported that reading briefs takes up a large percentage of the time they spend preparing to decide each case. In fact, along with a relatively short memorandum prepared by a law clerk, some judges read nothing more than the parties' briefs in preparation for oral argument. Thus, the briefs serve a critical role in informing the court about the nature of the case and the law needed to resolve it.[32]

Like the lower court decisions under review, the briefs often serve as a judge's starting point in analyzing a case. One judge described a typical process:

> I start off by reading the district court decision—if it is a district court case, of course. Then I read the briefs, and how intently I read the briefs depends upon the issues. Oftentimes, you get into a case a little bit, and there are some issues raised that you simply know have no merit. So you can ignore those, and you go through, looking for some justifiable issue in the case, and many of them have none.
>
> If I find a case has some weight to it, then I will read the cases that the parties agree control and reread the district court opinion, if I need to, to see if the district court was asked to address those cases, and basically come to a preliminary view of how I think the case shakes out.

The briefs generally provide one of the first indications of which cases are important. As one judge said, "I don't usually go beyond the brief. In other words, I don't go look for cases. But I will read the cases that [the briefs] say control and see if I agree."

How much the judges rely on the briefs is, at least in part, a function of how much time the judges give themselves to prepare for oral argument. One judge reported that he begins his preparation almost as soon as the briefs arrive at his chambers; in that chambers, the judge keeps notes on the briefs but then pri-

---

31. *See, e.g., Miller v. Fairchild Indus., Inc.,* 797 F.2d 727, 738 (9th Cir. 1986) (court of appeals will not ordinarily consider matters on appeal that are not specifically and distinctly argued in appellant's opening brief).

32. In addition to the parties' briefs, courts occasionally receive amicus briefs submitted by parties other than the litigants. Amicus briefs are admitted at the discretion of the panel hearing the case, and there is some disagreement over when an amicus brief is appropriate. One judge stated that he rarely believes amicus briefs are appropriate, as he viewed them as little more than a political attempt to lobby the court. That view, though, appears to be in the minority, and amicus briefs regularly are admitted in high-profile or controversial cases.

marily relies for his preparation on memoranda from clerks and discussions with his clerks. In contrast, another judge reported,

> I don't [look at the case when it first comes to my chambers]. My first real contact with the case usually is when I read the briefs. I am a late brief reader. Normally, picking those briefs up—it used to be just a week, but now that my calendar is getting heavier, it's likely to be ten days before. Most of those days are just spent reading the briefs. I will normally read the disposition below first, then the briefs. If I have a bench memo [from a clerk], I will read that. In that order.

Because he came to the cases so soon before oral argument and conference, that judge did not have the time to carefully review many cases or to enter into a substantial dialogue with his clerks prior to issuing his preliminary vote in conference. Accordingly, that judge had no choice but to rely heavily on the briefs' descriptions of which cases are important and what those cases said. A third judge read and reread the briefs and focused a great deal of attention on them. As his clerk explained,

> What he does before going to oral argument is he reads the entire set of documents three times. He may not read the appendices—which may be very thick—listings of records and things like that, but he will read the briefs and the reply briefs and the supplemental briefs three times. The first time through, he reads them in detail to pick up the arguments and the cited relevant facts. He will do this from anywhere from a few days to perhaps a week or two weeks before oral argument. . . . He rereads them the night before [oral argument]. He will have already made marks on the briefs about questions and concerns and circled and starred high points or low points, as the case may be. Then, the next morning around 7:00 or 7:15, which means . . . from two to two and a half hours before oral argument, he goes into his office and he scans the briefs a third time. So he will have gone through the various parties' written arguments three times before either party steps before the bench to make oral argument.

In fact, along with a clerk's memorandum, the briefs are often both the first and last things that a judge reads prior to oral argument and conference. As one judge said, "Within a week or less of oral argument, I read the briefs again. Pack up and send the briefs [for the last three days of oral argument] to remote chambers, and I keep [the rest with me], and I will read the briefs once again on the plane."

Because briefs often play such a critical role in their deliberations, judges find it especially frustrating when the briefs are of poor quality.

Sometimes it is hard to understand what it is that the appellant says went wrong, and that is very frustrating when you cannot understand what the issue is that you are asked to decide. . . . Sometimes you have to [rely on the appellee's brief]. Sometimes you have to look to the appellee's brief to see how the appellee can characterize the [case] and then go to the reply brief, if there is any, to see what the appellant says in response that may help you understand a little better.

Consequently, appellate judges often rely on the lower court opinion to provide a more neutral analysis. That does not, however, mean that the briefs do not play a significant role in the judge's decision-making process. Neither, however, does that mean that all judges rely heavily on all briefs or even read all of the briefs in all cases. According to one judge:

[When I look at the briefs], I generally try to start with the appellant. I try to start with the ruling of the district court that we are reviewing to understand what the district court ruled. Then I look at the appellant's brief to try to figure out what it is that the appellant says the district court did wrong. Sometimes I do not even have to read the other side's brief very thoroughly, because it is clear from what the district court said and what the appellant says went wrong that nothing went wrong.

Although judges use briefs in different ways, the role of the briefs remains important because it shapes the way that the judges and clerks view the issues, rules, and facts of the cases.

Oral Argument

The oral argument rests at the apex of the appellate judicial process because it represents the disputants' lawyers opportunity to formally present their cases before the panel of judges. Prior to oral argument, the judges have seen briefs written by the lawyers, which may have presented important questions, noticeable oversights, or manipulative interpretations of the issues. In the oral argument, however, the lawyers have the chance to present their arguments in a face-to-face manner and to shape their discussions to the judges' particular concerns. At the same time, the judges have the opportunity to clarify points that are unclear or of concern. The oral argument is also the only portion of the appellate judicial process in which the lawyers representing the litigants are able to clash in person and to respond almost immediately to the arguments of one another. If the appellate judicial process were a drama, the oral argument would be its peak.[33]

---

33. *Cf.* Milner Ball, *The Play's the Thing: An Unscientific Reflection on Courts under the Rubric of Theater*, 28 STAN. L. REV. 81 (1975).

The main purpose of the oral argument is to allow the judges to question the attorneys and to give the attorneys a chance to reinforce the arguments made in the briefs. The dialogue between the judges and the attorneys is, therefore, the most pervasive aspect of the oral argument. Although the oral argument generally allows the judges to seek clarification, the utility of oral argument depends on how judges use it within their decision-making processes. As one Ninth Circuit judge explained,

> A lot . . . depends on where in the learning curve you think oral argument belongs. I am willing to read the briefs and go to oral argument and ask the questions that occur to me. That may mean that I am not really through thinking about the case and that it may well be that as I get to dealing with it later, I find other things. The disadvantage of that is once in a while a question will come up that I now wish I had asked at oral argument.

Oral argument allows the attorneys the opportunity to inform the court. According to one judge,

> The interaction, the questioning process, I think is very helpful. You may walk in knowing how you should come out. But then you can ask the lawyer that you think you are going to come out on his or her side some very tough questions to make sure that you understand the issue and that you come to the right conclusion.

The attorneys are in a unique position because they have lived with the case for far longer and far more intimately than any other participant in the appellate process. The oral argument, therefore, provides judges an opportunity to gain that experienced and knowledgeable perspective. One judge said, "You are dealing with people who know more about the case than we do or our law clerks do, at least it should be so if the lawyers are doing their work." Another judge explained that he uses oral argument to explore the intricacies of the record because the attorneys' expertise enables him to save the effort of hunting down needlelike details within the proverbial haystack of papers: "If I have a record question, I save it for oral argument. The lawyers are supposed to know that, and you can ask them that and then fill it in."

Oral argument serves to clarify issues as well as to allow judges to build a sense of confidence that the way that they are looking at a case is correct and that they have not missed some important legal precedent or factual detail: "It gives you an opportunity to reevaluate arguments as you listen to them. Sometimes you have missed something with your eye contact with the case that you get with your ear contact with the case. It provides that benefit." Another judge explained,

My participation in oral argument is simply to learn what the heck is going on and give the lawyers an opportunity to react to my tentative views of the case. I am a big believer in letting people know what you are about to do. And one of the district court judges, now on the appellate court, used to issue, when he was in the district court, tentative rulings, tentative findings, tentative orders. He would send those out to the parties and then two weeks later he would have a hearing. And he would say, "Okay, now you know where I am coming from. What am I missing?" So it would give the loser a real opportunity to get up on his or her feet and say, "Wait, this is what you missed." And it would give the other side an opportunity to participate.

So, in oral argument, frequently I will just say to the lawyers, "Look, here is what I think tentatively. What am I missing?" And then I let them inform me. And I really try to keep a very open mind until the whole process is over. Sometimes oral argument confirms what I already think about the case. Sometimes it completely changes the complexion of things, and I will realize, "Boy, I sure missed that."

As the caseload continues to increase, the information function of oral argument has increased in importance. As one judge stated,

I find each oral argument is very valuable to me. . . . On the heavy cases, it is valuable because if I could spend four months on a case, I suppose that anything a lawyer would tell me would be just sort of a confirmation of everything I knew, and I wouldn't change my mind much. But the more we're pressed, if you miss something and you sort of fall off on an aspect of the case, the moment you open your mouth, you're going to be told that you have. Or if you ask a question, you might get an answer that may steer you in another direction or sharpen up your point of view on something you are not clear about.

Finally, as one judge put it, oral argument helps the judges to see the "parameters of the issues" so that they do not allow their minds to wander from the issues before them. He explained that the oral argument can thus limit the scope of an opinion.

The oral argument's many benefits, however, may have a high cost. Judges spend at least one week of each month hearing arguments, potentially at the expense of time spent on other aspects of the judicial process. However, the number of appeals decided without oral argument is increasing at an astronomical rate. As table 3 demonstrates, the percentage of appeals terminated on the merits after oral argument, relative to the percentage terminated after submission on the briefs only, has fallen from approximately 63 percent in 1981 to approximately 35 percent in 2000, a reduction of almost half. The reduction is far more pronounced in some circuits. For example, in 1982, the Fourth Circuit terminated 86 percent of its appeals after oral argument, but in 2000 that number had dropped to approximately 21 percent (the lowest of any circuit). Other circuits showed similar declines. In 1981 the D.C. Circuit terminated 91 percent of its appeals after oral argument, but in 2000 it heard arguments only in approximately 45 percent of its appeals terminated on the merits. Similarly, in 1981 the Ninth Circuit terminated approximately 75 percent of its appeals after oral argument, but in 2000 it heard argument only in about 39 percent of its appeals terminated on the merits. Even the Second Circuit, which saw one of the smallest declines in appeals terminated after oral argument, heard arguments only in approximately 60 percent of its terminated appeals in 2000, compared with 84 percent in 1981.

It is not certain that a decline in the frequency of oral argument harms the judicial process because oral argument is not always a useful mechanism for clarifying how the law applies to the facts of a particular case. The judges uniformly reported that oral argument was valuable on occasion, but the percentage of time that judges reported that oral argument was constructive ranged from almost never to 99 percent. According to one judge,

> I would say as much as half of the time my vantage point, the way I look at a case, is changed in some respect by what I learn in oral argument. It does not mean I go from affirm to reverse, . . . but it does mean that something has happened in oral argument that has caused me to think about that case somewhat differently.

One judge answered that the oral argument is valuable to his decision-making process as much as 25 percent of the time but stated that he does not know which cases fall in that useful category until after argument.

> The problem is that I can't predict which 25 percent. Again, I have a couple of colleagues who would like to limit oral argument much more than we do. The reason that I have [not] been in favor of that is literally I can't necessarily tell you which 25 percent of the cases it is going to be. It is often unexpected. Much of it depends not only on the issues that are presented on the state of the record, but frankly it depends on the skill of the lawyers.

One judge suggested that judges' backgrounds and the way that they decide cases affect how valuable they find oral argument:

> Some judges just don't like oral argument, and they would just as soon do away with it. [I] get a lot of . . . requests [from other judges to compact] the

[five-day] calendar to four days or three days. There are others who like oral argument, and their decision-making process is [made] more comfortable [by] being on the bench. It seems, although I am not sure this is invariably true, that judges who come up through the trial practice and district court judges have a tendency to appreciate oral argument perhaps more than some who have been in the ranks of the professors or have been largely office lawyers. It may be that it has something to do with the way you honed your skills, where you feel comfortable.

Some judges find oral exchange to resonate with their own, personal decision-making styles:

> A lot of what takes place at oral argument is dialogue with the lawyers. My own way of thinking is very oral—I bounce ideas around and see how they work when you actually have to talk about them. I listen to the lawyers, and also, if I have an idea, I will try it out orally. Sometimes it makes sense when you are just sitting in your chair and when you try to say it, it sounds stupid. And I will listen to the other judges' questions and their exchanges with the lawyers and the lawyers' responses. Sometimes something . . . did not make sense to me in the briefs and then, when the lawyers start talking, I understand why they were involved with a particular detail that they were, why it mattered.

Other judges find oral discourse less useful to their deliberative styles. Even though some of those judges were litigators before coming to the bench, they reported that the oral discussions of the issues with the attorneys are rarely useful simply because the way that they think about issues is not substantially helped by oral discussion with attorneys. As one judge described, "I am probably less interested in oral argument than others because I tend to be more of a writing judge than a talking judge." Another judge explained that because the record in appellate cases is fixed, nothing that the attorneys can say in oral argument should be new to judges who are adequately prepared.

Another important purpose of oral argument is that it forces the three judges on the panel to come to a case prepared to discuss it. Without the structure of oral argument, coordinating the judges to prepare themselves to discuss a particular case may be the single most important element in enabling the judges to decide cases in groups. As one judge put it, oral argument "rarely changes my perception of the case. I think [that] before I go to oral argument, I know that case about as well as I am ever going to until we get the opinion written."

Because the judges all are prepared to discuss the case at the same time, the oral argument allows them to coordinate their schedules and discuss cases in

TABLE 3. Percentage of Appeals Terminated on the Merits in the U.S. Courts of Appeals after Oral Hearing by Circuit

Year	D.C. Circuit			1st Circuit			2nd Circuit			3rd Circuit			4th Circuit		
	Number of Appeals Terminated on Merits	Number after Oral Hearing	Percent after Oral Hearing	Number of Appeals Terminated on Merits	Number after Oral Hearing	Percent after Oral Hearing	Number of Appeals Terminated on Merits	Number after Oral Hearing	Percent after Oral Hearing	Number of Appeals Terminated on Merits	Number after Oral Hearing	Percent after Oral Hearing	Number of Appeals Terminated on Merits	Number after Oral Hearing	Percent after Oral Hearing
2000	629	281	44.7%	792	349	44.1%	1,965	1,181	60.1%	1,657	471	28.4%	2,423	512	21.1%
1999	669	290	43.3%	610	364	59.7%	1,863	1,270	68.2%	1,707	506	29.6%	2,644	602	22.8%
1998	633	339	53.6%	740	429	58.0%	1,721	1,168	67.9%	1,740	507	29.1%	2,569	658	25.6%
1997	732	344	47.0%	696	428	61.5%	1,688	1,096	64.9%	1,873	555	29.6%	2,387	720	30.2%
1996	695	363	52.2%	773	432	55.9%	1,834	1,125	31.3%	1,985	532	26.8%	2,885	740	25.6%
1995	703	396	56.3%	786	498	63.4%	1,889	1,186	62.8%	2,011	598	29.7%	3,009	842	28.0%
1994	775	346	44.6%	753	451	59.9%	1,947	1,229	63.1%	5,152	651	30.3%	2,537	835	32.9%
1993	816	365	44.7%	832	546	65.6%	1,702	1,160	68.2%	1,817	556	30.6%	2,264	800	35.3%
1992	723	386	53.4%	767	489	63.8%	1,500	1,072	71.5%	1,671	521	31.2%	2,140	849	39.7%
1991	691	350	50.7%	737	505	68.5%	1,608	1,151	71.6%	1,607	442	27.5%	2,109	815	38.6%
1990	605	343	56.7%	713	479	67.2%	1,243	957	77.0%	1,500	388	25.9%	2,159	737	34.1%
1989	820	391	54.3%	762	512	67.2%	1,136	890	78.3%	1,561	502	32.2%	1,882	743	39.5%
1988	897	440	49.1%	674	435	64.5%	1,114	915	82.1%	1,505	525	34.9%	1,877	799	42.6%
1987	1,010	464	47.9%	634	398	62.8%	1,178	898	76.2%	1,272	476	37.4%	1,756	810	46.1%
1986	656	426	64.9%	610	360	59.0%	1,230	983	79.9%	1,312	563	42.9%	1,729	860	49.7%
1985	591	443	75.0%	575	382	66.4%	1,217	979	80.4%	1,318	573	43.5%	1,584	727	45.9%
1984	525	496	94.5%	491	378	77.0%	1,257	992	78.9%	1,350	533	39.5%	1,028	689	67.0%
1983	591	545	92.2%	396	268	67.7%	1,095	899	82.1%	1,251	532	42.5%	743	680	91.5%
1982	607	548	90.3%	373	279	74.8%	1,139	927	81.4%	975	490	50.3%	708	609	86.0%
1981	532	484	91.0%	465	277	59.6%	1,108	931	84.0%	845	404	47.8%	1,389	634	45.6%

Note: The data in this table are derived from Tables S-1 to *Judicial Business of the United States Courts* (published by the Administrative Office of the United States Courts) for 1992–2000 and Tables S-1 to *Statistical Tables for the Federal Judiciary* (published by the Administrative Office of the United States Courts) for 1981–91. Information regarding the Federal Circuit is unavailable.

TABLE 3—Continued

Year	5th Circuit — Number of Appeals Terminated on Merits	5th Circuit — Number after Oral Hearing	5th Circuit — Percent after Oral Hearing	6th Circuit — Number of Appeals Terminated on Merits	6th Circuit — Number after Oral Hearing	6th Circuit — Percent after Oral Hearing	7th Circuit — Number of Appeals Terminated on Merits	7th Circuit — Number after Oral Hearing	7th Circuit — Percent after Oral Hearing	8th Circuit — Number of Appeals Terminated on Merits	8th Circuit — Number after Oral Hearing	8th Circuit — Percent after Oral Hearing	9th Circuit — Number of Appeals Terminated on Merits	9th Circuit — Number after Oral Hearing	9th Circuit — Percent after Oral Hearing
2000	3,896	1,162	29.8%	2,617	1,059	40.5%	1,598	791	49.5%	1,871	678	36.2%	4,728	1,856	39.3%
1999	3,730	1,100	29.5%	2,524	1,166	45.2%	1,484	783	52.8%	1,815	752	41.4%	4,479	1,616	36.1%
1998	3,552	1,354	38.1%	1,943	996	51.3%	1,415	839	59.3%	1,856	792	42.7%	4,337	1,624	37.4%
1997	3,438	1,213	35.4%	2,116	1,059	50.0%	1,564	802	51.3%	1,832	851	64.5%	4,841	1,889	39.0%
1996	4,038	1,258	31.2%	2,090	1,061	50.8%	1,628	879	54.0%	2,101	826	39.3%	4,415	1,844	41.8%
1995	3,806	1,235	32.4%	2,240	1,139	50.8%	1,737	921	54.0%	2,105	792	37.6%	4,410	1,869	42.4%
1994	3,658	937	25.6%	2,331	1,111	47.7%	1,811	1,096	60.5%	2,165	941	43.5%	4,654	1,884	40.5%
1993	3,359	887	26.4%	2,280	1,092	47.9%	1,656	911	55.0%	2,061	809	39.3%	4,664	1,618	34.7%
1992	3,020	888	29.4%	2,139	1,101	51.5%	1,604	906	56.5%	1,971	890	45.2%	4,061	1,636	40.3%
1991	2,692	734	27.3%	2,525	1,269	50.3%	1,369	765	55.9%	1,904	859	45.1%	3,727	1,705	45.7%
1990	2,659	759	28.5%	2,395	1,175	49.1%	1,334	751	56.3%	1,808	771	42.6%	2,984	1,523	51.0%
1989	2,539	803	31.6%	2,428	1,217	50.1%	1,287	695	63.9%	1,446	756	52.3%	2,899	1,698	58.6%
1988	2,332	771	33.1%	2,302	1,173	51.0%	1,110	739	66.6%	1,137	692	60.9%	2,696	1,683	62.4%
1987	2,204	710	32.2%	2,231	1,148	51.5%	1,218	786	64.5%	1,402	698	49.8%	2,545	1,601	62.9%
1986	2,157	804	37.3%	1,905	1,114	58.4%	1,136	752	56.2%	1,343	682	50.8%	2,640	1,679	63.6%
1985	2,019	848	42.0%	1,742	1,142	55.6%	1,190	790	66.4%	1,308	718	54.9%	2,286	1,418	62.0%
1984	1,723	778	45.2%	1,592	1,068	67.1%	1,169	758	64.8%	975	627	64.3%	2,152	1,389	64.5%
1983	1,535	719	46.8%	1,390	1,060	76.3%	946	698	73.8%	816	511	62.6%	2,014	1,533	76.1%
1982	1,575	819	52.0%	1,149	921	80.2%	787	650	82.6%	756	490	64.8%	1,961	1,481	75.5%
1981	1,329	692	52.1%	1,276	952	74.6%	897	701	78.1%	620	396	63.9%	1,514	1,122	74.1%

(continues)

TABLE 3—Continued

	10th Circuit			11th Circuit			All Circuits		
Year	Number of Appeals Terminated on Merits	Number after Oral Hearing	Percent after Oral Hearing	Number of Appeals Terminated on Merits	Number after Oral Hearing	Percent after Oral Hearing	Number of Appeals Terminated on Merits	Number after Oral Hearing	Percent after Oral Hearing
2000	1,582	562	35.5%	3,758	850	22.6%	27,516	9,752	35.4%
1999	1,608	509	31.7%	3,594	966	26.9%	26,727	9,924	37.1%
1998	1,576	551	35.0%	2,828	958	33.9%	24,910	10,215	41.0%
1997	1,379	410	29.7%	3,294	985	29.9%	25,840	10,357	40.1%
1996	1,837	548	29.8%	3,045	980	32.2%	27,326	10,588	38.7%
1995	1,851	545	29.4%	3,255	1,059	32.5%	27,772	11,080	39.9%
1994	1,657	529	31.9%	2,779	1,037	37.3%	27,219	11,047	40.6%
1993	1,552	506	32.6%	2,758	972	35.2%	25,761	10,222	39.7%
1992	1,608	611	38.0%	2,393	1,013	42.3%	23,597	10,362	43.9%
1991	1,678	565	33.7%	2,371	1,069	45.1%	23,018	10,229	44.4%
1990	1,560	670	42.9%	2,062	926	44.9%	21,022	9,479	45.1%
1989	1,512	526	34.8%	2,143	995	46.4%	20,115	9,728	48.4%
1988	1,140	526	46.1%	2,093	970	46.3%	18,877	9,668	51.2%
1987	1,175	478	40.7%	2,004	957	47.8%	18,629	9,444	50.7%
1986	1,235	500	40.5%	2,307	1,103	47.8%	18,264	9,826	53.8%
1985	986	475	48.2%	2,070	1,012	48.9%	16,886	9,507	56.3%
1984	946	544	57.5%	1,661	787	47.4%	14,869	9,039	60.8%
1983	969	462	47.7%	1,055	653	61.9%	12,801	8,560	66.9%
1982	836	503	60.2%	1,308	702	53.7%	12,174	8,419	69.2%
1981	1,048	458	43.7%	1,231	658	53.5%	12,254	7,709	62.9%

an informed manner. One judge said that the oral argument "allows us to come to focus on the issue. There are three people focusing on the issue. The three decision makers are focusing on the issues at the same time." Another judge explained,

> What I like about oral argument is that it focuses my attention on the case at the same time that the attention of the other two judges is focused on it. It seems to me that it makes our conference better and more likely to deal with the problems that are most troubling to the lawyers. As far as analytically illuminating the briefs, [oral argument is of value] only occasionally.

One consequence in omitting oral argument from the decisional process is that judges may not feel the same pressure to familiarize themselves with the case and therefore may not be as well prepared to decide the case. One judge stated,

I don't prepare differently if a case is argued or not argued. I read the briefs and go to oral argument and exp[ect] to discuss it that day. But I don't think the discussions are quite as good because we have not had the argument to think about the case just before we have our conference.

Because oral argument enables the judges to clarify issues, it may save time in the decision-making process. As one judge put it,

We have cut oral argument back in the amount of time that we give each case, and so I think that the relative benefit of oral argument compared to the time it takes to listen to the case is enormous. It takes me more time to decide the case if it does not need to be argued than it takes to hear it.

Conversely, because oral argument appears to serve its rule-clarification purpose relatively infrequently, some judges expressed that the excessive use of oral argument might be highly time-consuming, and some judges have suggested that oral argument may not be valuable in certain classes of cases.

I do [think we hear oral argument too frequently]. I think there are certain classes of cases—and I am thinking primarily about many criminal cases [principally ineffective assistance of counsel cases]—that come up on some constitutional issue with which we are confronted, and it appears to me that it is no more than a delay in the process. . . . It just seems to me that we tolerate that far too often.

Nevertheless, as will be discussed in chapters 5 and 6, other collateral benefits of oral argument may warrant oral argument in at least some cases where there may not be significant doctrinal benefits.

Waiver and Sanctions

One issue commonly raised by law clerks was that the lawyers do not provide an adequate review of a case's legal precedents and issues. The appellant's lawyer's job is to point out where the lower court erred, and the appellee's lawyer's job is to point out why the lower court did not err. To do so, attorneys must point to specific legal doctrines and cases as well as provide explicit citations to the record below. When the attorneys fail to accomplish those goals, judges and law clerks are often left to do substantial research to supplement the poor legal analysis provided by the parties.

The judges, however, have at least two methods at their disposal to shift the burden of locating legal and factual precedents back onto the attorneys. First, the judges have at their disposal a doctrine whereby a panel may deem an argument waived if it is insufficiently argued or supported in the parties' briefs. For example, the Ninth Circuit has a formal doctrine that states that the court will not ordinarily consider matters on appeal that are not "specifically and distinctly" argued in the appellant's opening brief.[34] Second, where an attorney performs his job so poorly that the court cannot adequately review the case, the court may impose sanctions against the attorney. The judges on the courts of appeals, though, are slow to consider issues waived or to impose sanctions because they do not view those solutions as efficient means to increase justice. One judge stated,

> Nobody worries about us throwing a case out on a waiver on a nonconstitutional, insignificant matter. I mean, some people would complain. The trouble is that these things get so complicated that in some of these cases I think the judicial process demands that if you are going to use the waiver, you have got to take the consequences. That is, if we throw a case out on a waiver, the Supreme Court is going to nail us, or we are going to have twice as much work when we could have used three lines [in the disposition] and taken care of it.
>
> It is kind of a hard thing to call. On some cases I have been there and we have used waiver and knocked them out and nothing has happened. In other cases, we have said, "Look, we are not going to do it. It is not responsible. It is not going to work." Even though we could kick it out, we decided this is the way we want it. Because, after all, we are trying to decide the case, trying to finish it, stop it. We are trying to find the truth and . . . justice. . . . If the waiver does it and we are willing to stick by it, fine.

A further problem that judges reported was that sanctions and waiver may not, in fact, be effective as deterrents to bad lawyering. First, the judges seemed pessimistic that word would reach the legal community because the number of lawyers who repeatedly represent cases on appeal in the circuit is relatively small. Second, the judges expressed concern that the attorneys who would be most likely to receive sanctions or to have their client's legal arguments waived were also the lawyers least likely to learn from those experiences.

The Central Staff

Staff attorneys provide judges with what is often the first introduction to a case's facts, legal issues, and rules. Staff attorneys' duties include the responsibility to prepare an inventory sheet for each case that comes before the court. These sheets include summary information such as whether the case is civil,

---

34. *See Miller*, 797 F.2d at 738.

criminal, or other; from what court or body the case is appealed; the judge who issued the appealed decision; a one- or two-paragraph description of the case's facts and legal controversy; and a list of legal questions that the case presents. The inventory sheets also contain information about related appeals or other related cases that the court has heard.

Many judges use these inventory sheets to provide a quick entree into the rules and facts of a case. As one judge said, "The first thing I do is look at the inventory sheets that the staff does . . . just to get the very bare-bones idea of what the case is about." Another judge explained, "I start by reading the [inventory] sheet. . . . I need to get that into my head before I read the briefs." Still another judge related, "The first thing I do is to take a look at the inventory sheets for the whole calendar. I take a look at all of them and kind of get acquainted with what issues are going to be coming up." Other judges reported using the inventory sheets as a checklist to make certain that they have prepared themselves on each issue.

Law Clerks

In many chambers, law clerks bear primary responsibility for preparing the judge to decide a case as well as significant responsibility for drafting the opinions. While the judges read the briefs and attend oral argument to gain a firm understanding of the case, the clerks provide the research and close readings of the cases that allow the judges to become informed beyond the limits that time puts on the judges' ability to be familiar with the case. As one judge put it,

> Since [the clerks] have only one-third of the caseload that I have, they are expected to know infinitely more about that case than I do. They are supposed to be the world's greatest authority on everything that is in the record and the briefs in that case, so they probably spend more time reading records, reading briefs, and reading supporting cases.

Law clerks aid judges in preparing to make decisions in four important ways: (1) researching the legal issues in a case and writing bench memoranda to summarize their findings; (2) creating a bench book of case materials; (3) serving as a sounding board for a judge's thoughts and arguments; and (4) researching, drafting, and checking citations for opinions. These aspects of the judge-clerk relationship will be explored in chapter 4.

Furthermore, clerks and staff attorneys have prepared and updated handbooks, including summaries of various legal areas. For example, in the Ninth Circuit, one judge's permanent law clerk prepared and annually updates a handbook on standards of review that consists of a comprehensive collection of paragraphs outlining the proper standards of review to be applied in numerous areas of law common to the circuit. Other handbooks include subject matters such as legal summaries of jurisdiction, habeas corpus, and court procedure.

The Factual Record from the Lower Court

Judges themselves rarely review the entire appellate record. Because the record is produced in the district court, there is only one copy, which presents the judges with potential coordination problems that only are made more serious when the judges retain chambers in more than one city or even more than one building within a circuit.[35]

Because there is only a single copy of the full record, the attorneys retain the responsibility of copying relevant portions of the record for each of the judges. The appellant's attorney submits the excerpts of record with the opening brief, and the appellee's attorney may submit additional documents in supplemental excerpts of record in the response brief. The law clerks review the submitted excerpts of record, and the judge has the discretion to review the full record (or to require clerks to do so). Because the attorneys rather than the court prepare the excerpts of record, the judges still have occasion to view the full record.

In the Ninth Circuit, there is an informal custom that the judge who has writing responsibility in a case is responsible for becoming suitably acquainted with the full record of the case. In some chambers, that means that the law clerks must acquaint themselves with the full record in each case. As one judge explained, "I want [my law clerks] to know the whole record and bring to my attention anything in it that I should know about that was not highlighted in the briefs or included in the excerpts." The majority of judges on the Ninth Circuit, though, do not require their clerks to comprehensively review each case's full record. One judge stated that his clerks go through the full record only "as to anything that there is even the remotest question about, including an item where, as I call it, the condensed explanation simply does not make sense, it does not hang together, there is something factually missing." In those chambers, the clerks must identify issues where a review of the excerpts of record would be insufficient. One judge explained that he would prefer to personally review the full record in every case but that the time constraints caused by the caseload have spurred him to delegate the responsibility to his clerks. Moreover, he reported that the delegation to his clerks includes the delegation of the responsibility to select which portions of the record require a detailed review:

---

35. Issues relating to the geographic dispersion of judges within a circuit are considered in chapter 5.

I do not have an absolute rule [about the use of the full record]. I have left that to the judgment of the law clerk. And different groups of law clerks do it somewhat differently. In general, I think they are selective, as they ought to be. They go through the record when it is significant. I think it would be wasteful to say "Now, you start at page 1 and read through every page of this record" when there is only one little issue that makes any difference. I expect them to know the case. I cannot do it anymore. I used to be able to go to the record. When I had a case assigned to me, I would go to the record, I would go to the briefs, then I would do my own research, but none of those things is possible anymore. I have to depend upon them to do it, and I have to depend upon their integrity and thoroughness in doing the job, and I tell them that.

Moreover, in some chambers, the judges do not ordinarily order the full record from the lower court without a specific reason. As one judge explained,

I don't [order the full record as a rule]. I think by and large that it is counterproductive. I have the excerpt of record, which is what the lawyers think I need. If it turns out that I need some part of the record, then I ask the lawyer to quote it to me at oral argument. If he or she is prepared, they should be able to open that record and give me what I need. I have not found that to be an inordinate process that creates a lot of problems.

There are some cases— extraordinary cases— that I think I need to see the record before I go on the bench. Most of the time I do not. Most of the time I can read the district court's decision, and most of the lawyers are good enough to put [the documents] in the excerpt of record on which the case really turns. When they miss it, I have to ask them the question at oral argument. I think that is a much better use of my time and my law clerks' time rather than getting a record for every case. Some judges disagree. They feel that they have to have the record in the case. I believe I have to have the record to write an opinion, but that is different than oral argument.

Another judge explained that because most cases simply do not require a review of the entire record, the extra burden on the lower court caused by ordering the record is unjustified:

We have the excerpts of record, which are supposed to contain the key rulings of the district court, the docket sheet, and the key documents that are necessary to decide the case. [To order the full record] is a tremendous burden on the district courts. We are part of a system, we are part of a big system, it is not just us, we are part of the system of justice. The district courts are part of our system, and it is a tremendous burden on those offices for judges to ask for entire written records of documents that were filed with the district court when the parties are supposed to give us the key documents. So I do not ask for the whole record, because I presume that we have what we want in the excerpts.

Another judge simply stated, "You can tell right away which ones you are going to need records on. Any administrative hearing, if you don't have the record, you are going to be lost. And most of them we get the records anyway."

One judge who does not regularly order the record explained his criteria for doing so:

> Basically, if the clerk or I think there is something that we need to know that is not being answered by the excerpt of record, we will order the record. In sufficiency of the evidence cases, almost always we will order the record. Those you simply cannot do from the excerpt.

One problem with ordering the full record only as needed is the sometimes sizable delay in its receipt. The full record comes from the district court or agency from which the appeal is taken, and, as one judge pointed out, some district courts and agencies can be frustratingly slow in responding to requests for the whole record:

> We order the record because it takes a long time to order the record. If you need the record—you get to preparing the case and the excerpt doesn't have it, and you say, "I wish I had the full record." When you decide you are going to order the record then, it takes two weeks. So we basically order it because you never know which case is going to require it. When you get to that point at midnight [when] you are sitting there working, you say, "I wish I had the record." You say, "As a matter of fact, I do have the record."
>
> So that came out of a bitter experience of not ordering the record and finding I can't get it tomorrow. It takes two weeks, so now we just always order it. We make sure that somebody on the panel has ordered it because [of] delays—if another judge has it on our court, it is not a big deal. It can be gotten in a day or two. But if it has not ever been ordered up from the district court, that is what takes a long time.

Judges sometimes order a single document from the record and request that the district court fax it directly to chambers. Although that can substantially cut the time it takes to order a record, a two- or three-day delay can result. That is significant given the dense schedules chambers keep and given that a clerk may well have moved on to another case by the time the needed document arrives.

The failure to review the full record can result in a judge overlooking a document that may have important consequences for the proper decision in a case but was not included in the excerpts of record. Moreover, in some *pro se* cases,[36] the court will waive the requirement that the appellant submit excerpts of record. In those cases, judges who wish to see any documents from the record, including the transcripts of the proceedings or the orders being reviewed, often must look to the original record. Yet several clerks indicated that they had worked on cases without excerpts and the other judges on the panel had not ordered the record or requested any of the documents from the record. That is particularly troubling because it means that at least some judges make decisions about sufficiency of the evidence, jury instructions, and the like without seeing the evidence or instructions being reviewed.

Because judges often are reluctant to go beyond the excerpts of record and to review the full record, the appellate judicial process might be improved if the court were to shift the record-reviewing responsibility more firmly onto the attorneys, perhaps by creating a rule that resembles the rule concerning the appellant's brief that says that any argument not made in the appellant's brief is considered waived. In the context of the record, that rule would say that the court will not consider any item from the full record that is not included in the excerpts of record attached to the parties' briefs. A version of that rule has been adopted by the California courts of appeal. Under the California Rules of Court, the parties may stipulate parts of the record that are to be incorporated into the clerk's record for appeal. Where such a stipulation is made, the court will not consider documents in the trial record that are not included in the stipulated clerk's record.[37]

The California rule resonates with the view that the responsibility for presenting the record to the court lies with the attorneys. One judge expressed that view as follows:

Q: Does your chambers order the full record as a matter of course?

A: No. Not unless it is [regarding] something [about which] the record is going to be determinative. I would say if the lawyers do a good job of preparing the excerpt, then I rarely need the full record because if you look at it as a haystack and there is a needle in it, it is up to the lawyers to find the needle and tell you where it is. It is not up to me. I won't lift a finger to go through a three thousand–page transcript to find out if there is an error in there. That is not my job. It is up to the lawyer to show me where the error is.

---

36. *Pro se* cases are those in which defendants represent themselves.
37. *See* California Rules of Court, Rules 4–12.

One judge said that he would support adopting some form of the California rule and suggested that the resistance to adopting such a rule derives from some judges' political agendas:

> If I had a political agenda, I might take a different view. I might say, "Well, it is my duty to see that no immigrant is repatriated without full search of the record." Or, "No capital . . . judgment is ever executed without full search of the record." But I don't think that is the law, or . . . should be. I think the appellate lawyer . . . has the duty to show by line and page where the trial judge made a mistake. If there is a default in presenting that to the appellate court, the appellate court should get on with its work.

For whatever reason, though, almost all of the judges I spoke with about a California-like rule expressed serious reservations about how such a rule would apply in federal appellate proceedings. One judge said:

> We have vacillated back and forth. We had a rule similar to that at one time. . . . And there have been a lot of times where we have said, "Look, the rules are going to say, 'You put it in the excerpt, or we are not going to consider it.'" The first thing that happens is you get a desperate case and you realize that you have got to go out of the record. So now you are making orders to submit it and put it in the excerpt. It is hard to be a judge and recognize that these rules are like bar examinations, they are like rules of the road. They are kept to keep society in order in an attempt to keep our court in order. But they are not the truth. All they are are the ways, the manner in which we attempt to get to the truth and justice. So, if the rule is precluding that, it is a nice little rule and you can just cite it. "We are not going to consider your case because you did not put in an excerpt." What did that do for justice? Zero.

Another judge explained,

> It is a little bit like raising children. You can have as many silly rules as you want, but what if they don't do it? Now what do you do? Are you going to say, "I am not going to decide this case on the justice and the right way because they did not put it in?" I guess you could.

V. Procedural Rules and Agenda Setting

While formal doctrinal rules play a significant role in maintaining the balance between autonomy and interdependence, formal procedural features also play a role. By establishing which judges hear which cases and which judges have responsibility to write opinions in each case, formal procedures serve to set the court's agenda.

Screening Panels

Before judges become involved in cases, the central staff begins the process of screening to determine, based on criteria set by the judges, the type of judicial process that the case will receive. A case designated for full-dress treatment will receive the detailed attention of a panel of judges who bring the full attention of the chambers onto a case. Ordinarily, full-dress treatment provides the attorneys the opportunity to argue the case orally. In screened cases, however, judges often do not use the same decision-making process. They rarely utilize the full services of their law clerks; they rarely require their law clerks to write detailed bench memoranda; and they rarely engage their law clerks in the detailed discussions common to full-dress cases. Instead, in screened cases, the staff attorneys play a more central role, drafting memoranda and sometimes presenting the case to a panel of judges for decision. Moreover, screened cases virtually never receive detailed written opinions but more commonly receive a summary disposition that can often be little more than a single word, *affirmed.*

Because of the summary attention given to screened cases, judges take a conservative approach to screening cases, even in the face of a caseload crisis. As one judge explained,

> We really sort of take a very cautious approach towards cases that are screened out for screening panels because we recognize that those are not going to get . . . the attention probably that the other cases get. . . . It is a triage type of business. . . . I think we probably err in terms of sending things to panels rather than keeping them in screening, which is fine. Because with that we have over a thousand cases that go to screening each year that the panels agree are just no-brainers. . . . I think the screening process works pretty well.

Even with this cautious approach, the screening process has the potential to disadvantage certain types of appellants. As Thomas Davies has pointed out, the screening process can create an agenda-setting bias that makes it more likely for criminal appeals to be screened and for civil cases to receive full-dress treatment.[38]

---

38. *See* Thomas Davies, *Gresham's Law Revisited: Expedited Processing Techniques and the Allocation of Appellate Resources,* 6 Just. Sys. J. 372, 395 (1981).

Panel Assignment

A case designated for full-dress treatment is assigned to a panel of three judges. This raises at least two procedural questions: (1) who puts judges on panels with one another? and (2) which cases are assigned to which panels? The power to place particular cases before particular judges is potentially highly significant, as there may be predictable biases in certain classes of cases. In all of the circuits in which I interviewed, however, those two potential problems are disarmed by a system of random assignment. First, judges are randomly assigned to panels. In theory, that means that, over time, each judge should sit with each other judge on the circuit an equal number of times.

Second, cases generally are assigned randomly to panels. There are limited exceptions to this random method of case assignment. For example, cases that are related to one another, either by facts or issues, may be assigned to the same panel in an effort to avoid unneeded repetition of effort and to avoid potential intracircuit conflicts. Similarly, because some cases demand more attention than others, cases must be assigned so that more time-consuming cases are distributed to maintain an even caseload distribution.

In the Ninth Circuit, case distribution is accomplished by a system of weighting in which staff attorneys review cases prior to their assignment to panels and assign to the cases a weight, which the staff attorneys use to more evenly distribute cases among chambers. That weighting system, however, introduces another potential problem, as some classes of cases are systematically assigned lower weights than others. One staff attorney, for example, informally reported that criminal cases are systematically assigned lower weights than civil cases. Consequently, the assignment of cases to panels can create biases similar to those noted earlier with respect to the screening process.

Opinion Writing

Two aspects of opinion writing are affected significantly by formal procedural rules: (1) the determination of which judge is assigned to write the court's opinion; and (2) the determination of whether to publish a written opinion in a case.

Assignment of Opinions

Which judge authors an opinion is determined by the court's chief judge, or, in the chief's absence, by the active judge on the panel who has been on the court the longest. In circuits where the responsibility for preparing draft bench memoranda is split among the judges on a panel, assigning judges must divide responsibility for cases before they have an opportunity to review the cases in any significant detail and before they see which judges express strong feelings about the cases. In those circuits, while the opinion-writing responsibility is separate from the responsibility for drafting bench memoranda, judges rarely split those two responsibilities in practice. In fact, some judges reported that they can sometimes be irritated when opinion-writing responsibility is assigned differently from bench memorandum-writing responsibility because they and their clerks already have placed disproportionately protracted preparation time into cases for which they had bench memorandum responsibility.

Although some judges allow their brethren to request responsibility for particular cases, many judges simply randomly split the bench memorandum responsibility so that the case weight is evenly distributed. Assigning judges who ask for their colleagues' preferences and those who split cases according to their own preference both are expected to divide the cases so that the judges have relatively even case distribution, and politics is expected not to enter into the process. As one judge explained,

> If they want to do it randomly, that is fine. If they want my law clerks to indicate cases or issues that intrigue them, I turn that over to the law clerks, and I take no part in that. I do not care what piece of the pie I get. I work under the assumption that each presiding judge is trying to be fair and trying to equalize the load—also fair in terms of sending out cases of some novelty or cases that are slam-dunks that are not going to require much research or writing.

Publication of Written Opinions

Whether the court writes and publishes an opinion also has significance because (1) only a written or oral opinion provides the litigants with an explanation of the reasons for a panel's decision; and (2) in most circuits, only a published opinion may be cited as precedent. Under local court rules, judges on the courts of appeals have the discretion to resolve cases without published opinions. In some circuits, that means issuing summary dispositions that generally resolve the case without providing any analysis or reasoning. In other circuits, that means issuing brief memorandum dispositions that provide some limited reasoning but are not as in-depth as opinions. These memorandum dispositions are not published and, depending on circuit rules, carry no precedential weight and cannot be cited as authority.

Every year since 1990, when the Administrative Office of the Courts began to keep statistics regarding publication of opinions, the percentage of appeals terminated without a published opinion has increased. In 1990 the courts of appeals terminated 68 percent of appeals without issuing a published opinion. In 2000 approximately 80 percent of appeals were terminated without published opinion. Although most circuits have seen some decrease in the percentage of appeals terminated with a published opinion, the decline in publication has been far more pronounced in some circuits. Whereas the Third Circuit has seen almost no change in the percentage of appeals terminated with a published opinion (publishing opinions in approximately 20 percent of all terminated appeals with relatively little variation), the Eleventh Circuit has fallen from publishing an opinion in approximately 32 percent of all terminated appeals to publishing in less than 15 percent of terminated appeals. More typical is the Ninth Circuit, which increased the percentage of appeals terminated without written opinion from approximately 70 percent in 1990 to approximately 84 percent in 2000. (See table 4.)

Most commentators who have considered the decline in published opinions have decried it as a harmful practice that undermines the legitimacy of the judicial process as well as the ability of lawyers and the public to know and apply the law.[39] As William M. Richman and William L. Reynolds have observed, "The pernicious impact of the increased use of parajudicial personnel and the reduction of oral arguments has been exacerbated by recent developments in opinion publication."[40] Indeed, in the mid-1980s, federal appellate judges themselves began to note the potential harmful effects of nonpublication.[41]

A decline in the percentage of cases decided with published opinions does not necessarily indicate a decline in the quality of justice. Indeed, merely because a case is deemed worthy of full-dress treatment and not screened out does not necessarily mean that the case is worthy of a written opinion. As one judge explained,

> Many of the memos that we send out are not that easy, they are not simple. They are not the type of thing that you can sit down and . . . have a staff attorney tell you, "Here is what the story is" [in] fifteen minutes. I mean, you really have to apply yourself. Just because it is [ultimately resolved in an unpublished] memo does not mean it should have been a screener.

---

39. *See* Martha J. Dragich, *Will the Federal Courts of Appeals Perish If They Publish? Or Does the Declining Use of Opinions to Explain and Justify Judicial Decisions Pose a Greater Threat?* 44 Am. U. L. Rev. 757, 775–81 (1995); *see also* Lauren K. Robel, *The Myth of the Disposable Opinion: Unpublished Opinions and Government Litigants in the United States Courts of Appeals*, 87 Mich. L. Rev. 940 (1989); William M. Richman & William L. Reynolds, *Appellate Justice Bureaucracy and Scholarship*, 2 U. Mich. J. L. Reform 623, 632–33 (1988).

40. Richman & Reynolds, 1988, *supra* note 39, at 632.

41. *See, e.g., National Classification Committee & National Motor Freight Traffic Assoc., Inc. v. United States*, 765 F.2d 164, 172–75 (D.C. Cir. 1985) (Wald, J., separate statement) ("serious questions continue to be raised about the circumstances in which it is appropriate for this court to dispose of cases in such a truncated manner"); Posner, 1985, *supra* note 13, at 122–23.

Instead, the criteria for determining whether a case should be resolved with a published opinion or an unpublished memorandum disposition include, among other things, such issues as whether the case involves a new or evolving area of law, whether the case carries substantial political or practical importance with ramifications for parties not before the court, and whether the lower court had published an opinion.[42] One judge reported that some of his brethren occasionally published opinions in cases that presented a clean example of the application of the mainstream rule. He explained that in many substantive areas, one or two cases from many years ago established a rule, and recent published cases contain examples only of exceptions to the rule. All of the cases that are simple applications of the rule are resolved in unpublished memorandum dispositions. He said that there is a consequential danger of an attorney misunderstanding the case law as indicating that the rule has been consumed by the exceptions. To avert that result, that judge reported that some judges will occasionally publish a clean application of the rule to remind the public that the rule still holds force.

The decision to dispose of a case as an unpublished disposition may at first appear to be merely an issue of efficiency—a judge wishes to avoid the difficult task of justifying a result in a detailed, published account. Judges with whom I spoke, however, had a different and more subtle view of the process. Unpublished dispositions serve to avoid cluttering the case law with numerous ordinary cases that merely repeat the rule and that may run the risk of confusing the rule with seemingly contrary statements that an attorney might mistake for a revocation of precedent. By limiting publication to instances where the published opinion adds some significant aspect to the case law, the rules also limit maverick judges' and lawyers' ability to create exceptions to a doctrinal rule that the panel had no intention of suggesting or allowing.[43]

Moreover, by limiting publication to significant cases, judges can focus greater attention on those cases that merit such attention. Accordingly, circuits that publish a lower percentage of terminated appeals also have a higher percentage of published dissents. For example, in the twelve months ending on September 30, 2000, the Ninth Circuit, which published a written opinion in only 15.9 percent of its cases, published a dissent in approximately 17.4 percent of its written published opinions. In contrast, the Seventh Circuit, which published in 43.5 percent of its cases, published a dissent in only 7.5 percent of its written published opinions, and the D.C. Circuit, which published in 40.2 per-

---

42. If a lower court did publish an opinion and the appellate court is reversing, it may be necessary to publish an opinion to remove the binding precedential aspects of the lower court opinion with which the appellate court takes umbrage.

43. Even if one were to conclude that it is justified to publish selectively, the question still remains whether the courts are choosing to publish in all cases where publication would be justified.

TABLE 4. Percentage of Appeals Terminated on the Merits in the U.S. Courts of Appeals without Published Opinion

	D.C. Circuit			1st Circuit			2nd Circuit			3rd Circuit		
Year	Number of Appeals Terminated on Merits	Number without Published Opinion	Percent without Published Opinion	Number of Appeals Terminated on Merits	Number without Published Opinion	Percent without Published Opinion	Number of Appeals Terminated on Merits	Number without Published Opinion	Percent without Published Opinion	Number of Appeals Terminated on Merits	Number without Published Opinion	Percent without Published Opinion
2000	629	376	59.8%	792	462	58.3%	1,965	1,523	77.5%	1,657	1,385	83.6%
1999	669	419	62.6%	610	277	45.4%	1,863	1,320	71.0%	1,707	1,382	81.0%
1998	633	359	56.7%	740	370	50.0%	1,721	1,207	70.1%	1,740	1,486	85.4%
1997	732	457	62.4%	696	339	48.7%	1,688	1,230	72.9%	1,873	1,572	83.9%
1996	695	406	58.4%	773	397	51.4%	1,834	1,264	68.9%	1,985	1,715	86.4%
1995	703	432	61.4%	786	370	47.0%	1,889	1,306	69.1%	2,011	1,657	82.3%
1994	775	522	67.3%	753	351	46.6%	1,947	1,288	66.1%	5,152	1,787	83.0%
1993	816	557	68.2%	832	318	38.2%	1,702	1,133	66.5%	1,817	1,482	81.5%
1992	723	443	61.2%	767	323	42.1%	1,500	982	65.4%	1,671	1,346	80.5%
1991	691	427	61.7%	737	228	30.9%	1,608	1,018	63.3%	1,607	1,305	81.2%
1990	605	338	55.8%	713	272	38.1%	1,243	716	57.6%	1,500	1,210	80.6%

Note: The data in this table are derived from Tables S-3 to *Judicial Business of the United States Courts* (published by the Administrative Office of the United States Courts) for 1992–2000 and Tables S-3 to *Statistical Tables for the Federal Judiciary* (published by the Administrative Office of the United States Courts) for 1990 and 1991. Information prior to 1990 and information regarding the Federal Circuit is unavailable.

TABLE 4—Continued

	4th Circuit			5th Circuit			6th Circuit			7th Circuit		
Year	Number of Appeals Terminated on Merits	Number without Published Opinion	Percent without Published Opinion	Number of Appeals Terminated on Merits	Number without Published Opinion	Percent without Published Opinion	Number of Appeals Terminated on Merits	Number without Published Opinion	Percent without Published Opinion	Number of Appeals Terminated on Merits	Number without Published Opinion	Percent without Published Opinion
2000	2,423	2,194	90.5%	3,896	3,223	82.7%	2,617	2,155	82.3%	1,598	903	56.5%
1999	2,644	2,382	90.1%	3,730	3,010	80.7%	2,524	2,067	81.9%	1,484	842	56.7%
1998	2,569	2,327	90.6%	3,552	2,522	71.0%	1,943	1,544	79.5%	1,415	699	49.4%
1997	2,387	2,109	88.4%	3,438	2,672	77.7%	2,116	1,733	81.9%	1,564	810	51.8%
1996	2,885	2,605	90.3%	4,038	3,150	78.0%	2,090	1,578	78.9%	1,628	863	53.0%
1995	3,009	2,678	88.9%	3,806	2,974	78.1%	2,240	1,850	82.5%	1,707	916	53.6%
1994	2,537	2,199	86.6%	3,658	2,924	79.9%	2,331	1,860	79.7%	1,811	857	47.3%
1993	2,264	1,927	85.1%	3,359	2,560	76.2%	2,280	1,876	82.2%	1,656	869	52.4%
1992	2,140	1,794	83.8%	3,020	2,191	72.5%	2,139	1,667	77.9%	1,604	756	47.1%
1991	2,109	1,765	83.6%	2,692	1,953	72.5%	2,525	1,985	78.6%	1,369	650	78.6%
1990	2,159	1,837	85.0%	2,659	1,803	67.8%	2,395	1,827	79.6%	1,334	610	45.7%

(continues)

TABLE 4—Continued

Year	8th Circuit			9th Circuit			10th Circuit			11th Circuit		
	Number of Appeals Terminated on Merits	Number without Published Opinion	Percent without Published Opinion	Number of Appeals Terminated on Merits	Number without Published Opinion	Percent without Published Opinion	Number of Appeals Terminated on Merits	Number without Published Opinion	Percent without Published Opinion	Number of Appeals Terminated on Merits	Number without Published Opinion	Percent without Published Opinion
2000	1,871	1,235	66.0%	4,728	3,978	84.1%	1,582	1,211	76.5%	3,758	3,313	88.2%
1999	1,815	1,094	60.3%	4,479	3,770	84.2%	1,608	1,219	75.8%	3,594	3,102	86.3%
1998	1,856	1,078	58.1%	4,337	3,627	83.6%	1,576	1,140	72.3%	2,828	2,304	81.5%
1997	1,832	1,008	55.0%	4,841	3,969	82.0%	1,379	1,019	73.9%	3,294	2,843	86.3%
1996	2,101	1,293	61.5%	4,415	3,534	80.0%	1,837	1,365	74.3%	3,045	2,529	83.1%
1995	2,105	1,330	63.1%	4,410	3,480	78.9%	1,851	1,333	72.0%	3,255	2,757	84.7%
1994	2,165	1,248	57.6%	4,654	3,755	80.6%	1,657	1,120	67.5%	2,779	2,289	82.3%
1993	2,061	1,181	57.3%	4,664	3,836	82.2%	1,552	998	64.3%	2,758	2,292	83.1%
1992	1,971	1,082	54.8%	4,061	3,222	79.3%	1,608	988	61.4%	2,393	1,812	75.7%
1991	1,904	1,048	55.0%	3,727	2,836	76.0%	1,678	1,085	64.6%	2,371	1,663	70.1%
1990	1,808	1,063	58.7%	2,984	2,104	70.5%	1,560	1,027	65.8%	2,062	1,408	68.2%

TABLE 4—Continued

	All Circuits		
Year	Number of Appeals Terminated on Merits	Number without Published Opinion	Percent without Published Opinion
2000	27,516	21,958	79.8%
1999	26,727	20,886	78.1%
1998	24,910	18,663	74.9%
1997	25,840	19,761	76.5%
1996	27,326	20,771	76.0%
1995	27,772	21,083	75.9%
1994	27,219	20,200	74.2%
1993	25,761	19,029	73.8%
1992	23,597	16,606	70.3%
1991	23,018	15,963	69.3%
1990	21,022	14,298	68.0%

cent of its cases, published a dissent in 8.3 percent of its written published opinions. (See table 5.)

A challenge to the system of selective publication recently has arisen as a result of advancing technology. Whereas unpublished dispositions previously have not been readily available to the public at large, online computer research services such as Westlaw and Lexis have begun to post online unpublished dispositions. Consequently, many of the advantages of the unpublished disposition have become questionable. For example, lawyers searching for relevant precedents online might find unpublished dispositions similar in fact or law to their own cases. Because the judges put far less effort into writing and editing their unpublished dispositions, their reasoning often is less tightly written, and phrases sometimes indicate broader statements about the law than the writing judge or other panel members would allow in a published, citable opinion. However, when attorneys locate unpublished dispositions online that seem to bolster arguments, there is a temptation to cite these unpublished dispositions to the court to say, "It is not precedentially binding, but this court confronted the issue and decided it this way." That danger, though, does not appear to have come to fruition.[44] As one judge said,

---

44. *But see* Mark D. Hinderks & Steve A. Leben, *Restoring the Common in the Law: A Proposal for the Elimination of Rules Prohibiting the Citation of Unpublished Decisions in Kansas and the Tenth Circuit*, 31 WASHBURN L.J. 155 (1992); Daniel N. Hoffman, *Nonpublication of Federal Appellate Court Opinions*, 6 JUST. SYS. J. 405, 414 (1981) (arguing that unpublished opinions are less available to less powerful and wealthy litigants).

TABLE 5. Percentage of Published Opinions with One or More Dissents

	D.C. Circuit			7th Circuit			9th Circuit		
Year	Number of Written Published Opinions	Number of Published Opinions with Dissent(s)	Percent of Published Opinions with Dissent(s)	Number of Written Published Opinions	Number of Published Opinions with Dissent(s)	Percent of Published Opinions with Dissent(s)	Number of Written Published Opinions	Number of Published Opinions with Dissent(s)	Percent of Published Opinions with Dissent(s)
2000	253	21	8.3%	695	52	7.5%	718	121	17.4%
1999	250	26	10.4%	642	46	7.2%	701	122	17.4%
1998	274	23	8.4%	716	29	4.1%	701	108	15.4%
1997	275	28	10.2%	754	38	5.0%	849	129	15.2%
1996	289	40	13.8%	765	36	4.7%	864	107	12.4%
1995	271	36	13.3%	791	46	5.8%	927	124	13.4%
1994	253	44	17.4%	954	72	7.5%	893	114	12.8%
1993	259	33	12.7%	787	56	7.1%	819	94	11.5%
1992	280	33	11.8%	848	49	5.8%	833	120	14.4%
1991	264	39	14.8%	719	55	7.6%	888	117	13.2%
1990	267	25	9.4%	723	51	7.1%	877	85	9.7%

Note: Year means the twelve-month period ending on September 30 of the listed year. The numbers of written published opinions derive from data in Tables S-3 to *Judicial Business of the United States Courts* (published by the Administrative Office of the United States Courts) for 1992–2000 and Tables S-3 to *Statistical Tables for the Federal Judiciary* (published by the Administrative Office of the United States Courts) for 1990 and 1991. These figures include both signed and unsigned written reasoned published opinions. These figures do not include unpublished opinions and orders or published opinions that the Administrative Office of the Courts considers to be "without comment"—that is, opinions that do not "expound the law as applied to the facts of the case and [that do not] detail the judicial reasons upon which the judgment is based." The number of published opinions with one or more dissents was ascertained by searching the Westlaw CTADC, CTA7, and CTA9 databases for: sy("dissent!" or "dissent!") & da(aft 9/30/_ and bef 9/30/_).

It has not changed the way we do [memorandum dispositions]. There is no sense having the practice if you are going to let people cite them to you and read them. If they get some help out of it, that is fine. But we don't want to get to the place where they cite them because then we have got to spend a lot of time in our writing of those that we don't want to spend. It is not efficient for us to do it. Once we have made the initial decision, it is not worthy of publication. I see the problem, but the noncitation rule stops it.

Thus, because attorneys have respected the court's internal formal rule regarding citation, at least one potential problem of the online publication of unpublished dispositions has not arisen. Other problems, though, may not be as simple to remedy. For example, one benefit of the unpublished disposition is that the case law is not cluttered by numerous recitations of simple cases that add little to the court's precedents. As online services become more and more the research tool of choice within the legal community, the presence of unpublished dispositions mixed in with published ones undermines the cleanliness of the case law. The online services have not yet met that potential problem by separating published and unpublished materials into distinct databases.

VI. Conclusion: The Organizational Role of the Court's Formal Features

The appellate courts' formal features help to maintain the balance between autonomy and interdependence by setting the boundaries of the acceptable decisions that judges can make. The formal features of the court have at least three significant organizational dimensions: (1) the application of the up-looking and intracircuit doctrine of stare decisis; (2) the down-looking standards of review; and (3) the application of procedural rules to resolve agenda-setting issues. In place of the coordination provided by a central office, which in typical multidivisional organizations would be responsible for creating rules that regulate the variation in the work of subdivisions, the appellate courts' formal dimensions are set externally by the Supreme Court and other governmental rule-making entities, as well as internally by other panels of the same court and, with respect to procedural rules, by agreement among judges.

The doctrines of stare decisis and the standards of review enforce these externally and internally created formal rules by requiring judges to follow particularized legal rules and precedents and by limiting the issues that appellate judges can address. The formal enforcement mechanisms of these doctrines, however, have been weakened by the increased caseload because, as a function of the number of cases decided, the Supreme Court and en banc court of appeals panels consider a only relatively small number of cases each year. Consequently, the judges on the courts of appeals reported that they are not seriously concerned about the possibility that they will be overturned if they do not strictly follow applicable precedent. Instead, judges follow legal precedents because they feel that it is their job to do so and that justice is best served when they do. This cultural enforcement of the doctrine of stare decisis, which is considered in detail in chapter 6, cannot take the place of the formal enforcement mechanisms. Because judges follow precedent based primarily on their personal beliefs in the importance of the rule of law and of the doctrine of stare decisis, judges have more autonomy than would be the case were the formal enforcement mechanisms more effective.

Furthermore, the effectiveness of the formal doctrines of stare decisis and the standards of review hinge in large part on each judge's ability to learn the law and facts necessary to independently review each case. Judges learn the applicable precedents and the facts relevant to a specific case from at least five sources: (1) their own legal and personal expertise; (2) other judges' legal and personal expertise; (3) the research, insight, and expertise of the law clerks and central staff; (4) the input of the parties' lawyers through briefs and during oral argument; and (5) the record of the lower court. Changes in the ways or frequency that judges are able to utilize each of these methods can reduce a judge's autonomy by reducing the judge's independent knowledge of a case.

For example, because judges learn the law and facts from multiple sources, the limitation or reduction of one of these sources (such as the reduction of oral argument or limitation on the briefs) can be overcome by the reliance on other sources (such as personal expertise or law clerks and bench memoranda). All of these sources, though, are not equally effective. The parties' briefs, while sometimes containing thorough and well-cited summaries of the applicable law and facts, are intended to advocate for one party's position and, therefore, cannot be relied on to present the law and facts neutrally. Similarly, although the oral argument provides the judge an opportunity to ask the lawyers specific and probing questions that efficiently draw out legal or factual details that may not have been included in briefs or in the excepts of record, the lawyers' presentation of that information again generally is intended to persuade the judge rather than to neutrally present information. Conversely, law clerks' bench memoranda generally are intended to present the law and facts in a more neutral fashion (although, as I discuss in chapter 4, law clerks too can take argumentative positions), but clerks generally are less familiar with the record and the applicable precedents than the lawyers arguing the case. Accordingly, although a law clerk's bench memorandum can provide much of the information a judge requires to decide a case, the reduction of opportunities for the judge to learn from the lawyers (such as the reduction of oral argument or limitations on the briefs) takes from the judges a potentially valuable source of information.

Similarly, a judge who has personal experience in a particular factual matter or has legal expertise in a specific area is more likely to formulate a definitive conclusion to a particular case and thus is potentially less likely to be swayed by the other actors in the judicial process. Although judges can rely on their legal and personal expertise to help them form judgments about how a case should be resolved, such expertise cannot take the place of thorough case-specific legal and factual research, which judges rarely perform themselves. Without such research and without the assistance of lawyers' briefs and arguments, clerks' bench memoranda, or information from other chambers, judges could not be certain that their knowledge of the law and facts is complete.

The relative availability of methods for learning of the applicable legal precedents and relevant facts thus is a critical organizational dimension of the appellate courts. Courts vary in the sources of legal and factual information made available to the judges, and this variation can affect the balance between autonomy and interdependence. Changes in the availability of these sources, though, also can remedy an imbalance that results from other, potentially problematic changes. For example, because of the increasing number of cases, judges have less time to review the full record on appeal and rely more on the lawyers to provide excerpts of the factual record that contain all materials relevant to a case. As a result, judges may have to rely on other judges to find important facts in the record because only one of the judges on a panel (at most) generally reviews the full record. The adoption of a California-type rule, which provides that judges will consider only documents that lawyers submit in the excerpts of record, can force lawyers to submit more thorough and manageable excerpts of record and can equalize the access to the relevant record among the judges on a panel. Accordingly, by enabling judges to more easily learn all of the relevant facts through their own chambers' research, such a rule would increase judges' autonomy and decrease dependence on other chambers. Although adopting such a rule may increase autonomy, judges expressed concern that such a rule would result in a decline in the court's ability to resolve some cases justly, and such a change thus would put procedure ahead of substantive justice.

Finally, a court's procedural and agenda-setting rules also serve to limit judges' autonomy by forcing them to accommodate their decision-making processes to a formally dictated process. For example, the agenda-setting rules regarding when cases will be screened can determine the number and types of cases a judge must decide. Because all of the appellate courts generally assign cases to panels without regard to subject matter, judges are less able to exercise undue influence on the development of precedent on any particular topic. In some courts, though, the opinion-writing assignment also has a greater element of randomness (because writing responsibility is assigned before a detailed review of the cases is undertaken). A collateral benefit of this relatively random assignment is to protect the court from having any one judge become too influential in an area of law by retaining writing responsibility in a particular type of case. Randomness in assigning opinion-drafting responsibility therefore can shift the balance from autonomy to interdependence.

Similarly, procedural rules set the agenda for how and when judges must prepare for oral argument, how often judges hear cases orally, which judge will write the court's decision, how long judges have to prepare to meet with their brethren to issue their preliminary vote as to how a case should be resolved, and whether that decision will be a published opinion (and thus whether a case will result in a new legally binding precedent). By determining which judges decide which cases, the legal and factual issues that a judge has the autonomy to decide, and the process that judges must follow in deciding cases, the formal aspects of the court serve as the fulcrum on which the judges' autonomy and their interdependence are balanced.

CHAPTER 4

The Internal Structure of the Appellate Judicial Chambers and the Role of the Law Clerk

The court's organizational structure plays a major role in maintaining the balance between each judge's autonomy and his dependence on other organizational actors. Structure affects the process by which judges work toward resolving cases and affects both the methods and frequency of interchamber communication. However, whereas the court's formal features have a relatively direct impact, directly limiting judicial autonomy and requiring a degree of interchange among the chambers, the court's structure has a more subtle effect. Structure does not impose formally determined requirements on the judges, but rather acts on the judicial process by influencing the court's actors to act and interact in particular ways. For instance, how the court is structured influences the frequency and formality of judges' interchanges with one another, causes judges to favor certain forms of communication, and affects how judges prepare to decide cases. The structural context of the appellate judicial process, therefore, may have a strong yet indirect effect on the way that the court functions.

It should not be surprising that the court's structure strongly affects a judge's behavior. Organizational theorists long have understood that an organization's formal and informal structures can significantly influence the behavior of the individuals within the organization. In fact, Max Weber's early conceptualization of the importance of the bureaucratic form to modern organizational success was itself a realization that organizational structure has a significant bearing on the behavior of the organization and of the individuals within the organization.[1]

---

1. *See generally* Max Weber, *Bureaucracy* in Max Weber, Economy and Society 956 (1978).

I. The Concept of Organizational Structure in Organizational Theory

To the organizational analyst, the concept of *structure* has two different although related meanings. First, *organizational structure* "refers to the design of the organization and the lines of authority that link the divisions of the organization and the divisions with the central office."[2] That definition highlights the formal linkages between organizational subunits, focusing on the formal bureaucratic role of individuals in the organization rather than on their individual characteristics. This definition concentrates on the organization's formal social structure in the sense that a "formal social structure is one in which the social positions and the relationships among them have been explicitly specified and are defined independently of the personal characteristics of the participants occupying these positions."[3] Accordingly, the first meaning of *structure* adheres to the commonly understood sense in which an organization can be charted.

A second meaning of *organizational structure* focuses on the individual actors' informal relationships with other individuals within the organization.[4] In that sense, an organization's structure consists of the "networks of networks" within the organization.[5] That second meaning concentrates on the organization's informal social structure, in which individuals' roles and relationships are functions "of their personal characteristics and the interactions that occur among them."[6]

Because of the court's peculiar multidivisional nature, a complete understanding of the court's organizational structure requires an investigation of both the internal structure of the individual judges' chambers and the more general structure of the court as a whole, including the interaction among the judicial chambers. In a sense, the microprocesses of judges working with their staffs to decide cases are the locus of autonomy, whereas the interaction among the judicial chambers is the locus of interdependence. Both of those processes are affected to some degree by the court's formal and informal structure. This chapter considers the relevance of the internal structure of the individual appellate judge's chambers and emphasizes the role of the law clerk within the judicial process. Chapter 5 considers the relevance of the court's structure in interchamber communication.

----

2. Neil Fligstein, The Transformation of Corporate Control 16 (1990).

3. W. Richard Scott, Organizations: Rational, Natural, and Open Systems 17 (2d ed. 1987) (emphasis omitted).

4. Barry Wellman & S. D. Berkowitz, *Introduction: Studying Social Structures* in Social Structures: A Network Approach 1, 2–4 (B. Wellman & S. D. Berkowitz eds., 1988).

5. *Id.*

6. Scott, 1987, *supra* note 3, at 17.

II. Law Clerks

Individual judicial chambers consist of loosely organized relationships between judges and their staff and among the members of the staff. Judicial chambers are small suborganizations consisting of a single judge, one or two secretaries, two to four law clerks, and, occasionally, one or more law students serving as interns. Because there is great variation in the ways that judges utilize and interact with their staffs, the nature of the relationships between judges and their staff can reveal much about a judge's decision-making process. Chief among those relationships is that between judges and their law clerks.

Who Are the Law Clerks?

It is widely accepted that the first American judge to use law clerks was Justice Horace Gray.[7] In 1875, as a justice on the Massachusetts Supreme Judicial Court, Justice Gray began the practice of employing at his own expense a recent graduate of the Harvard Law School each year referred to him by his half brother, the esteemed Professor John Chipman Gray. When Justice Gray was appointed to the Supreme Court in 1883, he brought with him a young law clerk and continued the practice of hiring a new law clerk each year.

In 1885 the institution of the law clerk was endorsed in the Attorney General's Annual Report: "it would greatly facilitate the business of the Supreme Court if each justice was provided by law with a secretary and law clerk. ... The labor of the Judges of the Court in investigating questions and preparing their opinions is immense, and while the heads of Departments and Senators have this assistance, I do not think there is any good reason that the judges of this Court should not also have it."[8] Congress acted on this recommendation the next year, authorizing one clerk for each justice,[9] and by 1888 all nine justices

---

7. See JOHN OAKLEY & ROBERT THOMPSON, LAW CLERKS AND THE JUDICIAL PROCESS: PERCEPTIONS OF THE QUALITIES AND FUNCTIONS OF LAW CLERKS IN AMERICAN COURTS 10 (1980) ("Although proof of paternity is rarely conclusive, the available evidence seems indisputably to bestow the mantle upon Horace Gray of Massachusetts as the first American judge to make use of law clerks"); *see also Fredonia Broadcasting Corp., Inc. v. RCA Corp.*, 569 F.2d 251, 255 (5th Cir. 1978) ("Historically, the practice of employing federal judicial law clerks began in 1882 when Justice Horace Gray was appointed to the Supreme Court"); Nadine J. Wichern, *A Court of Clerks, Not of Men: Serving Justice in the Media Age*, 49 DEPAUL L. REV. 621, 624 (1999); ROBERT A. CARP & RONALD STIDHAM, JUDICIAL PROCESS IN AMERICA 75 (1990); Paul Baier, *The Law Clerks: Profile of an Institution*, 26 VAND. L. REV. 1125, 1129–30 (1973); Chester Newland, *Personal Assistants to Supreme Court Justices: The Law Clerks*, 40 OR. L. REV. 299, 300–301, 305–6 (1961).

8. Attorney General's Annual Report, 1885, quoted in DANIEL MEADOR, APPELLATE COURTS: STAFF AND PROCESS IN THE CRISIS OF VOLUME: AN APPELLATE JUSTICE PROJECT OF THE NATIONAL CENTER FOR STATE COURTS 15–16 (1974).

9. Meador, *supra* note 8, at 16; Newland, *supra* note 7, at 301.

employed a clerk.[10] However, most of the justices retained a single clerk for as long as the clerk was willing to remain. Justice Gray's model of annually replacing his clerk lived on, though, because his successor, Justice Oliver Wendell Holmes, Jr., continued the tradition of taking graduates from the Harvard Law School for one-year stints.[11] Over the next twenty years, it became the custom on the Supreme Court to employ clerks for one-year terms, in the style of Justice Gray.[12] Congress authorized law clerks for the U.S. circuit judges in 1930, and the institution subsequently has grown steadily.[13] Judges on the courts of appeals currently are authorized to have three or more clerks. Some judges hire just two clerks, and others choose to hire a fourth clerk instead of a second secretary. The chief judge of each court is authorized to hire an additional law clerk.

Law clerks' roles in the judicial chambers vary widely. Law clerks are responsible only to their judge, and judges choose to use the services of their clerks in widely diverse ways. Law clerks often assist the judge in preparing to decide cases by providing research assistance and serving as a sounding board. In many chambers, law clerks draft judicial opinions. Because law clerks play an integral and varied role in court organization, the scope of their duties will be discussed throughout this book.

Law clerks are selected by the judges for whom they work. Clerks do not have to undergo Senate scrutiny, as judges do. Instead, judges have the discretion to hire whomever they wish. Most judges hire clerks for one-year terms, although some judges hire clerks for longer periods, and still other judges have a "permanent" clerk who remains with the judge for an undefined period. Judges seek different qualities in their clerks and therefore apply diverse criteria in their hiring. Some criteria, though, are common to most judges.

First, judges generally prefer law clerks who have graduated from the most prestigious law schools. All judges find themselves with many more applicants than they have positions. Although judges generally hire three law clerks, some judges receive hundreds of applications. The judges readily admit that these applicants are generally excellent because, as one judge said, "The law schools do a good job of letting the students know that the clerkships are very competitive."

Although judges have different ideas of what they seek in a clerk, they employ very similar criteria to sift through the applications. Most judges seek clerks with excellent law school grades. Most seek some indication that the stu-

---

10. Oakley & Thompson, *supra* note 7, at 16.

11. *Id.*

12. *Id.*

13. 46 Stat. 774 (1930).

dent has some diversity of legal experience, which generally translates to a strong preference for students who have served on the school's law review. Some judges seek a certain jurisprudential or political bent, preferring students who either demonstrate political leanings similar to or different from those of the judges. One judge spelled out his process, which was fairly typical:

> I wish I could tell you that it is a very orderly, scientific process. There is a rough screening that is done by looking at their academic achievements— grades and writing capacity, their ability to juggle several things in law school. Somebody who has just got good grades would be more likely to be passed over for someone who has good grades and has done law review, and has . . . done writing assignments of some kind.

There is some variation among judges about the importance of law review. Some judges view it as absolutely necessary because it helps to develop writing and research skills. Others claim that although law review really has little effect on how well the student will do as a law clerk, it does serve as an indicator of commitment and of excellence, and therefore as a good screening criterion in a judge's first cut. One law clerk suggested that law review participation demonstrates to the judge that applicants are willing to do huge amounts of work for nothing more than the promise that it will ultimately help them later.

One judge stated that he requires his law clerks to have some post–law school experience:

> I only hire clerks that have at least one year of legal experience after law school. I do that [because I] value experience and maturity beyond law school. . . . That experience is valuable to them and to me. The experience that they gain—they have been out in the real world. They have seen real clients. They have had the interaction in an office, either that or another clerkship. . . . They have seen reality. It is not all academic. . . . When you go out into the real world, you find that formula, the way it ought to be, is not the way it is. So then once you come in with that sort of leveling process, then one can be a little more mature. It does not always work.

Some judges ask their current clerks to sift through the applications to find applicants with backgrounds similar to those of the current clerks. One clerk reported receiving instructions to "find a duplicate" of himself. The judges generally seek the same things in their clerks year after year, and using the clerks in the screening process is one way of accomplishing that practice.

Once the first cut is made, however, the process becomes more difficult and less predictable. The judges often rely on connections to law professors or former clerks for guidance in the form of strong references:

[I]t has a lot to do with the enthusiasm and almost the unique approach that one of their professors might take about them. I recall that one clerk that I had just a few years ago, one of the best clerks I ever had, I got a call from a professor I know at [a non–Ivy League law school, who] said, "I want to recommend you the best student I have had in twenty years."

Networking is among the most common techniques used. Judges who have academic backgrounds often have connections with former colleagues and take their recommendations very seriously:

I was a teacher for [many] years, so I have good friends in the law school, and some of them know what kind of person would be most compatible with my views and the way I write and think. So those people, if they have good students, will call me, and I rely most heavily on recommendations of people I trust on the faculty.

One law clerk explained that at many schools, including the one he attended, it is well known which judges use which professors to assist with the law clerk hunt. This clerk explained that at the beginning of the first year of law school, some students will immediately seek to form a relationship with certain professors known to have relationships with particular judges. Another law clerk described the experience of a friend who could not find a job after law school. A professor took an interest in him and telephoned a judge and arranged for the student to serve as the judge's law clerk.

Judges almost always interview candidates before hiring them. Judges ordinarily limit the number of students they interview, but the interview in many cases is the most important step in the process. Many judges indicated that they seek candidates who will get along with the judge and with the other clerks. One judge explained: "I interview no more than ten people out of the batch, and that is just to see whether there is someone I would like to spend a lot of time with." Another judge indicated that the most serious problems he had with his clerks were when his clerks did not get along well with one another. The interview process is, in part, an effort to avoid that problem.

Some judges use other, less common methods for their clerk selection. For example, one judge delegated his selection process to a committee of law professors with whom he had a long-standing relationship. The judge seemed quite satisfied with this method.

The Role of the Law Clerks

Law clerks aid judges in preparing to make decisions in four important ways: (1) researching the legal issues in a case and writing bench memoranda to summarize their findings; (2) preparing case materials into a bench book; (3) serving as a sounding board for a judge's thoughts and arguments; and (4) assisting judges in writing opinions.

Bench Memoranda

Most judges in most circuits have clerks assist in preparing for oral argument and conference by writing detailed memoranda discussing the facts, issues, and legal authorities relevant to each case. These bench memoranda resemble briefs in their structure and comprehensiveness, but unlike briefs, these memoranda are not meant to advocate for a particular party. As one judge explained,

> [The bench memorandum] must contain everything that is relevant to the decision making on both sides of every issue. But also, I want them to recommend a result to give the bench memo some focus. Other than that, I want it as short as they can make it. When they don't make them very short, frequently they are ten to twenty pages in a difficult case, more than that, and I think that is far too long. It is one of the hardest things to get law clerks to do. But, on the other hand, it must include everything that is relevant to all the arguments that are made and why they reject those that they reject. They are to include everything that is in the briefs submitted by the parties and do independent research because they are going to have to come up with an ultimate recommendation, and the parties do not think of everything.

Several judges likened the bench memorandum to a road map of the case. One judge, for example, stated, "The clerks do bench memos for me on [complex cases], and they operate as a kind of road map into the case. What they are supposed to accomplish in that bench memo is to enable me to speed through the decisions, the pertinent possible records, and the briefs." Similarly, another judge said,

> I start off each case with their writing a bench memo, and I like to feel that the bench memo is a road map for me. It tells me everyplace they have been and where I need to go. And it tells me the places I can skip because they are not important. Lawyers . . . tend to be verbose and write much more and put much more in the record than is necessary to make out their case. The clerk is supposed just to go over all that ground and then hopefully it spares me the trouble.

The bench memorandum helps the judge to understand and recall what is involved in each case. Because the judges see so many cases, it becomes difficult for them to recall all the details of any given case. One judge explained,

> My main interest in getting a memo prepared is [that] the volume of cases
> is such at this point that it is hard for me to remember [each individual
> case], spontaneously remember it, the facts and issues, whatnot. It helps
> me a lot if I can have just a little summary that gets my mind on track. . . .
> I did not used to use memos, but I started using them five or six years ago
> just for that reason.

Some judges find bench memoranda helpful in identifying issues that need
to be discussed and therefore serve as a starting point for judge-clerk discussion:

> I assign one of my clerks [to the case]. I have him read all the cases, all the
> briefs, and do backup research. I want to know the cases that the parties are
> relying on, the contrasted issues, and what cases are really pivotal or dispositive, and then I have them go to the record. . . . I have them look elsewhere to find cases and do other research. I then have them prepare a relatively short bench memo. It is supposed to be short—sometimes it is long.
> And sometimes it is easier to be long than short, but I try to get them then
> to cite what the main issues are and where the case law is going and essentially give me a recommendation. Then, after I have read the briefs, my
> clerk and I will . . . have an intense—probably three-hour—discussion on
> [the case].

Judges commonly use bench memoranda as springboards for conversation. As
one judge put it, "The law clerk will generally put a position in the bench
memo, and then the exchange would be oral from that."

Another purpose of the bench memorandum is to organize the law clerk's
research and present it to the judge in a meaningful way. Some judges reported,
therefore, that the bench memorandum helps to ensure that they have not
missed any important cases as a result of the parties' or the judges' own oversight:

> I always like to have a bench memo, whether I think the questions and
> answers are clear or not, because I may think they are clear, but I may have
> overlooked some authority that causes me to be in error, and I want my law
> clerk to find it before I commit myself. . . . One thing about being an experienced senior lawyer is often you know what the law was ten years ago, and
> you are not sensitive to some change that has occurred. So I will get a pretty
> thorough, independent analysis and critique of my own tentative impressions in a case where I am the writing judge from my own law clerk.

Similarly, another judge said,

> I tell my law clerks basically that the one thing they should be able to do just coming out of law school is research. They may not have any judgment, but they ought to be able to write, and they ought to be able to do research. So I expect them to find everything. I don't want any judge to ever come up and say, "That is very interesting, but what about this case" that they haven't found. Their job is to do that research. That is their main job.

While many judges use the bench memorandum as a tool, others do not have their clerks draft bench memoranda. For example, some judges explained that, although potentially helpful, bench memoranda require more of the clerks' time than such memoranda are worth to the judge. Because some judges place the bulk of their energy into preparing opinions and less energy into preparing for oral argument and conference, some judges prefer to use their clerks' energies in the same fashion. One judge reported,

> I used to utilize a bench memo when I first started, . . . and the clerks have a tendency to spend so much time preparing bench memos that it is counterproductive. I would rather have them interacting with opinions than I would [have them] preparing [a bench memo], which is really nothing more than a summary of the arguments in the case. And since I read the briefs, . . . I no longer have bench memos.

Some judges believe that careful reading of briefs and oral reports can take the place of bench memoranda. For those judges, the bench memorandum has no purpose. As one clerk explained,

> Because he reads the briefs so many times, we don't have to do . . . bench memos. . . . Because he says it is better for us to spend our time working on the opinion, doing research as necessary instead of giving him these memos. . . So that means . . . his initial preparation is done entirely by him. We do not have any input, we do not give him a recommendation on how we should handle the case, we don't give him a memo on authorities. He chooses his own questions to ask at oral argument. We do not supply him with anything. We read the briefs so that we know what is going on at oral argument. But we do not communicate . . . really about them before oral argument. He might make a passing comment here or there about, "What did you think about this argument?" But generally, we do not really talk about it before oral argument.

According to another judge,

There is already too much paper around here. We sit down and discuss the case and try to figure out how it ought to be decided and why. And sometimes it is clear from that discussion that more investigation on a particular subject is required, especially when it is a case under state law where I may not know very much about the law. [Under those circumstances], you have to do a little more investigation so I may send them off on some research assignments, or sometimes I will send them off to try to find something in the record, and they will bring that back over the course of the week before argument.

That judge explained that he expected clerks to report orally on research assignments.

Some judges also perceive that using clerks to draft long, detailed bench memoranda leads to longer and less well written opinions and dispositions. One judge explained,

[The use of bench memoranda] leads to overwriting of dispositions and opinions. People are sorely tempted to take a bench memo and turn it into a disposition. That is [why] we get long, horrendous dispositions. You can tell a bench memo—if it looks like it is not written by a circuit judge but by a first-year lawyer.

In some cases in some circuits, the judges pool their clerk resources and share bench memoranda in a manner reminiscent of the pooling of petitions for certiorari in the U.S. Supreme Court.[14] All but one of the judges on the Ninth Circuit participate in a bench memoranda pool on every case on every oral argument calendar. In such a pooling system, the judges on a panel split the responsibility to produce a bench memorandum in each case among their three chambers. Then, rather than each chambers preparing to hear the case independently, one chambers produces a bench memorandum and sends it to the other chambers. Similarly, the judges on the D.C. Circuit share the preparation responsibility in cases that the staff attorneys dub "complex cases" so that the clerks from each of the three chambers have responsibility for one-third of the issues presented to the court.

The judges use the shared bench memorandum system in an effort to increase each judge's efficiency, and many judges reported that the system accomplished just that. By dividing the work of the bench memorandum among the chambers, the judges and the law clerks avoid duplicating the basic work of reviewing the record and the facts, checking the parties' research, and

---

14. This chapter discusses how the pooling process affects the way that judges work within their chambers. Chapter 5 considers the impact of the pooling process on the interaction among chambers.

providing an initial analysis of the case. Several judges explained that by requiring clerks to write one-third as many bench memoranda, the pooling process frees the clerks to work on other important aspects of the judicial process, such as drafting opinions.

The perception that the shared bench memorandum system saves judges and their clerks time critical to the accomplishment of their purpose has spawned a desire on the part of at least one D.C. Circuit judge to utilize a pooling system on more than merely the complex cases. He stated,

> [If I could change something in the way we use clerks], I would do in every case what we do only in our blockbuster cases—the cases that are complex cases. In complex cases the chambers pool their resources. So we will get three clerks, one from each chamber, working together on the bench memo. They will divide up the issues evenly among the three chambers. [Without pooling], there is a lot of duplication, as you can see, because the two colleagues that sit with me will have the clerks doing the same thing [I have my clerks doing]. I think there is . . . much to be gained from the three clerks' exchange that would result [from increased pooling]. It does happen in our complex cases.

Nevertheless, some judges on the Ninth Circuit expressed the view that sharing bench memoranda creates more work for them and for their clerks. Prior to the pooling process, many judges used their own or their clerk's judgment to determine whether a bench memorandum was called for in a particular case, and clerks only wrote memoranda in cases that called for it. One cost of pooling, however, is that judges lose control over the use of their clerks. As the Ninth Circuit's lone dissenter from the pooling process explained,

> Participating in bench memo [sharing] shackles us to other chambers to set some external deadlines that I don't like to follow. It causes a loss of control over my staff over a substantial portion of their time. This happens many months out of the year. It is not like it is just there and then it is gone. It is kind of a constant call on their time, with which I have no control. I don't like having anything sent out of my chambers that I don't personally review. I don't think I am capable of reviewing the bench memos and approving them. I don't want to take on that burden.

Moreover, as one judge explained, each memorandum now requires more work because it must represent the chambers:

> The idea was efficiency, and, of course, when we first do our things inside chambers, they were just what the judge wanted. When we started doing them for other chambers, they got much longer, much more complex.

> There was a sort of a competition. You had to have a very excellent memorandum go out because it is representing the chambers, and so, instead of having three or four pages of analysis, we would get twenty or twenty-five pages that looked very much like the first draft of an opinion. So, initially, perhaps there was some idea that it would save time. In fact, it has not, because so much more time is put in on bench memoranda than . . . in those early days.

In fact, the Ninth Circuit's sole holdout from the pooling process cited the increased amount of work as one of his reasons for not participating in the process.

Overall, the judges who participate in the shared bench memorandum process feel that the system increases efficiency as long as most of the judges on the circuit participate. As one Ninth Circuit judge said, "I think [the sharing of bench memoranda] basically works, and I think the reason that it works is because the vast majority of the judges do it." One serious problem with the shared bench memorandum system, though, is that although all of the judges on a court may participate in the pooling process, the judges vary substantially in how they view the purpose of the bench memo. Consequently, the nature of the bench memoranda produced by the chambers varies, and that variation can make a bench memorandum that is extremely useful to one judge virtually without utility to another judge. That variation was a common complaint about the efficacy of the pooling system. As one judge explained,

> I think that [the pooling system] is fine so long as some discipline is exerted over the clerks so they don't spend too much time on the case undirected by a judge. I think that the main problem with the bench memo process is that [its] purpose . . . is kind of inconsistent. On the one hand, the purpose of it is to have the law clerks provide guidance to the judges on what the case is about, to help them understand what it is they need to decide and what the controlling law is. On the other hand, the law clerks really . . . should [not] be working on spinning their wheels on things that the judges don't feel are important. Yet if the judges try to give some guidance writing their bench memos, then the purpose of the bench memo to help the judge is lost. . . . The function is a little ambiguous, and I think that the way that different chambers treat the bench memos varies from chambers to chambers as to the role of the judge.

Accordingly, the efficiency of the pooling system may be somewhat undermined by the variation among judges' work habits. At one extreme, judges who emphasize the bench memorandum as a tool for preparation may produce long and detailed memoranda that may overwhelm the resources of judges who are not accustomed to such detailed accounts. One judge, for example, explained that if a bench memorandum is too long, he cannot effectively use it, and he will need his law clerks to produce a shorter version for him, editing out information that the clerk considers of less relevance: "[The law clerks] look over the bench memorandum. It comes in, and they have several instructions. One is if the bench memorandum is long, I will not review it. They will have to get a bench memorandum that fits our standards, and so they will do so." Conversely, bench memoranda produced by clerks whose judges do not emphasize memoranda may be brief and may have little utility to judges who require complete and detailed analyses. As one judge said, a bench memo "may be worthless. It will be used by me for whatever it is worth, and I have sort of an idea that a bench memo is a tool to make a repository, sort of an audit, of the factual [and] legal aspects of the case." A more extreme version of that problem can occur when judges place so little importance on bench memoranda that they delegate responsibility to law students who are serving as temporary externs. Although some judges reported having had excellent work from student externs, many judges expressed frustration at colleagues who use externs to produce bench memoranda because the work was not of as high quality as that produced by law clerks and was supervised by law clerks rather than judges. According to one judge,

> I will tell you what I don't like is bench memos from externs. I find those are universally unreliable, and when I see a bench memo from an extern I tend to say, "Uh-oh"—you know, "battle stations." I have gotten a lot of stuff—and this is not to put law students down—but somebody halfway through his or her second year just is not up to speed. I am sure there are exceptions, but most of the extern bench memos I get are not good. And I don't trust those or rely on them at all. It is like we start all over again.

The variation in the bench memoranda, therefore, limits the amount that sharing can increase efficiency.

Efficiency, though, is not the sole potential benefit of the shared bench memorandum system. Shared memoranda provide judges with an additional viewpoint. As one judge explained,

> I do send the bench memo out to the other judges without any comments by myself, figuring they are entitled to a fresh look at the work of the law clerk. If I have time at the conference, [I will] go ahead and indicate what my feelings are with reference to the bench memo and any conclusions which might arise.

By having a memorandum on a case prepared by a law clerk from another chambers, the judge has access to an additional voice that is not advocating for any party. In the Ninth Circuit, several judges expressed the view that the law clerk did not work for a single judge but worked for the panel; accordingly, they stated, the work of the law clerk should be neutral and should provide the other judges an entirely neutral perspective into the case. The following interchange is illustrative:

> Q: What do you think of that process [of sharing bench memos]?
> A: I like it. I really like it. I know that some chambers do not exchange bench memos. And chambers differ. My view is—and I know this is different from some other judges—is that the product, the bench memo, is, because we submit it under the clerk's name, [it] is the product of a law clerk to the panel. I may, in fact, disagree with what the bench memo says, so I encourage independent thinking on that. I like it, and I think it is nice to have two points of view. When another chambers prepares the bench memo, we have our comment memos internally. I think that is helpful because there are different perspectives on things.

A related benefit of the shared bench memorandum system is that the judges have an opportunity to communicate with one another prior to the oral argument. That communicative aspect of the pooling system will be discussed in chapter 6.

Because judges in a shared bench memorandum process must focus on the bench memorandum long in advance of oral argument, some judges focus their preparation early in the process. As one judge explained,

> I think . . . you will find two, generally speaking, different approaches to the decisional process. One of which is a sort of front-loading—the judge gets ahold of the case very early and sort of guides it from then on within his own office. The other one is a back-loading business in which the judge has a pattern in which the case is prepared and he is prepared for the decision, but his own participation comes very late in the process.

Where judges front-load, they emphasize the preparation of the bench memorandum as critical to their thinking processes. Front-loaders are characterized by high involvement in the bench memorandum preparation and generally require their law clerks to prepare at least some independent memoranda in those cases for which they do not have writing responsibility. Front-loaders, therefore, enter the oral argument at the height of their preparation and rarely require much research or time to prepare opinions after the argument. For example, one judge characterized the bench memorandum as the "critical document" for the decisional process because, he explained, he starts his preparation with the bench memorandum and looks to it throughout his decision-making process. During his preparation, he goes through the bench memorandum and makes corrections, which sharpen his own thinking about the case. The bench memorandum also is the last document he looks at prior to oral argument and conference. Finally, he reported, his opinions often reflect the structure and reasoning of the bench memo. In fact, he stated that his decisional process "ends up with the bench memo being the basic document."

Some of the judges who characterized themselves as front-loaders indicated that they ordinarily prepare a preliminary opinion or memorandum disposition prior to the oral argument and, after conference, often make only small changes to accommodate other judges' requirements. Because judges almost always know in advance for which cases they will write dispositions, front-loaders produce comprehensive draft dispositions early in the process and can avoid the overlap between two calendars that can confront back-loaders. Front-loaders thus can quickly produce opinions and circumvent a major cause of delay.

Back-loaders, conversely, do not characteristically have heavy involvement in the bench memorandum preparation process but rather rely on the completed bench memorandum for preparation for oral argument. Such judges become significantly involved in cases only while preparing the dispositions after argument. For example, one back-loading judge reported that he does not even read the briefs or begin to consider the case until just before the oral argument. Accordingly, he reported, he has not yet read the briefs during the time his clerks write and send out the bench memoranda. As a result, he ultimately may disagree with the clerks' interpretation of the case, although this possibility does not concern him.

In circuits that do not use the shared bench memoranda system, judges must prepare to decide every case without knowing in advance whether they will be responsible for preparing a disposition in any particular case. Consequently, judges are restricted in how they prepare to decide cases because they must, internally, prepare each case on the calendar so that they may participate in oral argument and conference. Only once they are assigned a particular case can they begin to focus their full attention on that case. As one D.C. Circuit judge explained, judges must have a relatively high level of preparation for each case prior to argument rather than focusing their chambers' attention on just one-third of the calendared cases. That process makes it virtually impossible to be a front-loader because judges cannot spend the extra time on the cases for which they have disposition-preparation responsibility until after conference. As one front-loader on the Ninth Circuit explained, not pooling bench memoranda would require him to change the way that he and his clerks perform their work and would lead to greater delay and more overlap between calendars.

However, the benefits of the shared bench memorandum system come with an expensive price tag. First and foremost, the shared bench memorandum system may cause judges to excessively delegate significant aspects of their decision-making responsibility to other judicial chambers. In terms of the multidivisional model of the court, excessive delegation of preparation constitutes a weakening of a judge's autonomy and an increase in judicial interdependence.

The one judge on the Ninth Circuit who does not participate in the bench memorandum sharing process explained the serious delegation problem:

> Probably most of all, I don't [participate in the bench memorandum sharing process] because I think it's a cheat. You talk about the redundancy of having three sets of clerks look at it, but the redundancy is part of the process of appeal. Otherwise, we would only have one judge. . . . They have three judges, three offices, with three sets of staff and three chambers, three sets of computers with three sets of files, three sets of facilities in all respects, because they . . . want us to do the work three times. If they would only want us to do the work once, we would have appeals with only one judge. I think having a process where essentially the heavy load of the work is done by one law clerk in one chambers is a shortcut of the process. It is essentially a cheat of the system, abrogation of our responsibility to do independent work.
>
> And all the reasons people have for sharing bench memos, I think are exactly the reasons we ought not to do them. It is a duplication of work. It's not, in my judgment, a sin to duplicate work: it's a required virtue. I've told my colleagues. This is not a secret.

Many judges who participate in the pooling process do so with some hesitation. Others expressed a skepticism about accepting information from bench memoranda without some check internal to the chambers. For example, one judge reported that he expects shared bench memoranda to contain errors but that the process of locating and correcting errors serves to sharpen his own analysis of the case:

> Do I accept everything that is in somebody else's bench memo at face value? Not really. But it is a good starting place. I read everything, including bench memos from my own chambers, with a very open mind and an eye toward something that may have been missed. And the first time I read a bench memo from anybody, . . . I am sort of tracking if I think it is right. If it is right, then I would probably rely on it a lot in terms of having to go back to it . . . to refresh my recollection and things like that. If I think it is off base, we will either go back and rewrite them in my chambers or I will send a memo out to another chamber saying, "Geez, you know, I think there is another take on this case you might have missed." So that I rely on bench memos a lot to sort of get the wheels and the gears going. Sometimes

bench memos are—and not very often—pretty good. But sometimes they are, what a friend of mine . . . calls "fruitful error." I mean, just because they are wrong does not mean they are no good. Sometimes they are wrong, but by thinking through why they are wrong, you realize what is right. So at the very least they are fruitful error.

The recognition that some bench memoranda may mischaracterize or miss entirely important legal or factual aspects of a case leads to a serious potential problem when judges overrely on an erroneous or incomplete analysis. That problem is exemplified by one judge's admission that if a case "is not assigned to me [for bench memo responsibility], I am likely to do a more superficial job with the excerpts." That judge's frank statement demonstrates the potential for overreliance inherent in the shared bench memorandum process.

The use of shared bench memoranda may have an unexpected collateral effect. Because it allows judges to know in advance that they likely will have primary responsibility for particular cases, it allows them to focus their attention on those cases. Consequently, judges may not focus sufficient attention on the cases for which other judges are responsible. That would suggest that courts that use a pooling process would have more unanimity among the judges. Although the variation among the circuits is small, that hypothesis does not appear to be borne out, at least regarding the Ninth Circuit, which generally uses a pooling process; the D.C. Circuit, which uses a pooling process in only a small number of complex cases; and the Seventh Circuit, which does not use a pooling process. For example, in the twelve months ending September 30, 2000, the Ninth Circuit had dissents in 2.6 percent of its terminations on the merits, whereas the D.C. Circuit and the Seventh Circuit each had dissents in 3.3 percent of their terminations on the merits. However, in the twelve months ending September 30, 1998, the Ninth Circuit had dissents in 2.5 percent of its terminations on the merits, the D.C. Circuit had dissents in 3.6 percent of its terminations on the merits, and the Seventh Circuit had dissents in only 2.0 percent of its terminations on the merits. (See table 6.)

Although there are other potential explanations of the differing dissent rate among circuits, most judges in the Ninth Circuit have in place safeguards to prevent them from becoming overreliant on other chambers. For example, most judges on the Ninth Circuit have their own clerks produce supplemental research on cases for which they do not have primary bench memorandum writing responsibility. However, as in clerk usage more generally, judges vary in how they use clerks to provide supplemental review of such cases.

Some judges who participate in the bench memorandum sharing process use their clerks to prepare a less formal but still detailed memorandum independent of the bench memorandum, called either chambers memoranda or mini-memoranda. The chambers memorandum is ordinarily less exhaustive

TABLE 6. Percentage of Terminations on the Merits with One or More Dissents

	D.C. Circuit			7th Circuit			9th Circuit		
Year	Number of Appeals Terminated on the Merits	Number of Opinions with Dissent(s)	Percent of Opinions with Dissent(s)	Number of Appeals Terminated on the Merits	Number of Published Opinions with Dissent(s)	Percent of Published Opinions with Dissent(s)	Number of Appeals Terminated on the Merits	Number of Published Opinions with Dissent(s)	Percent of Published Opinions with Dissent(s)
2000	629	21	3.3%	1,598	52	3.3%	4,728	121	2.6%
1999	669	26	3.9%	1,484	46	3.0%	4,479	122	2.7%
1998	633	23	3.6%	1,415	29	2.0%	4,337	108	2.5%
1997	732	28	3.8%	1,564	38	2.4%	4,841	129	2.9%
1996	695	40	5.8%	1,628	36	2.2%	4,415	107	2.4%
1995	703	36	5.1%	1,707	46	2.7%	4,410	124	2.8%
1994	775	44	5.7%	1,811	72	4.0%	4,654	114	2.4%
1993	816	33	4.0%	1,656	56	3.4%	4,664	94	2.0%
1992	723	33	4.6%	1,604	49	3.1%	4,061	120	3.0%
1991	691	39	5.6%	1,369	55	4.0%	3,727	117	3.1%
1990	605	25	4.1%	1,334	51	3.8%	2,984	85	2.8%

Note: "Year" means the twelve-month period ending on September 30 of the listed year. The numbers of appeals terminated on the merits are from Tables S-3 to *Judicial Business of the United States Courts* (published by the Administrative Office of the United States Courts) for 1992–2000, and Tables S-3 to *Statistical Tables for the Federal Judiciary* (published by the Administrative Office of the United States Courts) for 1990 and 1991. The numbers of published opinions with one or more dissents were ascertained by searching the West-law CTADC, CTA7, and CTA9 databases for: sy("dissent" or "dissent!") & da(aft 9/30/_ and bef 9/30/_).

than the bench memorandum, covering the major issues raised by the appeal but not covering minor issues in significant detail. Chambers memoranda generally are not intended to exhaustively discuss all cases that have been decided on all points and only rarely discuss cases from other circuits if there is a case within the circuit. Also, the chambers memoranda are less well edited than the bench memoranda, with less attention given to proper citation form and to the exhaustive citation of multiple cases for a single legal proposition. Similarly, a clerk preparing a chambers memorandum generally does not perform a detailed review of the full record but reviews only the excerpts of record provided by the parties. Finally, and perhaps most importantly, because the chambers memoranda are not intended for distribution, the judge serves a less active role in editing and honing the legal arguments.

Because bench memoranda in the Ninth Circuit generally are not distributed until one week prior to the oral argument, those judges ordinarily have their clerks prepare the chambers memoranda without the aid of the bench memoranda. In some of the chambers, the judge prefers that clerks not look at the bench memoranda from other chambers while preparing their chambers memoranda, thereby ensuring an entirely independent look at the case. Where law clerks prepare chambers memoranda without the aid of bench memoranda, they prepare for all cases using the same process and the same degree of detail. As one judge said, "We read the briefs, and we make the same [preparations]. The only thing we don't [do] if there is another bench memo coming in [is that] we are not going to prepare a full-blown bench memo. A bench memo is only a tool, anyway."

In other chambers, whether a clerk uses the bench memorandum to aid in the preparation of the chambers memoranda is merely a matter of timing—if bench memoranda arrive prior to the writing of the chambers memoranda, clerks use the bench memoranda. As one judge described,

> I have my clerks prepare what I call mini-memos in as many . . . cases as possible. Occasionally, some months, we just cannot do it, and I will say, "Don't worry about this one, because we had one just like this one last month." In most of them, I try to get a mini memo from them that summarizes what it is the case is about so that they understand it better. . . . [Mini-memos] are independent [of bench memos]. Sometimes they will be [in response to bench memos] if the bench memos come in before they are written and they will say at the end that [the mini-memo] basically tracks the bench memo analysis or [it] does not. I want the clerks' independent point of view.

Where the bench memorandum is not available when the clerk prepares the chambers memorandum, the clerk generally will review the bench memorandum when it arrives and compare it to the chambers memorandum. One judge described the process:

> What we do is the same review. We will look at a case and say, "This is a bad case," or whatever. We will try to identify the issues, and we will do some independent research, and we will throw it against the bench memo to see how we are coming off. In other words, the bench memo is used as a guide to prepare our own internal memoranda, which may differ or may look at a different issue point of view. Or we may pick up an issue [the writing chambers] don't.

Regardless of whether the clerks have access to bench memoranda when preparing chambers memoranda, the purpose of the chambers memorandum writing process remains the same—to provide an independent, in-depth review of the case so that the research and analysis of the case is accomplished individually in each chambers. Those chambers that use the chambers memo-randum process lose much of the efficiency benefit of the pooling process, repeating almost all of the work necessary for the preparation of the bench memorandum. But those judges gain an additional perspective and an increased probability that they have been made aware of all of the relevant cases.

Other judges do not have their clerks prepare anything independently of other chambers' bench memoranda but instead have them review the bench memorandum and prepare a written critique of it in which they evaluate its arguments and present independent research only to shore up any omissions. These memoranda are called screening memoranda, comment memoranda, or shadow memoranda. As one judge explained,

> They do a screening memo on every case. The bench memos we get from other chambers are all . . . looked at very carefully by my clerks, and they will write me a two- to three-page memo on the bench memo and on the case. "Yes, the bench memo appears to be right"; "Yeah, the bench memo appears wrong"; "The bench memo missed this"; "The bench memo has missed that."

Similarly, another judge stated, "What I refer to as the comment memo is, once we have received a bench memo from other chambers, then internally one of the clerks will then prepare a draft memo commenting on the bench memo and adding any salient points that he or she thinks are critical." The purpose of the comment memoranda is to assure judges that the bench memoranda were thorough and to provide judges with an additional viewpoint from one of their clerks. Moreover, some judges use their clerks to screen the arguments and citations to cases and to the record so that the judge will not need to read unnecessary, repetitive, or irrelevant cases and documents. One judge remarked,

> [The clerks] review the incoming bench memos, and they write me critiques. . . . I want some independent verification from one of my law clerks that the bench memo has not overlooked something or has gone off kind of askew. I expect them to read the key cases, so they can narrow the field. So then I end up instead of having to read ten authorities in a given case, I might only have to read two or three because the rest are repetitive.

Some judges prefer to have their clerks prepare comment memoranda, but when bench memoranda are late or cases are very complex, the clerks will prepare a chambers memorandum without the aid of the bench memorandum. According to one judge,

> I have them do what we call a comment memo. Unless I am sitting [over] cases where the other judge has circulated a [proposed memorandum disposition instead of a bench memo], I don't usually have my clerks look at [memorandum dispositions]. So I will look at that and refresh my recollection on the case by looking at my memo and the briefs. And if I agree with the bench memo, that may end it. The [proposed memorandum disposition], that may end it. . . .
>
> Q. What do you expect the clerks to do in preparing that comment memo? Do they just read over the bench memo and then do a little bit of extra research?
>
> A: It depends on the case and how much time we have. But if it is relatively simple, then they will read the bench memo. They will skim the brief [and] the district court order to see if anything strikes them as funny. . . . If everything seems to be meshing, that may well do it.

Requiring clerks to draft comment memoranda in each case retains more of the efficiency benefits of the shared bench memorandum process because a judge's clerks need not repeat the entirety of the writing chambers' labors. However, the efficiency benefits are bought at the cost of an increased reliance on the research and judgment of other chambers, resulting in a greater potential for error through overly abundant delegation. Nevertheless, because the comment memorandum method provides a notable increase in efficiency balanced with some of the benefits of an independent review by the judge's own clerks, the comment memorandum process is the most commonly used system in the Ninth Circuit.

Less common than the use of the comment memorandum, but more common than the use of the chambers memorandum, is the process in which a judge relies solely on the bench memorandum for aid in his preparation, using his law clerks to fill in research gaps only as necessary:

> [I have my clerks prepare something for me in cases in which I do not have bench memo responsibility] only if after I have read the bench memo, I am concerned about things that are not addressed in the bench memo prepared by another chambers. . . . I go over each of the cases, whether we have prepared the bench memo or whether it has been prepared by somebody else, and discuss specifically the issues which are raised in the brief and the way they have been addressed in the bench memo. If at that time, any of us are concerned about some additional issues, then we do some independent research on those issues. Then we are pretty well ready for calendar.

Another judge explained, "Having read the bench memo, I then determine whether or not all the issues that have bothered me are actually addressed in the bench memo. If they are not addressed, we go back and get some additional research on those issues." Other judges ask their clerks to review a bench memorandum only if the bench memorandum disagrees with the judge's tentative view of the case. For example, one judge related,

> Sometimes, if it is a case assigned to another judge for [bench memo responsibility], I will dictate my tentative view, and I will say if the bench memo comes out the same as my tentative view I don't need any work from my law clerk. If it comes out different, I want an independent memo from my law clerk, analyzing the whole case.

Similarly, another judge said,

> Q: On the cases for which you don't have bench memo responsibility, do you have your clerks prepare anything in addition to what you are getting from the other chambers?
> A: Sometimes, especially when I disagree with the position taken by a law clerk or, presumptively, the judge—his or her judge. I discuss that matter with my law clerks and ask them to prepare just a brief, one- or two-page memo discussing a particular issue, taking a position on it. If they disagree, I will view their view versus the judge's who prepared the bench memo, and I will make up my mind.

Most commonly, however, judges who use the supplemental research method ask for additional research only if, in their judgment, the bench memorandum lacks sufficiently in-depth analysis of an issue that the judge deems important.

One judge, for instance, said that he rarely asked his clerks for additional research in cases for which he did not have bench memorandum responsibility: "I think that they are busy enough trying to get their own cases polished and properly researched that I don't impose on them."

The use of the law clerks only for supplemental research works most effectively with a back-loading strategy because, as discussed earlier, the bench memoranda ordinarily are distributed approximately one week prior to oral argument. Not coincidentally, therefore, all of the judges who reported using the supplemental research method also reported that they were back-loaders who emphasized the use of law clerks for opinion drafting rather than for preparation. Because the law clerks do not regularly repeat the preparatory work done by other chambers, the supplemental research method carries a substantial efficiency benefit for the judge's staff. However, such judges do not reap the advantages of having an increased array of viewpoints because they see only one memorandum written by one clerk, just as if these judges did not participate in the pooling process. Moreover, by relying primarily on other chambers' preparatory work, the judge relinquishes a large degree of control over what issues are emphasized and how thoroughly the research is accomplished. Consequently, the supplemental research method carries with it the most severe threat of trading a judge's autonomy and independence for efficiency through excessive delegation to other chambers.

Additionally, a potential cost of the pooling process is the development of author's pride in the bench memorandum. Without the pooling process, judges have told no one of their views, and other judges do not know how judges or their clerks are considering an issue. Once the bench memoranda are sent out to other chambers, however, the judge and the law clerks have invested in its result and reasoning, potentially making judges and law clerks less willing to surrender the position represented in the bench memorandum.

Especially when judges have worked diligently on bench memoranda, perhaps using the writing process to develop their own thoughts, there is a danger of becoming devoted to a position prior to oral argument and conference and therefore becoming less open to changes based on arguments of counsel or other judges. As one judge said,

> I regard [the bench memo] as a safety valve, because the risk is that—and I see this happen, frankly, in other chambers—the judge gets a theory going on the first pass of the case, and he prevails, and the bench memo is conformed to his views, and that usually creates problems down the road. Usually when that happens, somebody has missed an issue. [My clerks] are told to play it down the middle, make your own independent assessment of the cases, and indicate the pros and cons. I allow them to make a recommendation, but that is, I keep telling them, the least important thing that they

do. The most important thing that they do is to get out on the table all of the issues.

Another judge stated that it is relatively rare for judges who prepare bench memoranda not to be in the majority, possibly because judges strive for unanimity. However, he related that in his own experience, when he is presiding judge and his chambers have written the bench memorandum, even if the panel disagrees with the memorandum's recommendation, he will often side with the majority and assign the case to himself. Nevertheless, he said he usually regrets that decision because, "I usually stay in the same frame of mind." He went on to explain, "I work toward agreement on the cases, but . . . I don't know that it's worth the agony."

In an effort to abridge the potential problem of a judge becoming irreversibly committed to a position prior to conference, many judges do not review the bench memoranda prior to distributing them and then distribute them under the name of the law clerk rather than under the name of the judge or as a product of the judge's chambers. One judge reported, "I try to make sure that the law clerks don't invest too much time in it so they don't get author's pride in the particular result. Because then you have a very hard time, if the court disagrees with them, in getting any help from the law clerks." However, even that step may not entirely eliminate the problem because, as the lone dissenter from the Ninth Circuit's pooling process said, consciously or unconsciously, judges tend to show some deference to the outcome of the bench memorandum:

> I have had people in situations where [the panel reached a decision] and I said [to the judge who wrote the bench memorandum], "Do you want me to write the opinion?" The [other] judge said, "Well, to tell you the truth, I don't think I can get my law clerk to [do it]," suggesting the bench memo went the other way. So . . . I think the bench memos tend to put these people into [a] position, even though they are just law clerks' work. You have to go back to your law clerk and have the work done. It just causes a battle when it comes to getting a law clerk to change positions. He [has] committed himself to his own judge; that is why the judge is sometimes embarrassed. They come to conference and see the judges go the other way. I think it is totally shamefaced. [The clerk] wants to fight. Who needs that?

Moreover, the law clerks themselves may become more committed to the way that the bench memorandum came out because of an understanding that an incorrect bench memorandum will cause the judge embarrassment that, in turn, may embarrass the clerk with the judge. One clerk related that while reviewing a bench memorandum, he discovered a case that the bench memorandum missed and that potentially changed the result. That clerk's judge indicated to the other chambers that the missed case controlled the result. Several days later, that clerk's chambers received a reply from the other chambers' clerk that distinguished the missed case on grounds that that clerk's judge questioned. The clerk pointed out that admitting the oversight would have been highly embarrassing to the clerk who missed the case; therefore, that clerk had every incentive to work as hard as possible to distinguish that missed case.

Bench Books

In addition to writing memoranda that summarize major cases and discuss how those cases should apply to the facts, many clerks collect the major cases and documents from the record into a "bench book" for the judge:

> The law clerks, as part of the process of setting up the bench book . . . have extracted from the materials the opinion, or order, or whatever the dispositive issue is. And as early as they can, they get me copies of the crucial documents there are or crucial passages in the transcript. So I am reading all of the materials independent of the law clerks.

The bench book enables the judge to personally review the relevant cases and documents.

Law Clerks as Sounding Boards

Among the law clerk's most important functions is serving as what some judges and law clerks referred to as a sounding board. One clerk explained, "I think our main function is largely to be a sounding board so that there is someone the judge can bounce ideas off of about a case. [The clerk] is familiar with a case and familiar with the law, and he is also a confidential source." The judges use the clerks to filter and thereby clarify ideas. The clerks have researched the case and often have attended oral argument. Consequently, they are capable of identifying and responding to difficulties in the judge's arguments.

Moreover, because each clerk generally is responsible for fewer cases than each judge, clerks have more time to examine and consider each individual case. Accordingly, they occasionally are able to focus on more unusual aspects of the cases. Most importantly, though, law clerks are the only individuals educated in the law with whom the judges can freely discuss cases. As will be discussed in chapters 5 and 6, judges sometimes hesitate to discuss cases with other judges, and clerks thus may be the only court personnel in whom judges can confide.

Judges converse with their clerks throughout the appellate process. Prior to argument, some judges have a formal preargument conference with their clerks in which the judge and the clerks discuss the issues as a group. One judge described that conference as follows:

> For two full days before I go on the bench, [I] sit down with all of my clerks, and we will go through each case one at a time. And the clerk will present the case, "Here are the facts"—you know, the who, what, when, and why. "Here is what happened. Here is what the appeal is. Here is what the appellant says. Here is what the appellee says. Here is what I think ought to happen, and why." And then we will bat it around until I get a good sense that I am prepared for oral argument.

Another judge explained that he uses a similar preargument conference:

> Anywhere from two to three days [before argument], we go over each case and try to give it the amount of time [the case deserves], and there are no time limits. If it takes half a day to do one case, we talk half a day. And it is a real exchange, and I expect the clerk to come to that session as prepared as the advocate should be for oral argument itself. And that consists of a lot of testing of hypotheses, and what questions might be asked, and what is the best argument on this point, and what is the best argument from the other point of view. And there might be some further research—record research, legal research, or whatever comes about as the result of that. [All of my clerks are] there, and they are free to comment on each other, and I encourage that. I don't want anybody holding back. If a comment does not seem to make sense, then they are perfectly entitled to raise a question, and I expect them to do that.

In addition, between hearing argument in cases, judges occasionally bounce ideas off of law clerks. In one judge's words,

> The day we are in court and sitting, the clerk who has helped me prepare the case would be with me in court. And then there may be a break before we have our conference, in which case I may come back and talk to the law clerk. Or we may, more frequently, go directly to conference, and then I will want the law clerk to discuss what happened at the conference . . . and my writing assignments.

After the judges' conference, most judges will, at least briefly, discuss the results with the clerk. One judge explained,

> I have a discussion with [the clerks about] what happened in oral argument, what the other judges have said, or what the plan is about how we are

going to decide it or formulate a plan. Sometimes we discuss these things in conference. I sit down and discuss it with the clerks.

Often, any postconference discussion, whether in a formal conference or an informal conversation, serves as a preface to the clerk's role in drafting an opinion. As one judge stated,

> After [the judges] confer, I come back to my chambers. I meet with my clerks. I go over everything that happened in conference. I tell them which cases I will decide myself, who I have assigned other cases to, and the ones I have assigned to myself. The clerk who has been working on [those cases] starts working with me on drafting an opinion.

Even most judges who do not directly use the clerks in the drafting process will inform the clerks about what occurred in the conference.

Acting as a sounding board also includes helping judges to avoid error. One clerk asserted, "By and large, my perception is that we are here to keep the judge from doing something that is really stupid." Another clerk stated, "I think [our purpose is to] prevent [the judge] from making big mistakes." As a sounding board, it is the clerks' responsibility to critique judges' arguments so that the judges may clarify their positions or alter them if an error is discovered. Similarly, the way that clerks check their judges is through argumentation and discussion.

Clerks more frequently help judges tighten their ideas rather than change their minds. As one judge reported, "It is rare, if ever—and I cannot remember a case—where a law clerk would turn me around 180 degrees. But it has improved my thinking. It leads me to modify my position, to clarify it." That judge explained that clerks who disagree with the way judges intend to vote are expected to work as vigorously as possible to change the judges' minds. Another judge's clerk explained that his judge does not require him to write any type of memorandum unless the clerk disagrees with the judge's interpretation of the case. The clerk said that as a result, clerks are very hesitant to use up their "political capital" on a case. Clerks choose their battles, only voicing disagreement in important cases in which there was some chance that the judge would change his mind.

One judge described the process of discussion with the clerk as integral to the way that he decides cases. He works with the clerks closely throughout the decision-making process, expecting clerks to voice their opposition at any stage of the process.

> I expect them to tell me about it . . . or to write comments on my opinions. But of course, we are discussing this all along. We discuss cases beforehand. I solicit their views. We discuss the case immediately after the oral argu-

ment. We discuss the various opinions. . . . I expect them to tell me what they think.

Judges generally felt that free discussions should proceed as long as there is anything judges may not have taken into account. Subsequently, however, discussion should end because it has little value. According to one judge,

> [I expect them] to proceed vigorously to a certain point—either when I tell them, "Look, I understand what you are saying, I just don't agree," or until they are satisfied that I really have digested it and they have nothing more to say. I will sometimes say to them, "You have not persuaded me. What else have you got?" And they will go back and say, "That is all there is."

Only one judge did not seek disagreement from his clerks, stating that if his clerk disagreed with the judge's view on a case, he expected the clerk to "bend his ideas to mine." This judge explained, "I am not interested in disagreement."

Law Clerks and the Preparation of Opinions

It is now rare for judges to write the first draft of their opinions. Only two of the judges with whom I spoke indicated that they always wrote their own first drafts, and only three others indicated that they often or usually did so. In both chambers in which the judges always wrote the first drafts of opinions, clerks did not write bench memoranda and only aided the judge in research and served as sounding boards. In the three chambers in which the judges frequently wrote the first drafts of opinions, the clerks wrote detailed memoranda in all of the cases for which the judges were assigned cases. One judge who writes all of his own first drafts explained his writing process:

> About half the time, I have come back [from the judges' conference], and I have sat down at my word processor and written an opinion with fair dispatch. Certainly within a week of the argument I sit down and write. . . . The other half of the cases, I am apt to assign . . . further research to my clerks and say, "Let's pursue X and see what we can find out about X," whether it was a factual matter or a legal matter. And they will try to find some law about it.

Where the judge retains all first drafts, clerks still perform a significant role, researching, editing, commenting, and cite checking the opinions. One clerk reported that his judge's first drafts are usually very close to the published opinions:

He writes the first draft, and although it is a first draft, it is usually very complete. The [additional] research or any filling in of that [draft] on our part tends to be very minimal. . . . Once we have the first draft, we go through it. We check it for any stylistic comments we want to make, for any substantive comments we want to make. If there are any case cites, we go through the case and the pertinent parts to make sure that he has cited those cases accurately. We check the facts, make sure the facts and the statements [are correct]. And we hop on [Lexis] to make sure that all the cases he cited are still [good law]. We also look to see if there are any additional cases which he might have cited but has not cited. . . . We give it back to him and he incorporates these comments or does not incorporate them, as he sees fit.

That clerk's statement illustrates his limited role in influencing opinions written in those chambers. In essence, the clerk's sole role is to check the opinion for errors. As that clerk's judge stated,

Once I am done with the opinion, I give it to my clerks and say, "You're on. Is this opinion fully organized, well organized, accurate, inaccurate? Basically, tell me what is wrong. Tell me how it can be improved, criticized." I get their critiques back. I revise and send it to my brethren.

In short, a small minority of judges use their clerks as sounding boards, then pen opinions themselves and use clerks to help editing in a back-and-forth interchange of drafts.

All of the remaining judges with whom I spoke used their clerks to write a first draft of the opinions in at least a good portion of cases. One judge explained his process:

The law clerk will prepare a draft opinion, although that is not universally the case, but that is what normally would be the case—prepare drafts, submit it to me, and I would work it over in such ways as I saw fit and return it to the law clerk, and we go back and forth four or five times, probably, before all the bugs get worked out, depending on what kind of case it is.

Although many judges prefer to use their clerks to write first drafts of opinions, the amount of guidance that judges give to their clerks varies substantially. In the Ninth Circuit, where judges regularly share their clerks' bench memoranda, some judges work very closely with their law clerks on those memoranda, editing, shaping, and adding to them to such an extent that drafting opinions is no more than changing the tone. One judge reported that he used his law clerks merely to flesh out a well-defined outline:

After each oral argument, on every case, I write a memo on what the case was about and what we decided to do. Then on each case that I am assigned, I will write a little more extensive memo, which is, in effect, an outline for an opinion. It is what my decision is, how I want to approach it, and this kind of thing. And then I direct my clerk to prepare an outline of the draft for that particular opinion. And then I will go over that outline. I will work with the clerk on that if there are any changes—say, "Here is what we want to do or we don't want to do," or "I want to emphasize this and not that." And then [I] have the clerk initiate a draft. . . . Sometimes the cases are fairly easy, straightforward, where it is not something that I would have to really monitor along the way. At other times, these issues are pivotal, and if research discloses this or that, I will have to get involved and say, "All right, we're going to do this or do that," or "We might have to reverse, might have to decide other things." So, it is an ongoing interaction with the clerk.

Another judge gives his clerks a detailed memorandum that serves not as an outline, but merely as a guide as to which arguments and issues ought to be stressed:

When I leave the conference, I dictate a memo to file in which I record my own records, the discussions that occurred, the votes where each judge is concerned, comments where each judge is concerned. It may be a short memo or a long memo. In those cases that I have been assigned to write, well before I do that, I dictate the memo to file. I do it in the presence of the law clerk who is assigned to cover [that case]. If the law clerk has anything that he feels needs to be fleshed out or talked more about, then I do that. More often I discuss it in addition to dictating to the file. With regard to the cases which I will be authoring, I generally go into somewhat more detail with the clerk, indicating positions I think we should take, things that should be avoided, comments that need to be addressed by us, by the comments by the panel judges. So at that point I begin to give the structure to an opinion in a very, very general way and give directions to the law clerk. My general practice is to have the law clerk [write] a paragraph [on each case]. The law clerk may not actually get to the preparation of the draft for some time after that. . . . Then a draft is submitted to me. There may be— and what I urge my clerks to do is maybe some discussion of what they are to do or not to do. In any event, after what may be some preliminary discussion on the procedure, I see the draft. Depending on how the law clerk and I think, alike or not, . . . there may be a lot of revisions and a total restructuring, or there may be somewhat less. It just depends on if we are thinking on the same wavelength. It could be where I review the six cuts in a draft and resubmit it. . . . I prefer to work with a draft.

Still another judge indicates to his clerk at a postargument conference what types of things ought to go into a draft and then sets the law clerk free to write a draft that the judge later will revise:

> Usually the clerk will do the first draft. Before he . . . does it, I will talk with [him], or meet with [him] at the . . .conference [after oral argument] or at subsequent conferences as to what it is I think needs to be covered. I send out to those [clerks] the one piece of writing that does accompany each case for me. I will send out a postconference memo to the other two judges, describing what it is that we agreed upon or in terms of what the decision is going to be. This sort of acts as the framework for the decision I am writing or the other judges are writing. The clerk does the first draft. I will revise it, sit down with them, go over my revisions, ask them how things are that they don't understand. Or we will cover this or that. Then I will go back to as many drafts, this back-and-forth, as needed before we finally come out with a written final product.

By giving the clerks only some initial guidance as to how the opinion should come out and some of the reasons underlying that decision, the judge frees the clerk to structure the opinion and to emphasize some aspects of the reasoning over others. The clerk's discretion is increased where the judge provides less editing after the first draft is completed. For example, one judge explained his process:

> I assign the first responsibility to a clerk, and I assign that responsibility after discussing the case with them and telling the point of view of the panel and my point of view with respect to the major issues. The clerk then— who probably has written the bench memo and has a good understanding of the case—drafts a proposed opinion which is consistent with the decision of the panel and probably with the bench memo, too—at least much of the research done on the bench memo. I read it, and if it is the right result and the arguments are persuasive to me, I send it out without having really committed myself to the opinion as yet, but at least I send it out for consideration. If I get back a comment or an affirmation or a rejection, as the case may be, and if the case is affirmed by two other judges, I probably will go along with the case that I have prepared basically. But I have not yet really sworn off on accepting a contrary point of view. But if there is no contrary point of view, I probably would swear off and sign off the case.

Thus, judges fall along a continuum of control over the initial drafting of their opinions.

Regardless of where they are situated along this continuum, however, judges uniformly indicated that they felt that their drafting, editing, and revising processes ultimately produced opinions that represented the judges' views and style. The back-and-forth that judges have with their clerks—what several judges called "ping-ponging"—requires both judge and clerk to work extensively on opinions and to craft and hone the opinion's style. One judge explained that he feels a responsibility to edit the clerk's draft closely enough so that the opinion is stylistically as well as jurisprudentially the judge's own. He explained how that requirement places an onus on him:

> In the end, every opinion that comes out of these chambers has to be made my own. And sometimes it means writing the whole thing myself, sometimes it means very heavy editing. . . . A clerk who is so onto my style that I can make it my own with light editing . . . is my dream, but in reality it does not happen that way. Some years you get no clerks that can be that good, and some years you get one. It is rare that you get two.

Another judge stated that the ping-ponging of opinion drafts results in a clerk-drafted opinion that is indistinguishable from a judge-drafted one:

> Q: In those cases that you have the writing responsibility, how do you then go about preparing the disposition?
> A: Originally, I prepared the original draft of the disposition, and we work[ed] off of my draft. More recently, we worked off of a law clerk's draft. I review that, and we do revise substantially.
> Q: Do you think that change in the way that you have drafts done is significant to the product?
> A: No. I think the quality is just as good when they do it as when I do it— that is, when we get down to the bottom line. Of course, I am a great believer in communications, so we always have great communications sessions, and as I indicate to the clerks, everybody has an equal voice in the discussion. But they want to remember that there is only one vote.

Another judge stated that opinions were generally of a higher quality when the clerk prepared the first draft:

> It probably gets better organized, and no matter how comfortable the working relationship is—and I think it is very comfortable around here—

but if [I] do it first, there is a tendency for them to give more emphasis than is warranted to what [I] have written and less emphasis to the other points. I just find it easier that if they come back with a tightly, well-organized thing, and it is written, and then I can take it and put my own approach into it. . . . I am typically getting it back on disk and just throw it into my computer and fire it up on the screen and go to work on it. It is easier to insert my thought process, words, language, etc. into their draft than it is vice versa.

Even with extensive editing, clerks who draft opinions often have extensive discretion in how they choose to structure the draft and what they choose to emphasize.

One clerk referred to his role in opinion writing as "complete authority." While that statement seems a bit strong in light of the judge's reported close editing, the clerk explained,

You get your marching orders from that postconference meeting. And the judge . . . will himself draft a postconference memo which is sent out to the other judges with outlines, usually very skeletal reasoning. And then we write it. . . . So the reasoning you use from there on, it is all up to you.

Another clerk indicated that he had a great deal of discretion in drafting an opinion. When writing, he starts only with the way the judges voted and their reasons for doing so—and sometimes the judge does not even give a clear reason for his vote. The clerk is responsible for deciding which arguments to use. The clerk felt that he had the strongest impact in this aspect of the judicial process.

Yet another clerk related that he too received little guidance in what to emphasize:

There are some pretty basic things like . . . whether they are going to affirm or reverse or remand or whatever. And if the attorneys have done their jobs, you know, obviously, what the judge has done is picked this up. So when you are writing this opinion, if everything is basically right, then you can basically pick one side, look at their briefs, look at their research, make sure it is right, and you follow that because that is what persuaded the judge to take that step. . . . But there are cases where the briefs are not as instructive, and that is where it is more difficult. Sometimes the attorneys did not do their work, or they did not focus on [the correct issues], and that is where I think you find even more need to interact with the judge because you are doing something different than what was in the [briefs].

III.   Physical Structure of Chambers and Clerk Usage

Physical design may strongly affect the interaction within a judicial chamber. A building's structure can reflect and symbolically represent social structure, and physical structure can affect social structure.[15]

When judges are appointed to the U.S. Courts of Appeals, they are given space in a federally owned building in which they can design their chambers. Within the limits of that area, the limits imposed by the structure of the building, and budgetary constraints, judges may use that space however they choose. Consequently, there is substantial variation in how judicial chambers are physically structured. The *United States Courts Design Guide*[16] provides suggestions as to how the chambers may be structured, but although generally respected, those guidelines are by no means mandatory. Chamber organization can reflect judges' personal work habits or priorities. One judge, for example, explained that he had organized his chambers around the books in the library, maximizing the number of volumes that could be kept at hand and ensuring ease of access for himself and his staff. As a consequence, his office is at one end of a long hall, with secretaries' areas separating him from each clerk's area along the hall. Books are stored along all of the walls.

There are three essential sections to every appellate judicial chambers: the judge's office, the secretarial office/area, and the clerks' offices/areas. However, there is much variation in how these sections are organized, how much space is allotted to each of them, and where they are located relative to one another. The three sets of areas generally are directly connected; however, there are numerous examples of disconnected chambers in which one or more of the clerks' offices is separated from the judge's office and secretaries' areas by as much as two floors. It is far from extraordinary for at least one clerk to have an office located down a hall from the main chambers in which the judge is located.

Even within the more standard design, in which the judge's office and clerks' offices are connected, there is substantial variation. In some chambers the clerks' offices connect directly to the judge's office. In others, the judge must walk through the secretary's office to get to the clerks. In some chambers, the clerks sit together in one large office, whereas in others, each clerk has a separate office. In still others, the clerks sit in officelike alcoves, separated from one another but without a door or wall to separate them from the main chambers. When clerks have their own offices, they often are connected to one another, and the judge must walk through one clerk's office to get to another.

---

15. Bourdieu hints at this when he states that the setting of a house can be articulated with "technical necessity." Pierre Bourdieu, Algeria 1960 135 n.6 (1979).

16. *See* United States Courts Design Guide (1991).

These variations accounts for differences in the way judges interact with clerks as well as in the way in which clerks interact with each other. That can be seen with particular clarity in accounts of how changes in the structural organization of the chamber affected patterns and effectiveness of social interaction. For example, one judge stated,

> [When] I started [here], we were in terrible condition. I was in one office, and the secretaries were across the hall, and one [clerk] was appended to that office, and another was down at the end of the hall, and another one was two floors away. That was really bad. And I think we were slow, supervision was slow . . . . I have changed because of that, because of the surroundings and that kind of thing. Things are much more efficient [since we changed the chambers' structure].

Another judge said,

> [In] my first chambers . . . the clerks were all in one place, and it was a very confined area, and the trouble with [that was] that they were so physically crowded that I could not talk to one of them without interrupting the other. And then the third one was still in another office. The reason I chose these chambers is that the judge that preceded here had arranged the chambers with the idea of heavy concentration on how to make the clerks' quarters more pleasant for them and more compatible with what the judge's needs were. . . . The clerks have separate offices . . . that open up onto each other. I can walk in there and literally see [them all] at the same time, ask, "Who is working on this?"

The location of the clerks in relation to judges can affect both how often and in what ways judges communicate with clerks. For example, one judge said that he almost always communicated with his clerks verbally because "they are sitting right outside this door. Why should I write to them?"

Just because the clerk's offices are not immediately connected to the judge's office, however, does not mean that the judge does not have adequate ability to communicate in person and to personally supervise the clerks. For example, in one chambers where the clerks have offices down the hall from the judge, one clerk indicated that the chambers' design gave the clerk more freedom; however, he noted that although physically separated from the judge, the clerks still were influenced strongly by his work habits. The clerks found that they should be quiet and talk in low voices because the judge was himself quiet and preferred a quiet work environment. The judge occasionally would come to speak with a clerk, often standing at the door until the clerk noticed him. That, the clerk concluded, could be somewhat awkward for the clerks. For example, a clerk related that on one occasion, when conversing about a case, a clerk said, "I will die if I don't speak with [the judge] soon." Just after he uttered those words, he noticed that the judge was standing at the door. The clerk said that this incident showed him that he had to be conscious of the judge's presence in spite of the separation between his office and that of the judge.

The judges who had clerks in offices that were not adjacent did not report that the separation caused any significant problems. One judge explained,

> I think it would be nicer if I were able to have a contiguous office, I suppose. But it is really not a big deal. I just go out the door and over there. . . . If it were set up otherwise, the secretaries would be between me and the clerks. . . . You know, we pick up the phone and talk a lot on this, that, and the other thing—a question here, and "What is this?" that sort of thing. So sometimes, it is just on the phone or intercom, just like you would [speak to] anybody [else].

One judge designed his chambers when he was allowed only three clerks. The addition of a fourth clerk necessitated his being housed in an office separate from the chambers. According to the clerk in that separate office, the separation had little effect on his interaction with the judge but caused problems because of its distance from the chambers library. The clerk also described a sense of isolation that made communication with the other clerks more difficult.

When the clerks are located near the judge, there is often more informal communication than when the judge must make a greater effort to speak with the clerks. In one chambers, the judge explained that he often began fruitful conversations with his clerks when he was in their office gathering a book from the shelf. Similarly, another judge described how his chambers functioned:

> We see each other all day long. I mean, usually I keep the door shut, but not to them, but just so the noise in the hall is not distracting. But it is an open-door policy around here. We have a situation that is quite adequate for us. It is very workable. We have got a good library, and of course, you cannot have the library in one room, it has to be spread out.

Because the chambers' books generally are spread among the offices of the clerks and, sometimes, the judge, the judge and the clerks informally interact while getting and replacing books. According to one clerk, those informal conversations often move into the judge's office and continue as significant discussion sessions. The clerks also must access books from one another's offices, and similar informal discussions sometimes ensue. Those conversations often turn to the legal matters on which the clerks currently are working. Thus, where the clerks are located can have an impact on how often they communicate with each other.

Moreover, clerks' locations can also affect how often judges see individual clerks, as demonstrated by the following interchange among three clerks whose offices are located along a corridor leading from the judge's office:

> *Clerk 1:*   I am the one in the corridor. I never see the judge.
> *Clerk 2:*   Right. Whereas I am the first person, so I see the judge all the time. I cannot sit there and chat on the phone.
> *Clerk 3:*   Well, none of us can really chat on the phone because his doors are open, and it is just very close quarters. So we do not have long conversations with people like I had in my other jobs.
> *Clerk 2:*   And, you know, the judge wanders by my desk on the way to [clerk 2] or [clerk 3], and I look up and so I am like, "Hi, Judge."

Differences in chamber organization can affect how clerks interact. Clerks often described their informal communication as "screaming" from office to office, as illustrated by this exchange from an interview with two clerks:

> *Q:*   Do you share an office, or do you each have your own?
> *Clerk 1:*   We have our own, but they are right next to each other. We have enough conversation going on most of the time.
> *Clerk 2:*   We can scream to each other.
> *Q:*   Is that how it usually works?
> *Clerk 2:*   As opposed to the intercom, yes.

IV. Conclusion: The Organizational Role of Intracircuit Structure

The appellate courts' structural features have two dimensions: the internal structure of the individual chambers and the structure of the interaction among chambers. This chapter focused on the first dimension and considered how the way that judges structure their chambers and use their staff affects how cases are decided. In particular, this chapter considered the impact of the law clerk on the judicial process.

Within the courts of appeals, there is substantial variation in the ways that judges use their law clerks and, accordingly, on how law clerk usage affects the balance between autonomy and interdependence. Nonetheless, there are cognizable patterns of clerk usage: judges use their law clerks for four primary types of tasks: (1) to assist judges in preparing to decide cases by preparing bench memoranda; (2) to prepare judges for oral argument by preparing bench books; (3) to provide judges a sounding board to test and discuss ideas; and (4) to assist judges in writing judicial opinions. Even within these four categories, however, judges' use of law clerks is highly idiosyncratic. Some judges use their clerks for some but not all of these tasks, and law clerks often perform extremely varied tasks within each of these categories.

How judges use their law clerks may protect judges' autonomy by ensuring that they have the preparation to understand the law and facts and ultimately to decide each case. But law clerk usage also may cripple a judge's autonomy by limiting what the judge knows and when the judge knows it. For example, front-loaders who emphasize and participate in the clerk's preparation of bench memoranda have significant involvement in a case from the beginning of a chambers' preparation for oral argument. Front-loaders, therefore, generally are well prepared to ask pointed and relevant questions in oral argument and to have a well-developed position in conference. Front-loaders have heightened autonomy at the beginning of the judicial process and can translate that independence into influence in conference and the opinion-writing stage. This heightened autonomy at the front end of the judicial process thus can translate into heightened interdependence at the back end. Conversely, back-loaders, who rely on their law clerks to provide bench memoranda with little or no judicial guidance and participate late in the decision-making process, must rely more on their instincts and their clerks' assistance in preparing for oral argument and conference. As a result, back-loaders are threatened by a greater potential for decreased autonomy when it may be most important (in oral argument, where judges have a chance to probe the issues more deeply, and conference, where judges must take an initial position that can determine for which cases they are assigned opinion-writing responsibility). Although some judges justified back-loading as a means of preventing them from prematurely committing to a position, back-loaders face the sirenlike appeal of never personally delving into a case for which they have not been assigned opinion-writing responsibility. Thus, back-loaders face the threat that they will sacrifice at least part of their autonomy by sacrificing their ability to make a fully informed decision. Because back-loading creates an increased potential for creating an imbalance between autonomy and interdependence, courts should be careful before adopting changes, such as a shared bench memorandum system, that provide incentives for judges to back-load.

Back-loading also creates potential overdelegation problems in the opinion-writing process (which is where back-loaders tend to focus their attention) because many back-loader judges delegate to their clerks not only the lion's share of the preparation of the bench memoranda but also the drafting of judicial opinions. Whereas front-loader judges who delegate initial opinion-drafting responsibility to their law clerks already have worked closely with clerks while preparing bench memoranda, back-loader judges may delve into case details only after law clerks have written initial opinion drafts. While this strategy may save some time, it also sacrifices a part of the judge's autonomy. And where the physical layout of judges' chambers further hampers communication with and supervision of law clerks, the problem of overdelegation may be increased.

Although some patterns of law clerk usage appear to lend themselves more than others to overdelegation, most judges who use law clerks in a manner that could result in the surrender of autonomy have adopted alternative methods to ensure that they have not overdelegated to their clerks. For example, many back-loaders require their clerks to prepare bench books that include the most significant cases and factual documents. As a result, these judges prepare quickly for oral argument and then focus their attention on the opinion-writing process. Accordingly, even where the threat that overdelegation to law clerks might shift the balance away from judicial autonomy, judges have instituted stopgap measures to maintain the balance. As a result of such defenses, most judges appear to have avoided the pitfall of overdelegation to their law clerks

However, although the autonomy of most judges does not appear to have been crippled by overdelegation to law clerks, another, perhaps more pernicious, problem may have emerged: the overdelegation of judicial responsibility across the subdivisional boundaries to other judges. That threat goes to the center of the balance between autonomy and interdependence and may affect the essence of how a judicial panel functions as a collegial group. The next chapter addresses this problem.

CHAPTER 5

Structure and the Interaction among Judicial Chambers

B ecause the courts of appeals are multimember, collegial courts, one of their most conspicuous features is that the judges must interact with one another to decide cases.[1] Unlike the interaction between a judge and his staff, the interaction among the judges is an interaction among equals, and no single judge can dictate how that interaction must take place. Instead, the way that the judges may interact is strongly influenced by the court's structure. This chapter considers how court structure influences the ways that judges communicate with one another and how the nature of that communication affects the way that individual judges do their work.

In the courts of appeals, each chambers functions relatively autonomously from other chambers, but because the chambers must function interdependently to produce the appellate judicial product, the chambers must have substantial communication with one another. Typically, the regulation of interaction among the subdivisions of a multidivisional organization is a management problem overcome with the guidance and strategic decision making of a centralized office. In the absence of such centralized management, however, the courts must overcome the problems of communication through less formal structural methods and strategies.

This chapter begins by discussing how the court's multidivisional structure affects interchambers communication and boundary spanning. It then considers the relationship between a court's size and its interchambers structure.

---

1. See Evan H. Caminker, *Sincere and Strategic Voting Norms in Multimember Courts*, 97 U. Mich. L. Rev. 2297, 2298 (1999) (noting that researchers have paid "insufficient attention" to the ways in which judges on multimember courts influence one another); Lewis A. Kornhauser & Lawrence G. Sager, *The One and the Many: Adjudication in Collegial Courts*, 81 Calif. L. Rev. 1, 10–17 (1993) (same).

I.   Direct Communication among Judges

How judges directly communicate with one another, and when and how often they do so, may have serious repercussions for judges' ability to function inter-dependently with one another.[2] By and large, judges on the courts of appeals rarely discuss matters with one another except in the limited forums of the conference and the exchange of proposed written dispositions. They do, when the occasion demands it, discuss issues such as the submission of a case without oral argument, whether to accept the submission of an amicus brief, whether more briefing is necessary in a case, and other housekeeping matters. However, interaction regarding the substance of a case is surprisingly rare. As one judge said, "In the great majority of the cases, I do not interact with the judges." This section examines the nature and frequency of direct communication among the judges on the courts of appeals.

The Basic Forms of Communication

As with virtually any other organization, judges have three basic ways of communicating directly with their brethren: face-to-face conversations, telephone conferences, and written memoranda. And as with any other organization, the choice of which method to use can significantly affect the formality of the communication, the communication's timing, the ability to record the conversation, and on the ability to bring in other judges whose participation is relevant to the discussion.

In 1977 Stephen Wasby observed that judges preferred written communication because, among other reasons, memoranda allow for precise communi-

---

2. The issue of interchambers communication has been left relatively unexamined. Only one researcher, Stephen Wasby, has empirically examined the problem in detail. In a series of papers, Wasby has described how communication was accomplished in the Eighth and Ninth Circuits. *See* Stephen Wasby, *Technology in Appellate Courts: The Ninth Circuit's Experience with Electronic Mail,* 73 JUDICATURE 90 (1989); Stephen Wasby, *Technology and Communication in a Federal Court: The Ninth Circuit,* 28 SANTA CLARA L. REV. 1 (1988); Stephen Wasby, *Communication in the Ninth Circuit: A Concern for Collegiality,* 11 U. PUGET SOUND L. REV. 73 (1987); Stephen Wasby, *Internal Communication in the Eighth Circuit Court of Appeals,* 58 WASH. U. L.Q. 583 (1978); Stephen Wasby, *Communication within the Ninth Circuit Court of Appeals: The View from the Bench,* 8 GOLDEN GATE U. L. REV. 1 (1977). The remainder of this chapter revisits the questions of communication discussed by Wasby. Although there is some overlap with the issues covered by Wasby, his data on the Ninth Circuit consisted of interviews from 1977 and 1986. The Ninth Circuit interviews for this study were conducted in 1996 and 1997. Thus, reliance on Wasby's data, as reported in his 1977 and 1987 articles, allows for analysis of how the Ninth Circuit has changed over a twenty-year period in which the caseload increased steadily and the court's membership increased to its present twenty-eight active judges.

cations and establish a permanent written record of the conversation.[3] Wasby reported, however, that some judges expressed a preference for telephone communication because of speed. By 1986, Wasby reported, the judges on the Ninth Circuit had increased the use of written communication and decreased the use of telephone communication.[4] This change came about in large part because in 1984 and 1985, the circuit began to use a computer network system called CCI that enabled the judges to instantaneously communicate in writing with any or all of the circuit's judges.[5]

Not surprisingly, the trend that Wasby observed in the Ninth Circuit toward written communication through the computer network system has continued in the years since he conducted his research. On the Ninth Circuit, all of the judges I spoke with indicated that they generally preferred written communication through the e-mail system. That trend also has taken hold in the First, Seventh, and D.C. Circuits, where all of the judges with whom I spoke reported a general preference for written communication.

The reasons that the judges gave for their preferences resembled those reported by Wasby. Written communication allows for relatively easy communication among three busy individuals because it allows all judges to come to the writing at convenient times and allow them to easily respond to other judges consistently and concurrently. As one judge explained,

> The real reason for communicating in writing is if I get an opinion from a judge in Idaho, and it takes me a while to get to it, and I start having a problem, I pick up the phone and call him and say, "That opinion you sent me . . . ," and he will say, "Remind me what that was about." Then we will have a blank telephone conversation, and he will say, "I will call you back." Then he gets back into the case and works on it and perhaps is interrupted a few times, and the next day he calls me back and he will say, "That problem you called me about . . . ," and I will say, "Remind me what that problem is." It's hopeless.

Telephone communication requires the three judges to accommodate their schedules to speak about a particular case, which proves less convenient than is written communication. As one judge said, written communication "is easier. You can send somebody a memo whether they are in the office or not. If you start trying to arrange to talk to people on the telephone, you can spend hours trying to just arrange it." That coordination problem is exacerbated when a court has a large number of judges. As one judge reported,

---

3. Wasby, 1977, *supra* note 2, at 15.
4. Wasby, 1987, *supra* note 2.
5. Wasby, 1989, *supra* note 2, at 92–93.

[Telephone conversations] are very difficult for judges. If you sat on the same panel all the time, it would be easier. But when you are working between panels, every judge has a different demand for the next day and the next week. To try to break into their preparation schedule and say, "Look, I want to sit down and have you be prepared to talk about this case next Wednesday," it is like [asking the other judge to] do another mini oral argument. It is disruptive.

Written communications also enable easy inclusion of all three judges on a panel because messages can be sent to more than one recipient. As one judge said,

Ninety-nine percent of the time, after conference, I communicate through the e-mails. One reason is mechanical. It forces me, as I should, to make that communication with both of the other judges, not just with one of them. And if I have a reaction to something that they have written, my reaction goes to both of them, not just to one of them.

Similarly, another judge explained,

[After oral argument,] there is a fair amount of talk over CCI [by e-mail], a fair amount of discussion back and forth in writing. I want to be sure that I would not go too far in excluding the third judge from the conversation. I think that is very uncollegial and that only creates problems later on. But normally, if I have second thoughts in a case, I will just send a memo, and the other judge will respond.

Moreover, the use of written communication enables judges to more easily include their clerks in the process by providing them a copy of incoming memoranda. For judges who wish their clerks to be involved in the discussion, telephone conferences would require judges either to include their clerks in the conference, which could irritate their brethren, or to summarize the conversation to their law clerks, which takes additional time and creates more potential for lost or mischaracterized information. As one judge reported, "One thing you have to do if you do it [orally] is you need to include the law clerk because if the discussion takes you off on a different tangent, it is easier if the clerk is there to see how it develops than try to explain it to him. It would be just a little clumsy." E-mail simplifies the communication process by allowing judges to send written communication instantly and simultaneously to multiple recipients (judges and clerks) over long distances. However, some judges reported the problem that instantaneous written communication raises the probability of judges sending out "zingers"—communications containing rude or incompletely thought out comments without adequate time given to edit-ing.[6]

> In the old days, when I used to dictate a memo, they would come back the next day and [I could see that] I really did not mean to say it quite this strongly. What I really meant was to inquire. Now, we would sit down and pound out something and it goes out. I think it is much less work and it is sometimes too informal—i.e., sarcasm, one-upmanship, those kinds of things. [Some judges] love to do this, but what they don't realize is that the world is watching and sometimes shocked by how they refer to each other. We did not use to have that when we sat down and dictated a memo to other judges. . . .
>
> I think it is less formal on the phone. You always have a chance to explain what [you] really mean by this, and the other guy says "What?" "Please let me explain myself," and [you] have a chance to interact, which you don't even have on the CCI except when you blast off and punch the button. Now it goes to thirty five judges, and sometimes I think some of those memos are too informal.

Although the interactive nature of a telephone conversation allows judges to explain their meaning with less risk of offense, telephone conferences are less focused than written communication and therefore tend to waste time. As one judge said,

> The phone conferences thus far are not very efficient because there is no structure [to the conversation]. If you just start yakking away about the case, you just waste time. If you structure it—we have done structured tele-phone calls which were very beneficial in difficult cases.

The preference for written communication does not mean that judges never discuss cases over the telephone. However, telephone conversations often are reserved for unusual communications, for example, when a case gar-ners unusually high interest from the members of the panel. One judge stated that he usually communicates by e-mail: "Talking by telephone is relatively hopeless—not invariably. If there is a really big, high profile-case . . . then, maybe I would call and talk. But the problem there is you really need a confer-ence call [to include all of the judges]." Similarly, if a case is highly complex, the panel may orally discuss the case.

---

6. Wasby observed that judges he had interviewed in 1986 had thought this would be a prob-lem. Wasby, 1987, *supra* note 2. It is possible that as judges become more accustomed to using the e-mail system, they will be less susceptible to sending messages prematurely.

A difficult case . . . would be so complicated and so demanding that we may talk about what we are going to do with [it]. I use any method to get to the truth and the resolution of the case to try to sort out what is the justice of the matter. . . . So when a case demands it, the participation of the full panel may be by memo, by phone conference, and, of course, by oral argument.

Conversely, judges may communicate by telephone simply to verify their understanding of prior written communications:

> Q: In preparing dispositions, do you often have an opportunity to talk with the other judges on the panel?
> A: Not unless there is some—if I get something from the writing judge that seems to be contrary to my notes at the conference, then I will talk to them.
> Q: And how is that communication done? Do you generally talk by telephone?
> A: Always by telephone first and confirmed in writing.
> Q: When you talk by telephone, do you usually include the third judge as well, or do you just talk informally on the phone?
> A: I talk informally on the phone just to be sure that my notes are incorrect or that my understanding is incorrect before I go ahead and discuss it with the third judge. I will then confirm whatever I have talked [about] with the writing judge and of course copy the other member of the panel.

Similarly, one judge explained that he would call another judge if he had a serious problem with a bench memorandum:

> If I think a bench memo is inaccurate, perhaps even deceptively inaccurate, I will say something just to the judge. . . . "This is simply for your benefit, but take a look at section 2 or pages 4 or 5. At least, your clerk . . . was dead wrong. At worst it is deceptive, and that doesn't help the process." But that has only happened once or twice.

Judges very rarely communicate about a case with judges who are not on the panel. Although judges, like other organizational decision makers, sometimes may find it valuable to bounce ideas off of one another, they rarely do so. One judge explained his reasons:

> One of the problems [is that] it is not very easy to have a conversation with another lawyer about one of the problems without having the other lawyer filled in on the background, the facts, law, and so forth. To get somebody

to the point where if you discuss it, it is going to be helpful and meaningful leads to a fair amount of education. They may have to read some cases and so on. They don't have the time to listen, to get to the point where you are. . . . The reason you talk to your law clerks about it is I nurse them. They have the same problems you [do], and they come up to you and bring you up to speed so they can talk about it. So to ask questions, you have to educate somebody. That is a problem. Even if I had other judges around, I would just find it too difficult, even if they are on the panel. The case I sat on a panel a month ago. . . . I was waiting for an opinion from another panel member and they said, "What do you think of X case?" I would not remember and they would have to remind me, kind of warm me up, and it would take a long time. Even then, I don't think I would [want to] be in a position where I would say, "Gee, I can't give you my best." . . . I just had not finished reading the cases. I am not where I was at the time of oral argument. . . . I mean, a completely off-panel judge with no familiarity with the case to the point where [he] can make a useful discussion partner is quite a substantial commitment of your time and substantial commitment of the other judge's time.

In sum, the trend toward using written communication has continued from 1977, when Wasby described the beginning of a shift from in-person or telephone communication to written communication, particularly by e-mail. On all four circuits in which I have data, written communication is generally the preferred form of communication because (1) it is more formal and thoughtful; (2) all discussion is preserved; and (3) it is easy to keep all three judges informed of the conversation.

The Timing of Communication

The timing and quantity of communication among judges, although not entirely independent from the form of communication, also is relevant to understanding how the court's structure affects judges' interaction with one another.

Preargument Communication

In both his 1977 and 1987 articles, Wasby noted that communication in the preargument stage of the appellate process was extremely limited and consisted primarily of housekeeping communications regarding the submission of cases without oral argument, requests for continuances, and the need for additional briefing. That does not appear to have changed.

Because the judges have individualized and often very different methods of preparing for oral argument, judges found substantive communication before argument to be difficult to arrange and often fruitless. As one judge explained,

> I never found [preargument discussions] very useful in terms of the time it took. You are still in sort of preliminary thinking. I would rather go into argument knowing pretty well what the case is about, but not so well that I knew absolutely what the questions were. I think a more profitable approach might be to write an opinion and circulate it to the others ahead of time. Of course, some courts do that, and then there is a very specific target for them to address. But the way we do it—I think my experience has been [that] the best way to get it done is get the opinion done and have it done as carefully as you can with a maximum amount of work on that case from one chambers. . . . Then you exchange memos and then have discussions if it might be helpful. But, you know, the number of cases in which you do that is so small that if you did it in every case, it would be an enormous waste, I think.

Moreover, some judges indicated that preargument communication could render the judges more likely to make up their minds prior to the oral argument and the conference. Those judges, therefore, felt that more communication before the oral argument could harm the appellate process. As one judge explained, "I believe that oral argument is an indispensable part of a decision-making process in any case of complexity. Too much interaction by the panel may have a tendency of closing down avenues that would otherwise be considered." Another judge explained that by not communicating his initial views of a case to his brethren, he has not committed himself to a view, and he can more readily change his mind without the embarrassment of admitting to his colleagues that his initial view was incorrect. When asked about communication with other judges before oral argument, he explained his view:

> A: The view that I [dictate] in my reading notes is secret—nobody knows it except me and my law clerk—so it is very easy to change my mind without embarrassment. The judges do not ordinarily exchange their views on outcomes before oral argument, so I don't commit myself then either. In a case where I am somewhat up in the air, it is not at all unusual for me to be persuaded by argument, and it is also my habit— I guess just the decision-making process that I developed in my law practice—if I don't have to make up my mind until a particular time about something, I don't. So usually I don't really make up my mind until I walk into the conference room about which view to take, and occasionally I am turned around in conference. That process of oral argument and conference are for me very genuine. Even if I think my

mind is made up, since I have not told anyone outside chambers, it is pretty easy for me to decide I was mistaken, and it happens.

Q: Do you think it would be an improvement on the system if there was more communication before oral argument among the judges?

A: No, I think it would be a detriment.

Q: Really? And that is because it would make it more difficult to change one's mind?

A: You would commit yourself more to your view before knowing as much. . . . Oral argument is often very educational. . . . So I think it would be a real problem if we communicated earlier. We would get more committed when we were more ignorant.

Q: That is interesting. Several judges have suggested that it might even be a good idea to circulate dispositions before you get to the oral argument.

A: It would make it quicker. It would make it easier to deal with the caseload. But I think we would get a lower quality of decisions because we would be less open to argument and conference process.

However, some judges reported that there are times when preargument discussion regarding substantive issues is appropriate, and in those situations, the judges reported that they did not hesitate to contact one another:

> I do not believe in springing on the judges, "Oh, look how smart I am. I just found this." Or "Here's an idea. I'll bet you didn't think of that." I want when we get to the conference, which is immediately after argument, for them to have given some thought to these problems. So I try to give them as much information ahead of time as I can. So if we found something that we thought they really ought to read and think about, we would call chambers, or I would call the judge and tell them, "This case has just come down. It has a real effect on this case. I want to make sure you are aware of it."

Similarly, several judges reported that they would call other judges to inform them if bench memoranda appeared erroneous or missed critical cases.

Oral Argument as a Communicative Device

In chapter 3, I discussed how the oral argument serves the formal purpose of providing judges the opportunity to discuss with lawyers the application of the formal legal rules to the particular facts of the case. Oral argument also serves a deeper organizational function by providing judges an opportunity to communicate not only with the parties' attorneys but also with the other judges on the panel.

Because communication before oral argument is relatively rare, in many cases the oral argument is the first time that the judges really have the chance to communicate to one another. As one judge said,

> When we ask our questions, that is the first time that the judges are exposed to each other personally on the case. And I suppose what it does, it sets up the conference. It sets up the fact that [one] judge is concerned about a certain area and another one is not. It is a very interesting process because then the lawyers may get involved in that. There is no way out of [the communicative function of oral argument] unless a judge just wants to sit and babble on from the bench.

Accordingly, Wasby has suggested that oral argument can serve a communicative function: "For some judges, questions which they ostensibly direct to a lawyer may instead be intended for a colleague, because a colleague may give more credence to a concession the lawyer makes than he would to arguments made directly by fellow judges."[7]

My data indicate that judges consciously use oral argument to directly address other judges, although they do so only rarely. More frequently, judges may use oral argument to ask the attorneys questions that may be of interest to other judges. As one judge described the process,

> To some extent what you are doing at oral argument is bank shots, like in pool, and we have to work with each other—well, with each of my colleagues, I pretty much have to work with them until one of us dies. So you try to avoid intense confrontations that would make that less pleasant. . . . Suppose you want to say that some particular idea is stupid. Usually you don't tell it to . . . the judge [who is a proponent of that idea]. What you will do is you will say it to the lawyer who is a proponent of the idea and let him try and deal with it. If he has a good answer, that's great—you really have not committed yourself. And if he flounders around unsuccessfully because it turned out that it really was a stupid idea, then if some other judge was thinking about deciding the case on the basis of that idea, he will probably think better of it. So you will never have the confrontation at conference. Conferences tend to be short, nonconfrontational, [and] somewhat summary. Most of the real conference takes place during oral argument.

---

7. Wasby, 1977, *supra* note 2, at 5; *see also* Wasby, 1987, *supra* note 2, at 99–100 ("A judge apparently asking a question to a lawyer may really intend it for another panel member and be trying to convince his colleagues to favor his view" [internal quotation marks omitted]).

Another judge similarly explained,

> If I have a feeling that one of the judges on the panel is antagonistic to a certain point of view on an issue, either from something they have written or a question they have, it is a chance for me to throw . . . off a question to one of the lawyers to give them a choice to orally expound the validity of their position. So if a judge hears it explained orally, it may help.

Even where judges do not consciously use oral argument to communicate with their brethren, the nature of the oral argument session can serve a communicative function. As a judge asks questions and the attorneys respond, the other judges pay close attention to the discussion, thereby offering them a preview of how the discussion at conference may proceed and possibly setting the tone of that conference. As one judge said, "I think [oral argument] is interesting, from my perspective, to listen to the questions of the other members of the panel and that, I think, helps frame the discussions later and certainly frames some of the analytic points of the opinion." The following exchange with another judge further clarifies oral argument's indirect communicative role:

> Q: Do you think the oral argument is used to communicate ideas with your brethren as well as with counsel?
> A: I think you certainly can gather from the questions that are asked from other members of the panel where they are coming from, or the issues that are bothering them.
> Q: Do you ever use oral argument in that fashion on purpose?
> A: I would use oral argument to rehash questions responded to, yes.

Other judges expressed the view that the oral argument should be seen not as an opportunity to communicate with other judges, but simply as an opportunity to learn more about the case. Even judges' acknowledgment that they enter into direct discussion with their brethren on the bench does not necessarily mean that oral argument is seen as communicative. According to one judge,

> It comes up that we start minidebates when we are on the bench, but it never crosses my mind that oral argument is a time for me to make my views known. My participation in oral argument is simply to learn what the heck is going on and give the lawyers an opportunity to react to my tentative views of the case.

One further purpose of the oral argument is to provide a structure to the interaction among the judges. Judges commonly noted that an important aspect of the oral argument is that all judges are focused on the same case in the same place at the same time:

> What I like about oral argument is that it focuses my attention on the case at the same time that the attention of the other two judges is focused on it. It seems to me that it makes our conference better and more likely to deal with the problems that are most troubling to the lawyers.

Similarly, another judge reported,

> The one thing you know is that during that ten or twenty minutes of argument, you have got everybody's attention focused on that case. That is a good time to raise, through questions to counsel or whatever, the points that seem to be driving the appeal and get the response, and it is particularly helpful if you have got good counsel out there. . . . And then you are going to retire to conference the case right after that, so everybody's attention ought to be drawn to it.

One consequence of waiving oral argument, therefore, is that there is no external structure to force the judges to focus on the case in the same way at the same time. Even requests for submission of a case without oral argument can cause inefficiency because they force judges to put aside what they are doing and concentrate on the submission requests. As one judge said,

> If people on the panel start asking for cases to be submitted, they normally need to do so some time in advance—that is, before I get to read the briefs, a suggestion [to submit] comes. That means I have got to go out and get the briefs, take a look at them. I will probably waste twenty minutes just deciding whether or not to agree to save the twenty minutes of argument.

By serving as a communicative device and by forcing the judges to interact over a case, oral argument serves an important structural function.

Conference and the Postconference Memorandum

Following the oral argument, the judges meet in conference, where they discuss the cases and issue preliminary votes. The conference provides the only formalized opportunity for the judges to engage in three-way oral discussion of the case. Immediately after conference, the presiding judge ordinarily drafts a memorandum that briefly summarizes the conclusions reached at the conference and any important reservations or notes indicated by the judges. As one judge explained, "The conference memo should give each person's position, where they stand, and why somebody disagrees and whatever is going on."

The conference memorandum primarily serves to remind the judges what went on in conference. Because only one of the three judges is responsible for drafting a proposed opinion or disposition, there sometimes can be a sizable delay between the conference and when the other two judges on the panel return their full attention to the case. The conference memorandum records what was said at the conference so that the nonwriting judges can later recall with greater precision what was decided.

The conference memorandum also serves as the basic instruction for what needs to go into an opinion or disposition. When a judge or law clerk begins to draft an opinion, the conference memorandum may indicate which issues need to be addressed and in what detail. As one judge explained, "I construe the conference memo as the first basic instruction to a law clerk that was going to do a draft. . . . In other words, the law clerk doesn't make the decision. The conference makes the decision. The law clerk is required to follow that decision."

Postconference Communication

Once the conference is complete, the judges retire to their chambers to write the dispositions that will terminate the case. As in the preargument stage, the judges again are separated from one another and work relatively independently from the influence of their brethren. Ordinarily, communication after conference is highly limited in its frequency and scope. The judges reported that, more often than not, communication after conference takes the form only of the distribution of a proposed opinion or disposition and brief responses to that opinion. As one judge described, "After conference, usually all you get is a draft disposition. It usually conforms with your discussions at conference and maybe a memo or two. In a great bulk of cases, it is a memo or two after conference, and it's over." There are times, though, when a writing judge discovers that, for some reason, the panel either was incomplete in its consideration of a case or erred in its determination. In those instances, judges reported that they often write the opinion or disposition in accord with the newly discovered information and attach to the proposed disposition a brief memorandum explaining the change. If that alteration is sufficiently major, on rare occasions judges may telephone their brethren to discuss the issue.

More often, after conference, communication is limited to discussion of particular aspects of a proposed written disposition prepared and circulated by one of the judges on the panel. Many judges expressed that, after conference, further communication is generally unnecessary until a draft opinion or disposition has been prepared and circulated.

> Ordinarily, unless something comes up that is a problem and is going differently from where I thought it was going, I do not [communicate with other judges] until I get a draft out so they have got some target to look at. I find that unfocused attention to issues very often is counterproductive, and unless it is going to have to be changed in a major way from the way we talked about it, or in case I need additional briefing, I usually don't communicate too much until I have something for them.

In part because of the detailed nature of the discussions at that point, the judges explained that they rarely, if ever, orally discuss a proposed disposition:

> By and large, the only time that the judges talk orally about the case at all is argument and conference. It is a rare case when we exchange a single word orally subsequent to the conference. Now, that is not to say there is no communication. The suggestions process is pretty important. The judge circulates a draft, and the other judges make suggestions, and that is serious communication. But we rarely talk about a case after conference.

Similarly, another judge stated,

> Once you get past the conference, you are at the point of dealing with the case in sufficient depth and at a sufficient level of detail so that oral communication is . . . a waste of time in most cases. You can deal orally at a more general level, but at a more detailed level often it is clearer if you do it in writing.

Some discussion may result if a change occurs in the state of the law prior to when the panel issues its opinion. In particular, a panel may briefly discuss a new decision from the Supreme Court or from another panel of the circuit. That communication, though, is often of highly limited scope, and the writing judge often will simply alter the opinion according to the new precedent and then attach to the proposed disposition a cover memorandum indicating the necessary changes.

The En Banc Process as a Communicative Device

If the court votes to rehear a case en banc, the judges of the court sit over the case together with all of their brethren.[8] In addition to allowing the court to

---

8. Note that in the Ninth Circuit, the judges hold "mini–en banc" proceedings with fewer than the full complement of judges. The mini–en banc still allows the judges to interact with a large number of their brethren in the en banc process and with all of their brethren through the memorandum exchange leading up to a vote on whether to rehear a case en banc. The Ninth Circuit's en banc proceedings will be discussed in greater depth in chapter 6.

resolve important substantive issues and to maintain the law of the circuit, the en banc process serves as a communicative device. When a controversial opinion is written, the judges communicate frequently over whether an en banc rehearing of the case is called for. That exchange serves to allow judges to discuss important issues and to become more familiar with the views of the other judges on the circuit. One Ninth Circuit judge explained,

> [The en banc process] has other functions: the exchange of memos that occur in connection with considering whether we should take a case en banc, probably more than the decision in the case, . . . bring[s] us together and give[s] the judges an idea of what everybody is thinking. So as a process, it is invaluable—in fact, essential—to maintain a circuit this large.

During the en banc process, the judges have the same opportunities to communicate among themselves as they do in an ordinary three-judge panel. However, because the judges are considering only a single case in an en banc proceeding, communication may be more in depth and meaningful. Also, as discussed later in this chapter and in chapter 6, the size of a circuit also can affect the nature of communication among judges on an en banc panel.

II.   The Clerk Network

The network of law clerks on an appellate court can serve as a powerful vehicle for interchambers communication. Just as information flows across chamber boundaries from judge to judge, so too does information flow across chamber boundaries from clerk to clerk. Communication through the clerk network may be directed by a judge, or it may occur spontaneously, undirected by a judge.

The literature on clerk communication thus far has focused almost exclusively on directed communication.[9] Directed communication occurs in two ways: (1) judges may use their clerks to circuitously contact other judges; and (2) judges may use their clerks to contact other judges' law clerks.

In the first type of directed communication, judges ask their clerks to contact other judges' clerks in the hope that they will, in turn, contact their judges. The directed judge-clerk-clerk-judge communication allows the judge to avoid directly discussing a matter with the other judge, but allows the judge to move

---

9. *See, e.g.*, Jonathan Cohen, *In the Shadow of the Law Clerk: Assessing the Role of Law Clerks in the Judicial Process*, 3 LONG TERM VIEW 99, 104 (1995); Sean Donahue, *Behind the Pillars of Justice: Remarks on Law Clerks*, 3 LONG TERM VIEW 77, 78–79 (1995); Wasby, 1987, *supra* note 2, at 121–24.

information across the boundaries that divide the chambers.[10] By and large, though, directed judge-clerk-clerk-judge communication is intended to avoid the significance of direct judge-judge communication, which may communicate more severe concern than is meant. For example, judges who have comments that may appear to nitpick at other judges' opinions may use the clerk network to communicate those concerns in an effort to avoid annoying the other judge. One clerk explained,

> [My judge] called me in and said, "I think [these comments are] too nit-picky. I don't want to be known as someone who is a pain to work with, so why don't you just go up to one of the clerks [and pass the criticisms on to him]." So I talked to the clerk, and the clerk said "Fine." . . . And then his judge subsequently said, "Yes, absolutely no problem."

As Wasby has pointed out, the line between judge-clerk-clerk-judge communication and clerk-clerk-judge communication may blur where one clerk has the responsibility of commenting on a draft or preparing a memorandum in response to another judge's draft.[11] Nevertheless, judges may wish to communicate their clerks' comments to other judges but find the remarks too insignificant to bother the other judges directly. In that instance, judges may use the clerk network to communicate the comments. For example, one judge stated,

> When an opinion comes in from a colleague and I am on the panel, that is one of the few circulations that will go first to the law clerk who worked on the case. That law clerk knows that he or she is to turn it over to me within twenty-four hours with his comments. . . . So they will then send in the . . . copy of the opinion on which they have made comments. I may then transfer onto my copies the suggestions that they have made that I think will work [or I may] send the thing back to them just saying, . . . "This one is too trivial to bother the judge with, but call the law clerk."

Judges may use the clerk network as a convenient way to send inquiries without bothering other judges. One judge explained that when he receives a memorandum from another chambers, he may find that something is "off the

---

10. Wasby has suggested that the use of clerks for directed communication is on the rise and that his data indicated that such communications were more common in 1986 than in 1977. Wasby, though, does not indicate what in his data suggests that to be the case. My data suggest that directed communication is relatively rare. Whether that means that directed communication is again on the downswing, though, is unclear, as Wasby did not report how often such communication occurred.

11. Wasby, 1987, *supra* note 2, at 121.

mark," presenting the "delicate choice of what do you do at that point." In those situations, this judge's preferred method is to use the clerk network:

> I prefer to handle it in the most professional way possible. [One way is by having] my law clerk call the other clerk who authored the memo and say, "Have you thought about this?" or "Did you take [a new Supreme Court case] into consideration?" More often than not, the other clerk will say, "Oh my goodness, I did not. Thank you." Two days later, you will get a revised bench memo. And that is the best way for that to happen, in my view.

Judges also use the clerk network to seek information from other judges' chambers without bothering the other judge. According to one clerk,

> The judge will say to me, "Find out how so and so thinks [about an issue]." And this has happened to me. One of the judges, if they have sitting coming up, and he wants to know, we have got a really tricky—either legally tricky or politically tricky—issue. The judge will come and say, "See if you can find out what so and so is thinking on this issue." And I have had other clerks call me [seeking similar information].

One judge said that he uses the clerk network to check his understanding of a point the other chambers had made. He believes that using the clerk network protects him from appearing as though he could not understand the point:

> Occasionally, I will get a comment from the judge about an opinion that I don't quite understand. I may occasionally say to a law clerk, "Call judge so-and-so's law clerk on this case and find out what they are really driving at," because I don't want to sound like an idiot when I talk to the judge, but I don't really understand what he is getting at.

One judge explained that he will use the clerk network to politely hurry-up the other judge if another chambers is slow in producing a disposition:

> [Clerk communication] probably takes place more after argument and after conference on something that seems to be hanging up, and we are not getting the dispositions out quick enough. Then I do ask the law clerks to check with the other chambers to find out whether there is anything we can do to assist or whether it just happened to slip through the cracks some way.

Judges also will use the clerk network to coordinate the caseload. That use is especially vital in the Ninth Circuit where, because judges divide primary responsibility for each case prior to oral argument, different judges may have writing responsibility for cases that are similar or related. As one Ninth Circuit judge explained,

> I hope that, if it is cost-effective in time, that they will communicate with the other law clerks, particularly if they discover—once in a while, we will get a case in which, because [of] the panel assignment . . . we will get four or five immigration cases on the same calendar. Or we will get four or five cases out of bankruptcy court. [And] the random distribution will produce a case where your office is working on one bankruptcy matter and my office might be working on one, and we discover there is probably a common issue. I think it is cost-effective in time management and every other way to have law clerks communicate. Some judges don't like it, don't want their law clerks to talk, but I have never found it a problem.

Similarly, because cases that are related may be assigned to different panels, a judge will use a law clerk to inquire about how a panel that has heard a case but not yet issued an opinion is coming out on an issue. Again, that type of communication is especially vital in the Ninth Circuit, where a formal rule states that the panel that has heard the case first, not necessarily the panel that issues its decision first, determines the binding precedent. As a result, without communication among the judges on different panels, a panel might issue a decision that contradicts the binding precedent as determined by a case that was heard first but decided later.

One difficulty that judges find in using their clerks to communicate with other judges is that communication between two clerks, like that between two judges, may leave out the third judge on the panel. As one judge explained,

> [Clerk communication] happens, but we are a little cautious on that because we like to make sure that this is a three-cornered hat, and nobody is cut out of the process. But sometimes I will say, "Well, call this law clerk and talk this over with him." So that happens.

In a second form of directed communication, the judge may intend to contact not the other judge but the other judge's clerk. Directed judge-clerk-clerk communication is intended to tap the other judge's clerk as a resource where he or she has some expertise relevant to a case. For example, one judge stated,

> I encourage [my clerks] to [communicate with clerks from other chambers] with discretion. My personal feeling is that the clerks of the judges are the clerks of the Ninth Circuit. You work for all of the judges. . . . More often than not, . . . we find a clerk with a particular expertise. In one case,

... [one] clerk [in another chambers] had just written [an] article ... on a certain First Amendment issue—freedom of religion issue. And I would say to my clerk, "We got this issue. Go down and talk to [the other clerk]." We had a lot of interaction.

Such communication also may result because another judge's clerk has developed expertise in the facts of the particular case before the panel.

More common than directed communication is undirected communication, where a clerk from one chambers communicates about a substantive issue with a clerk from another chambers without instruction from—and often without the knowledge of—both judges. How much undirected communication occurs, and its significance, depends first on judges' instructions to their clerks regarding such communication and second on the clerks' discretion in discussing cases.

Judges have a great range of sentiments about their clerks discussing cases with other chambers' clerks. On one end of the spectrum are judges who view the clerks as working not for a single judge but for the court as a whole. In those chambers, the judge does not discourage interchambers communication and may indeed recognize and harness its benefits. One judge, for example, explained that he asks his clerks to discuss matters with other clerks and that he tells his clerks, "If they can convince you that you are wrong, and you can convince me, then there is a good chance we are wrong. We'll just change." Another judge explained that the clerk network can serve as an efficient means of communication and may serve to avoid time-consuming difficulties later in the process:

> I encourage my clerks and have no objection to their calling up some other clerk who is working on the same thing and saying, "You are doing this. Why are you doing that?" and so on. I think it is a useful way, rather than have an official communication between judges. You get a lot of things done.

Another judge explained that he found that the process carried profound benefits for the court as a whole: "I like the interchange. Some of the other judges may not. [It is helpful to my work because it brings] fresh ideas, fresh cases. I suppose rarely does it change a result—very rarely, probably. But it is apt to foster unanimity, I think." Still another judge views undirected clerk communication as a responsibility of his clerks' job. His clerk explained that "another responsibility of the clerk is as a liaison to other chambers with other clerks. The judge likes to know what people are thinking about decisions or opinions or whatever." One judge tempered his hesitation to have clerks communicate with other clerks with the view that clerks should listen to clerks from

other chambers: "They are supposed to listen. They are not supposed to talk—
I mean, it is all right, but they are there basically to talk to me about it first and
see what I say about its outcome."

Although judges may not mind that their clerks communicate informally
with those in other chambers, the judges may view such communication war-
ily because other judges are sensitive about such communication. Judges,
therefore, may instruct their clerks not to communicate with other chambers'
clerks unless there is some compelling reason to do so:

> I don't object to [a law clerk's] calling [another chambers]. However, I
> know that other chambers are sometimes sensitive to that, so I ask them to
> use care in talking with other chambers. I really don't care if other cham-
> bers talk to my clerks, or vice versa, but some judges do care. And they care
> quite deeply about that, so I just advise [my clerks], unless it is an impor-
> tant point, not to call other chambers.

Similarly, another judge explained, "I leave [the amount of clerk communica-
tion] pretty much up to [my law clerk's] discretion. I don't prohibit it. On the
other hand, I don't necessarily encourage it because I don't want to place any
additional burden on the other chambers."

At the other end of the spectrum are judges who feel that their law clerks
should not communicate with other chambers' law clerks unless absolutely
necessary. Those judges expressed the feeling that such communications often
take the form of a law clerk lobbying another chambers for a particular position, which those judges felt to be wholly inappropriate. Even in those chambers where judges prefer that their clerks do not engage in interchambers communication, though, there is a recognition that the clerk network has a proper
role in that clerks must communicate for purposes of sharing the record and
other information pertinent to a case:

> I don't really like my clerks talking a whole lot to other chambers. I regard
> a lot of that conversation as simply politicking of judges, and I don't want
> to really be politicked by some person one year out of law school. So I don't
> particularly encourage it; in fact, I discourage it a little bit. There is always
> conversation. The clerks call up and say, "Do you have the record?" [or]
> "Can you find testimony of this witness on this point?" So you always have
> that sort of thing. But I certainly don't encourage them to call up and say,
> "My judge disagrees with your bench memo" because I don't think that is
> appropriate.

One concern for those judges is that the clerks will have the opportunity to broker an agreement about how a case should come out. One judge explained,

I don't discourage [clerk-clerk communication], but I suppose that there could be a court where the clerks broker an agreement, and that is not what I think this court is all about. I know there are some judges who are more restrictive about their clerks talking to other judges' clerks. I have no prohibition to that. But the point is that we are trying to advance the review of the case versus brokering a deal on the outcome.

Another concern is that clerks will be influenced by other chambers' clerks and, therefore, no longer will be capable of providing an independent view. According to one judge,

My preference is that there be no communication because I want my clerks to be independent of me, and I certainly don't want them influenced by other clerks or other persons. So I tell them not to communicate with other clerks concerning a bench memo that has come in where they might have a disagreement. I think that is a matter up to the judges.

Judges recognize that they ultimately have only limited control over their clerks' communication and there is no choice but to rely on law clerks' discretion of what is proper to discuss. Some judges, therefore, have resigned themselves to trusting in their clerks' judgment and satisfy themselves with providing their clerks some modest guidelines for interchambers communication:

I allow them to [talk to clerks in other chambers]. I don't prohibit them. I know some judges do, but I don't prohibit them. . . . I hired them because they are discreet, and they are the best and the brightest from around the country, so I don't expect that I am working with saboteurs. So I don't second-guess them. I give them a little lecture on appropriate decorum and so forth, but by and large, I guess I try to do everything I can to encourage an atmosphere where there is just a totally open discussion until the moment when we have our docket conference. But until that time, while the cases are being reviewed, and the bench memos or whatever are being prepared, as far as I am concerned I want no breaks on that at all.

Just as informal communication between judges depends, in part, on the personal closeness of the judges, so too does informal law clerk communication depend on personal ties. Some ties within the clerk community naturally grow out of law school ties. Many court clerks come out of relatively few law schools and consequently may know one another before coming to a court. Many others have had similar law school experiences that may aid the clerks in forming closer personal bonds. Another trend in the courts is that judges who are personally closer tend to have clerks who are personally closer, in part, because judges that are personally close may choose clerks who have similar interests or backgrounds.

III.   The Bench Memorandum as a Communicative Device

In circuits that pool their bench memorandum resources, the bench memorandum can serve as an important and rare opportunity to communicate across chambers boundaries prior to oral argument. As a communicative device, the bench memorandum sits between direct communication among the judges and a directed clerk-clerk-judge communication. At least on the surface, bench memoranda are authored by law clerks; however, in the majority of judges' chambers, the judge has at least some role in the preparation process. In fact, in some chambers, the bench memorandum is written in a back-and-forth process between the judge and the clerk that is highly reminiscent of the opinion-writing process. Indeed, some judges indicate on cover memoranda that the bench memorandum comes not from the individual law clerk but rather from the judge's chambers.

The judges on the Ninth Circuit generally deny that they use the bench memorandum as a communicative device. Rather, they maintain that the bench memorandum is, by design, nothing more than a tool to help them to prepare to decide cases. As one judge said, "It is not a persuasive tool because I am not necessarily persuaded myself. My opinion is preliminary in the sense that I am not wedded to it at that point." Judges who work diligently on the bench memoranda to produce a document that represents their own personal view of the case persistently maintain that it is not designed to convince their brethren of their point of view but only to provide a neutral analysis.

Conversely, several judges indicated that, although they did not use bench memoranda as an opportunity to argue their points of view, other judges did.

> At least one judge has told us that he does [use the bench memo to express his viewpoint]. He has indicated in our judges' meetings that no bench memo goes out unless it reflects his view of the case. He tells the law clerk from the beginning "We have got to reverse in this case. [The police] once again acted like storm troopers. This was a terrible search, abusive," and so forth. But that is one judge. I know that he does that so I read his bench memos very, very carefully because I know they reflect his views, not the law clerk's. I thank him for his candor. I would much prefer that to some judge who pretended not to.

Another judge said,

I . . . know from talking with other judges that they take a different view of bench memos. In some cases, they view that as the initial starting point for convincing the other two judges to go along with their point of view. At least at this point in my career, and I might change, but I don't think so, what I have encouraged the law clerks to do is to write for the panel and not for me.

Even where judges do not consciously use the bench memorandum as a communicative or argumentative device, it may indicate how one judge views the case. Accordingly, how much of a communicative role the bench memorandum plays is a function of the degree of guidance the judge provides to the law clerk in drafting the document.

Judges follow three basic models for preparing their chambers' bench memoranda. First, the judge may simply set the clerk to work on the bench memorandum without any guidance. In that first model, the judge provides the clerk with absolutely no input on the memorandum and generally does not even review it before distributing it to the other judges on the panel. One judge stated,

> I don't involve myself in the preparation of the bench memorandum. That is not meant to do anything other than provide an analysis of the issues, and I don't expect to have my stamp of approval on it, nor do I get involved in it. . . . It is just a law clerk functioning as a law clerk instead of to one judge, to three judges. I not infrequently disagree with the law clerk's bench memorandum.
>
> But if you assume, which we should assume, that this is not an assignment for writing an opinion but an assignment to give a bench memorandum, you also assume that the bench memorandum is to do nothing more than to give you an analysis of the issues before the court. And if you assume also that the bench memorandum is not supposed to be a first draft of some disposition, then I feel quite comfortable with the role I play. And, in fact, on the covering memorandum that goes out, it indicates that this is the work of the law clerk which I have not reviewed.
>
> The only limitation that is placed on them is length. . . . Other than that, they have no instructions from me as to how it is to come out or otherwise, only to do a good job in analyzing as best they can.

Similarly, another judge explained,

> I see the bench memo as being written for all three of the judges and not as an expression of the view of the particular judge. . . . I don't discuss the cases with the law clerks until after the bench memo is written. But I have

already read the briefs and come to my own point of view, so I can get their input where I have gone wrong, and they can get mine if they have gone wrong.

Conversely, some judges reported that they were irritated by the practice of allowing the law clerk to write the bench memorandum with no input from the judge. Those judges expressed frustration because they found that those memoranda sometimes had errors or omissions that an experienced attorney would have caught: "I get some [bench memos] that say [the judge has] not read the bench memo. I get memorandum dispositions where the judge says 'I have not read this.' So I feel like saying, 'Well, I am not going to read it either.'" Some of the judges who do not provide supervision responded to that concern by expressing their view that the bench memorandum provides a view of the case by an independent law clerk—an individual not representing any party to the action or any judge who ultimately will decide the case. One judge explained,

> Basically, what you want is some bright young clerk to go through and correlate the arguments with the parties to make sure they join on the issue, do independent research as needed, and come to a conclusion. It is a road map sort of thing. It is certainly not conclusive. When it comes out of my chambers, it doesn't represent my opinion, necessarily.

Other judges plainly admitted that they do not provide guidance merely as a matter of convenience, explaining that they simply have not begun to review the case at the time that the bench memoranda are due to be distributed:

> I don't guide them. The first one or two bench memos a clerk writes for me I will read the briefs and the bench memo and make a critique or corrections or anything necessary. After that, I don't. The truth is, the clerks are into the cases before I am, but they are generally not talking to me about it. They are just making do and getting out their bench memos because those are due just about the time I start reading the briefs.

In the second model, the judge provides the law clerk some guidance in preparing the bench memorandum. However, the judge views the memorandum as the clerk's work rather than the judge's, and therefore the judge does not require that the memorandum ultimately agrees with the judge's view of the case. Judges who follow the second model generally set their law clerks to work on the memorandum without providing any input. The judge then discusses with the clerk any difficulties as they arise. In that sense, the judge does not direct the clerk in preparing the bench memorandum but instead offers guidance to help the law clerk produce a quality bench memorandum. One judge explained his process as follows:

> I only am a sounding board for the clerks preparing the bench memo. It is their product. I don't tell them how I want it to come out. I mean, we may discuss the merits of the case, and I may indicate a feeling about the outcome or maybe even a strong feeling. But I need the clerk's independent review of the advocacy of the appellant and the appellee because, if not, I would just say, "Look, why don't you write this up?" I have lost the talent and the research ability of the clerk who is researching the matter for me.

Unlike in the first model, judges who operate in the second model will review the memorandum before sending it out to other judges. That review is relatively light, looking for significant errors or omissions. The judges in the second model do not insist that the clerk come to any particular outcome:

> I will have talked to my clerks with respect to issues that they are writing a bench memo on, that they are concerned about, and will read their bench memos when they are finished and before they are circulated. I don't try to make major changes in the bench memos because they go out under the names of my clerks. But if they really miss the boat, I will talk to them about it, and they often make changes in the bench memo before they circulate them.

Another judge explained,

> If the bench memo seriously disagrees with my preliminary thoughts, if it is one of my cases then I will go talk to the clerk and see where the problem is. But I don't force my clerks to write bench memos that reflect my views. If the clerk has a considered opinion and has thought it through, and I simply disagree with it, I will let the bench memo go out with the clerk's conclusions, and I will probably send a cover memo with my thoughts. . . . There is all kinds of room in this business for points of view. If we have got a sharp clerk who thinks it ought to come out one way, and I disagree, I will [send it out]. I think the judges ought to have the benefit of both thoughts.

In the third model, judges provide clerks with a high degree of guidance. Judges and clerks work together on the bench memorandum in a process reminiscent of the opinion-drafting process. Consequently, the bench memorandum generally reflects the judge's view of the case. That, though, does not mean that judges who use the third model view the bench memorandum as an argumentative device. Instead, judges in the third model view the bench memorandum drafting process as integral to their own decision-making process. As judges work with clerks, testing arguments and weighing precedents, the judges continuously hone their views. Consequently, by the time the bench memorandum is sent out, such judges generally are convinced that their perspectives are correct.

The third model prevents the awkward situation where the bench memorandum presents a view different from the judge's ultimate view of the case, and where the judge must argue in conference, and perhaps in a dissent, against the view that his chambers defended in the bench memorandum. According to one judge,

> It certainly is a bit awkward if I go to the panel and say, "I really don't agree with what is written [in the bench memo]," because they view it as a product of the chambers—and rightfully so. I usually explain this is what I try to do, and I may not endorse everything that is there. But I think it encourages some independent thinking and some pride in the work.

One judge described the awkwardness of such a situation:

> A very bright extern of mine wrote a bench memo . . . about seven years ago. I read it and said, "Well, it is a good piece of work, but I don't agree with it." And she said, "Well, what are you going to do?" I said, "I am going to send it out, and I am going to put a little note, as I do on all of them, that this reflects your views and not mine." Well, the panel . . . loved her bench memo, so I ended up writing a dissent, and they incorporated almost word for word everything in her bench memo. Well, the Supreme Court [recently] came out with a case [that] overruled [that] case. It took seven years for me to overcome my extern's brilliant bench memo, which was wrong.

A result of that potentially awkward situation is that, regardless of their level of involvement in the bench memorandum drafting process, some judges insist that the bench memorandum ultimately accord with the judge's view of the case:

> I am not very deferential toward bench memos, and I don't really care whether I disagree with a bench memo. It just does not cause a problem for me to disagree with my own law clerks or another judge's law clerk's bench memo. Other judges are more deferential toward bench memos in some cases, and occasionally I have had difficulty in conference, where I dis-

agreed with my own law clerk's bench memo, persuading the judges of my view instead of the bench memo's view. So I have leaned toward not having my law clerk sign the bench memos, just having them come out of my chambers and having them reflect the views of my reading notes.

If the law clerk comes out with a different view from mine, then what I will do is have the law clerk talk to me before the bench memo goes out. Sometimes when I dictate my reading notes, I dictate that it is not clear to me how an issue should be resolved or it could go either way, and my law clerk has independence on it. Sometimes my law clerk will talk to me and say, "Judge, you came out this way on the bench memo, but I think we should come out that way because of this and this authority." And I will say, "Well, show me." And I will look at it and the law clerk is right, and I say, "Go ahead and send it out your way." And sometimes the law clerk will say, "You came out this way but I think we should come out that way because here is how I evaluate this." I might agree with him and I might not. I might say, "Well, you have your view, and I have mine, and I want the bench memo to reflect mine."

At the other extreme, many judges do not mind sending out bench memoranda that disagree with their views. In fact, some of the judges expressed the perspective that disagreement with clerks is beneficial and that their brethren should enjoy the benefits of that clerk's viewpoint:

I kind of appreciate their independent take on the thing. I don't want them to be parroting my views. I like the fresh look. I am sort of doing my thing on the case, they are doing their thing on the case. And therefore we have sort of two fresh looks at it. Sometimes we completely agree, sometimes we don't. But then, after all, maybe I missed something, or maybe I will tell them, "Maybe you missed something." So I like the idea that they are off on their own.

Another judge concurred,

What happens not infrequently as a result of [the bench memo disagreeing with my view of a case] is I go one way and the panel goes the other. And they will use all of my arguments. And all my research. But they'll go down one road, and I'll go down the other. I think our bench memos are very good, very thorough, so that is quite possible. But my view of a bench memo is not to put forth my position but to explore the issues all the way down the line, so that when a decision is made, nobody is doing it in ignorance of what is out there.

Because the bench memorandum can serve a communicative function, it limits other preargument interaction. According to one judge,

> I think the bench memorandum has the tendency to limit our interaction. It also has the tendency to—some may in some instances interfere with the broader oral argument. I am not convinced that bench memoranda is a good process for us to pursue. It is one that has now been made, but I am not convinced that it is right. When I came on the court, we did not share bench memoranda or our early work. Having experienced both sides, I am not convinced we are, just as the decision-making process is concerned, better off with bench memoranda. I understand the efficiencies involved, but that is a separate issue in quality of decision making.

Overall, however, the judges on the Ninth Circuit were satisfied with the shared bench memorandum process.

IV.   The Role of Size in Interchambers Communication

It has been commonly observed that size constitutes a significant dimension of organizational structure.[12] As Peter Blau and Richard Schoenherr have said, "Size is the most important condition affecting the structure of organizations."[13] This section discusses two aspects of the courts' organizational size: geographic size and numerical size.

---

12. *See* John Kimberly, *Organizational Size and the Structuralist Perspective: A Review, Critique and Proposal,* 19 ADMIN. SCI. Q. 571 (1976); *see also* PETER BLAU & RICHARD SCHOENHERR, THE STRUCTURE OF ORGANIZATIONS 57 (1977) (discussing the importance of size in organizational analysis); *cf.* Wasby, 1987, *supra* note 2, at 127 (discussing the geographic and numerical size of appellate courts). I treat organizational size as a dimension of organizational structure. In so doing, I follow a long tradition in organizational theory. *See, e.g.,* W. RICHARD SCOTT, ORGANIZATIONS: RATIONAL, NATURAL, AND OPEN SYSTEMS 241 (1987) (citing Richard Hall & Charles Tittle, *Bureaucracy and Its Correlates,* 72 AM. J. OF SOC. 267, 267–72 [1966]). It is true that depending on what one means by *size,* treating size as a dimension of organizational structure may mask the fact that size may result from the interaction of other organizational characteristics, such as the interaction of technology and environmental conditions (such as demand). *See id.* Where organizational size is viewed as the result of such interaction, size is properly understood to be a dependent variable that may serve as an indicator for more elusive concepts such as organizational success. *See, e.g.,* Blau & Schoenherr, *supra,* at 57. My interest in studying organizational size, however, is to understand how size affects other structural dimensions, such as boundary spanning and collegiality. Consequently, it makes sense to view size as an independent variable that is itself a dimension of organizational structure, particularly given that court size is determined by the public dimension of the courts rather than by economic success or strategic planning.

13. Blau & Schoenherr, *supra* note 12, at 57.

Geographic Size

A court's geographic size can be measured in at least two ways: (1) the geographic span of the circuit; and (2) the geographic dispersion of the court's resources.

Geographic Span

The geographic span of a circuit includes the area over which the judges of the court exercise jurisdiction. With the exception of the Federal Circuit, each of the courts of appeals has a land-based system of jurisdiction in which they have the authority to hear cases arising within a span of territory. For example, the Ninth Circuit has jurisdiction over California, Oregon, Washington, Alaska, Hawaii, Idaho, Arizona, Nevada, and some American territories, including American Samoa, Guam, and the Northern Mariana Islands. The Seventh Circuit has jurisdiction over Illinois, Indiana, and Wisconsin. The D.C. Circuit exercises jurisdiction over the District of Columbia as well as over appeals from certain determinations of administrative agencies. The First Circuit has jurisdiction over Maine, New Hampshire, Massachusetts, Rhode Island, and Puerto Rico.

The circuit's geographic span itself does not appear to be a very significant factor in the judges' interaction. Although some judges reflected that the geographic span affects them by affecting the types of cases that come before the court and the lawyers who argue them, the judges overall dismissed the geographic span of the circuit as having any significant effect on the way that the judges interact or the way that they work.

The only way in which there was any hint that the court's geographic span might have an effect is in the diversity of the judges who sit on the cases. Virtually all of the judges on the courts of appeals were residents of a state within the circuit at the time of their appointment. Two judges on the Ninth Circuit believed that the circuit's large geographic span served as an advantage because the judges represented diverse areas with a variety of concerns and perspectives. Consequently, those judges suggested that a large geographic span enabled the judges to benefit from diversity in a way that a smaller court might not.

The notable exception to the rule that judges are drawn from within the circuit is that the judges on the D.C. Circuit and the Federal Circuit were appointed from a national pool. However, because of the specialized jurisdictions of those two courts, the diversity that might otherwise have derived from drawing judges from a nationwide pool is somewhat alleviated by the jurisdictional specialization.

Some of the judges on the Ninth Circuit believe that the circuit's large geographic span gives rise to a political issue of some significance. The judges suggested that the recent slate of proposals to split the Ninth Circuit may have resulted, at least in part, from the belief among some lawyers and politicians that judges from one region might not be capable of dispensing justice in a very different region. According to one judge, the view that judges represented specific areas led to the suspicion that judges from California were overly liberal on some issues and therefore were not adequately sensitive to issues that are important to residents of more conservative states, such as Idaho, Alaska, Washington, and Oregon. In that judge's view, such suspicions were unjustified because one of the important elements of having multistate appellate courts is to provide consistency to balance the regional district courts. Moreover, he thought that the idea that California judges were too liberal was absurd. Whatever the empirical truth, though, the judges on the Ninth Circuit thought that the diversity of judges drawn from large circuits was a benefit.

Geographic Dispersion and Cybercollegiality

More significant to the judges' interaction with one another is the court's geographic dispersion—the geographic distance between judges. Because all judges on most circuit courts do not retain their home chambers in the circuit seat, the judges are not in the same city most of the time. For example, the seat for the Ninth Circuit is in San Francisco, but only two active judges retain their home chambers there. Instead, active judges sit in Pasadena, California (four judges); Reno, Nevada (one judge); Phoenix, Arizona (three judges); Portland, Oregon (two judges); Boise, Idaho (two judges); Seattle, Washington (one judge); Woodland Hills, California (one judge); Los Angeles, California (two judges); Fairbanks, Alaska (one judge); and Billings, Montana (one judge). In contrast, in the D.C. Circuit, all eleven active judges sit in the circuit seat in Washington. Thus, where the Ninth Circuit is dispersed, the D.C. Circuit is compact. Between those extremes is the Seventh Circuit, in which five of the ten active judges sit in Chicago, the circuit seat. The remaining judges sit in Milwaukee, Wisconsin (two judges); South Bend, Indiana (two judges); and Lafayette, Indiana (one judge).

Although geographic span is related to geographic dispersion, judges in a circuit with a large span are not necessarily dispersed. For example, the Ninth Circuit could impose a requirement that judges maintain their home chambers in San Francisco. However, because judges are generally appointed to sit on the circuit in which they reside, there is a strong correlation between the circuit's geographic span and its dispersion. As one Ninth Circuit judge explained, although the travel to and from the circuit's seat and the places where the court holds argument is highly disruptive to his work, he keeps his chambers in a different city because "I grew up in this town. I cannot afford to live in any other of the urban cities [within the circuit]." He further explained, *

I am given the choice now. If I did not have any choice, I would have to pick somewhere and have to figure the monetary problem out. But I have a choice. I live here because I grew up in this town, and my family is here. And it is a nice place to live, and it is not a big overgrown urban city. But if we were all forced to move to San Francisco, I suppose we would all somehow figure it out.

Geographic dispersion may significantly influence the ways that judges interact with one another. For example, the Ninth Circuit judges rarely are all in the same place at the same time. Because the court hears arguments in a variety of cities, even if the court held all of its arguments in the same week each month (which it does not), the judges would not all be in the same place at the same time. Occasionally, the Ninth Circuit holds judicial conferences in which the judges gather to discuss issues and problems of the circuit, which may ease dispersion somewhat. But unlike circuits with a smaller geographic dispersion, the Ninth Circuit judges all gather together only at those relatively rare events.

However, that the judges retain their home chambers in geographically disparate cities does not necessarily mean that the judges do not have frequent gatherings. For example, in the First Circuit, the active judges sit in significantly dispersed cities including Hato Rey, Puerto Rico (one judge); Boston, Massachusetts (two judges); Providence, Rhode Island (one judge); Portland, Maine (one judge); and Concord, New Hampshire (one judge). When the First Circuit holds oral argument, though, all of the judges are in the same city at the same time. The First Circuit holds arguments for one week each month, at which time all six judges gather in Boston.

Geographic dispersion may significantly affect the court's functioning. As Wasby has explained, "Geography's principal negative effect was that face-to-face contact was more difficult."[14] As one Ninth Circuit judge said,

I think that [communication problems due to the court's geographic size] is our biggest problem. If we had not developed the CCI system in the early '80s, I think the circuit would have started to crumble by now, because I think what I see—I know that other judges don't agree with me, but I would say the majority tend to—it is very, very important for face-to-face communication, or at least over the phone, where the judges can talk through the issues in the cases and also continue to develop an understanding of the general philosophical orientation of the judges and what are the considerations that go into deciding cases. And you don't do that very effectively by sending verbal bullets back and forth.

---

14. Wasby, 1987, *supra* note 2, at 133 (quotation marks omitted).

Another Ninth Circuit judge explained that geographic dispersion makes it more difficult for the three judges on a panel to discuss cases:

> There is no question [that we would communicate more about cases if we all were in the same building]. If we were all in the same building, that would happen. [But] we have been functioning this way for a quarter of a century, at least. That was not changed based upon numbers. I don't think there is any question that if all of us were in the same building, it would be, for many reasons, easier to get together on issues and talk about things. . . . It would [be advantageous]. For example, if you have a really tough problem, you could ask the two judges to come into your chambers at a certain time, tell them what you want to discuss, and they can maybe talk about it. Now, the way it is, we have to do that by memoranda or conference call. So I think the process would be better served if we were all in the same building. I thought that right along. From the very beginning, I could see the advantages of being in the same building.

Because the judges rarely communicate by conference telephone call and never by video conferencing (a technology that Wasby thought to be on the rise in 1987),[15] geographic dispersion continues to contribute to the relative rarity of face-to-face contact. However, many judges indicated that the increasing relevance of instant communication through electronic mail went some distance toward moderating the negative effects of geographic dispersion. As one Ninth Circuit judge explained,

> [Geography matters] much less so now than when I first became a judge. When I first became a judge, we didn't have CCI. If I wanted to ask [another judge] something, and I could not get him on the phone in Hawaii, I would send him a letter. Maybe eight days later he would respond, and so forth. Now, we fax. We call. We CCI. I think the advent of computers and all the other [technologies that I use to] communicate—I am on the fax machine all the time with five or six judges on various issues, better than if they were upstairs. I don't see the judges upstairs. We will see very little of them. My communication with them is through faxes and on the phone.

Another judge explained that "e-mail gives you a chance to really . . . effective[ly] exten[d] the conference after oral argument."

Although advances in technology have enabled judges to communicate instantly over large geographic areas, such advances have not enabled the

---

15. *Id.*

judges to communicate as informally as judges can do when they work in the same building. That informal face-to-face communication can serve an important role in the appellate judicial process. In contrast to the collegiality formed by informal face-to-face communication, one judge characterized the new collegiality formed through e-mail communication as "cybercollegiality." He noted that cybercollegiality can overcome some distance problems. For example, the computer network has significantly affected the way that judges communicate with one another, and computer bulletin boards and computer voting also have created a level of collegiality. However, the judge said, that communication can often be more formal than in-person communication. In effect, cybercollegiality exists when judges maintain a close intellectual distance while retaining a far physical and social distance. As one Ninth Circuit judge explained,

> I think that if you are in proximity to the other judges, I think it does encourage a bit more of an interaction. There are some judges who believe ... that you should not have any interaction. There should not be any two-judge interaction, that if there is any deliberation or consideration of law, that it include all three judges. I think that is a bit harsh. I think, frankly, on working through a point, it is very helpful to sit down with one other judge, if there is a sticking point on a case—particularly if the difference is between two judges—to go into the other judge's chambers, sit down, and try to work through it. I think those are helpful sessions, but unfortunately, that is, I think, a weakness of the court in one respect is that there is less deliberation than if the court were a smaller court and sitting in one place. There are some benefits, too, but I think the deliberation tends to be more formal in exchange of drafts rather than informal.

However, it would be a mistake to overestimate the amount of informal communication among judges within a single building. Judges on both the compact D.C. Circuit and the dispersed Ninth Circuit indicated that they rarely had face-to-face discussions about cases even with judges who maintain chambers in the same building. According to one Ninth Circuit judge,

> My guess is that even if we were all in the same building, on the same floor, in the same corridor, we still would not talk to each other about the cases. It just takes so much time, and it is so inefficient in terms of reducing a final disposition. I don't think it would make a whole lot of difference. . . . I practiced law in a small town where, for many years, most of the lawyers were on one floor, on one corridor, in one building, and we communicated mostly in writing about the cases. It is efficient. For one thing, you are not always interrupting each other. You can say precisely what you mean

instead of roughly what you mean. And you create a record so people can go back to it. I don't think [being together] would make a whole lot of difference except we would get into more fights with each other. . . . That is not to say that I approve of the size of our circuit. It is just that on that particular issue, I don't think it is significant. We have eliminated the problems that the mail used to cause.

Another judge explained,

I don't think that the physical location of the judges makes any major difference. Even if we were all confined to one building and one floor, it would not make a major difference because of the personalities of the judges and their busyness would not permit them to be as social as perhaps they might be.

In fact, only three of the Ninth Circuit judges indicated that they have more informal interaction with judges located in the same building, and one of those judges stated that such informal communication is not always a benefit:

The blessings of e-mail and the telephone make it so that I can communicate on cases very well, as well as with judges who are near. I surely see face to face the judges near me more than those who are in distant cities, but I find that I communicate exactly the same with those near me as with those that are far. In fact, I think the distance helps because it keeps us from getting at each other's throats. If we were all in the same building, facing the same people with the same issue more often, we would be more inclined to get annoyed. The fact is, we see one another sufficiently so that the extra face-to-face contact is not necessary. We know one another's views and habits well enough.

Another judge explained, "It is very fine to have them all staying in the same place, but it is like a college dormitory. It is because of the relationships that you develop, not the information you exchange on the particular project."

Nevertheless, geographic dispersion carries negative effects that go beyond the inability to communicate informally with other judges in the same building. Geographic dispersion creates potentially enormous inefficiencies in the circuit's operation. First, the judges themselves must spend time and money traveling from city to city to hear argument, and communication over distance also costs the judges in time. As one judge said,

[Our large geographic size] causes us to be inefficient. Rather than being in a city where we could walk to the courtroom together and solve a matter, we have to do it by e-mail. We cannot face each other personally. Travel disrupts me terribly because I have got to pack everything up. I have got to figure out what I am going to do for the next week, what I need, how I am going to do it. I have got to bring part of my staff with me. I have got to stay in a hotel room—I mean, it is totally disruptive.

Another judge related that if all judges on the circuit were located in the same building, "I think that there would be an efficiency factor. . . . Because if we all reported every day to one building, then the mechanics of getting things done, I think, would be obviously much simpler, much faster, and probably more efficient."

Second, having judges sit in geographically disparate cities requires the circuit to maintain duplicate facilities, such as court libraries and support services. The money spent on those duplications is money not spent on upgrading equipment, hiring more staff to aid in the processing of cases, or more diverse library resources.

Geographic dispersion may also affect how judges use their law clerks. Judges who must travel to oral argument may bring one or more of their clerks. From the perspective of those clerks, travel is at best a mixed blessing. Many Ninth Circuit clerks looked forward to traveling, but it can prove to be a very trying experience. Because judges on the Ninth Circuit hear oral argument for one week each month for eight months each year, the law clerks frequently are working on the upcoming oral argument calendar while the judge is hearing oral arguments on the prior calendar. To make matters worse, the facilities in visiting chambers can be inadequate for clerks' needs. The time spent getting from place to place can be burdensome. And a traveling law clerk's duties can be onerous. Thus, clerks who travel can face severe inconveniences in their work.

In addition, the judge cannot have face-to-face contact with the staff who remain at the home chambers. However, as with judge-judge communication, advancing technology has provided some respite from these communication problems. As one judge said,

> [One of our colleagues] is not reluctant to dictate memoranda constantly. I just sat with [that judge] up in Seattle. I was receiving rather lengthy memos from him on a daily basis, and he was not with a secretary. . . . I said, "How are you doing it?" and he said that after he got out of conference, he would call his office in [another city] and dictate to his secretary or perhaps a law clerk or to both, and she would prepare a memorandum that was intended for me up in Seattle. And I got it the next morning, incidentally. Very lengthy memoranda. On the other hand, I did not write memoranda up in Seattle because I did not have a secretary with me, and it was just awkward for me to do so with my staff down here.

Moreover, geographic dispersion can weaken the efficacy of the clerk network as a means for informal communication across chambers. Law clerks get to know other clerks in the same building, leading to an informal exchange of ideas across chambers. Where the judges are spread out physically, the clerk network more closely relies on the relationships that predate the clerks' terms, such as those formed in law school.

Although geographic dispersion has some potentially invidious effects, it also carries some benefits. One Ninth Circuit judge said that distance increased collegiality because "absence makes the heart grow fonder." Another judge explained, "I would guess that we all get along much better because we don't see each other as often. If we saw each other more often, we would be more hostile to those we disagreed with and more friendly with those we agreed with, and it would tend to produce factions." One Ninth Circuit judge suggested that the efficiency benefits of having all of the judges in one place are outweighed by the benefits of dispersion:

> I don't know if [requiring all the judges to be in one city] would do anything for collegiality. If anything, it will make it worse because when you put twenty-six judges in the same building, they cannot get away from each other. So collegiality is a whole different issue [from efficiency]. If you wanted to have a mechanical body that worked under strict rules and you put them in one place with a mechanical system and said "Do your job and do it as fast and as much as you could," being in one place helps.

Another Ninth Circuit judge indicated that geographic dispersion had less to do with collegiality than with judges' attitudes toward their brethren:

> [Being in one place] is obviously efficient. But it is more than efficiency. It has to do with the decision-making process. But the assumption is that we could maintain our collegiality if we were together. Unless we had the same collegiality we have now, being in the same building would not appreciably help the decision process, it would only go to the efficiency process. Unfortunately, some judges who are in the same building have less collegiality than we have. I don't think that . . . has to do with setting. It has to do with attitude and how the court has functioned and what its traditions are.

Numerical Size

Another measure of the size of a circuit court is the number of judges. The circuit courts range in size from the First Circuit (six active judges) to the Ninth Circuit (approximately eighteen active judges, twenty-eight authorized positions). Between those two extremes are the Seventh Circuit (ten active judges) and the D.C. Circuit (eleven active judges).

Like geographic dispersion, numerical size can affect the court's institutional life because, as the number of judges increases, so do social distance and judicial isolation. In a small circuit, for example, the judges deal with each other regularly, sitting on panels together relatively frequently. That can carry advantages because the judges become more familiar with one another, leading to better communication regarding the development of circuit law as well as more informal communication regarding specific cases. As one Ninth Circuit judge said,

> I think for the practitioner, having a smaller court is somewhat desirable for predictability. And also, I think among the judges there is a bit more of a day-to-day collegiality in the sense that you are going to deal with the judge for many years, and they are right around the corner. Say it is a seven-judge court—it has more of a personality, and there are more of the types of [two judge] conferences . . . trying to talk over a case or work it through.

Conversely, in a larger circuit such as the Ninth, the judges do not have as much contact with all of their brethren. They do not sit with one another with the frequency of judges on a smaller circuit, such as the First. As one Ninth Circuit judge explained,

> One way [that a large court's size affects the decision-making process] is that you don't sit with any particular other judge on the court with sufficient frequency for his views or her views to affect yours much. There are judges that I have never been on a three-judge merits panel with even though I have been on this court for [several] years. We affect each other in the way we think about things only in the slightest degree.

Because a large number of judges turn out a large number of opinions, larger circuits also have potentially significant problems maintaining the consistency and predictability of circuit law. According to one Ninth Circuit judge,

> Because we have so many cases coming out so often, it is possible for people to decide [similar] cases the same week . . . . So it is possible in one week to have two cases come down that are absolutely opposite to each other. Or it may have come down last week, and you just haven't gotten to it. It is such a big circuit that handling your own cases, keeping up on your own cases, is just a huge job.

The consistency problem can be hazardous to the court's collegiality:

> I think [the large number of judges on the court] makes it harder for us to speak with a coherent voice and to maintain a body of law that is predictable and ascertainable. Stuff happens all the time. You know what really frosts me is I busted my tail on a very complicated . . . case—busted it. And then, a week before we—our panel—issued an opinion with my dissent, somebody else comes out, had the same issue, and preempts us. And everything just goes right down the drain. And I was like, "What the hell is this?" That happens a lot—we are working on an issue and another panel has it and the two panels don't realize that we have got the same issue. I have wasted a lot of time on that. And for some reason, the [central staff members] just don't spot that kind of stuff. And the en banc thing— all of a sudden the case will come out of nowhere and you really don't know what was happening on it for a year. Wham! There it is. So the more judges you have, the harder it is to keep everybody on the same sheet of music.

The large circuit's difficulties with collegiality are complicated by the increased probability of having maverick panels that decide cases contrary to circuit law. One Ninth Circuit judge explained,

> Because of the nature of combinations and permutations, you get streaks. So a panel will frequently be three judges at one end of the [philosophical] spectrum . . . or three judges at the other end of the philosophical spectrum. And when they look around the table, these are all pretty smart people, and they recognize that. And they recognize that if they are going to do anything aggressive or venturesome, this is the time. Our size makes that sort of panel much more likely than if we were smaller. There are far more of them. We can even get a panel like that on [a mini–]en banc. You can draw a streak. . . . A streak is like if you keep flipping coins you won't get head, tail, head, tail, head, tail. You will sometimes get four heads in a row, sometimes five heads in a row. And a head, tail, head, tail or tail, head, tail, head distribution is relatively unlikely. . . . [D]istributions that have groups or streaks are more likely overall, because there are more combinations that include groups and streaks. That impairs the collegiality of the decision-making process.

The combination of decreased collegiality and increased potential for maverick panels can result in what one Ninth Circuit judge described as a feeling of "disengagement."

> The court is big enough that if you are not careful, you can think, "Well, that is not my problem. It is not my case. It is not an area that I have a case

in, so I will just keep my head down and do my work, and the hell with it."
I think in a large court that that tendency will be stronger than on a smaller
court. . . . The nature of the job is that you get cloistered. So I don't know
that being spread out geographically has much to do with it. . . .

If another panel has gone off on a track and ignored the Supreme Court
authority and is raising hell, you think "Well, it's not my case. The chances
that I will have a case that will be impacted by that case are maybe pretty
small, so maybe I don't need to worry about it." . . . One of the problems
you have—and this is part of the disengagement—is any court of any size
can have a maverick on it. And any court of any size can have personality
clashes. But in a large court a maverick is very difficult to ride herd on, and
that is where the disengagement comes in. And you think, "Oh God, there
goes Judge X again. I took him to task last time and got an en banc call, and
we did all the work to straighten this guy out. Is it my turn? Am I the only
guy who is going to watch this fellow?" So the large court, I think, dampens
itself a little bit in terms of being able to corral its mavericks. . . .

If you are on a small court, and, say, there are only nine of you, this maverick would know with some experience that anybody that wanted to call
him to task on a clear deviation from the party line [would do so, and] you
could bring him to task. That maverick would be much less likely to go off
on his or her maverick road. We are big enough that it is pretty damn
difficult to get a case taken en banc. We have got certain judges who almost
constitutionally vote against it. So it takes something on the order of
mini en banc to get their attention. So the mavericks understand that the
odds are that they can get away with it if it is not too bizarre.

Thus, the one-two punch of large numerical size and high geographic dispersion can have a serious, negative effect on a court's functioning as a single collegial body.

Large numerical size, however, is not without its advantages. Key among
those, of course, is a large circuit's ability to terminate large numbers of cases.
That advantage, though, can also be achieved by having a large number of
smaller courts, although many judges do not necessarily prefer that solution. In
spite of the emerging culture of disengagement that results from increasing
geographic and numerical size, almost all of the judges remained committed to
the idea that it is better in principle to have a relatively small number of large
courts rather than to have a large number of small courts. One judge stated,

[The increase in the number of judges on the court has affected the
process] because you sit with fewer people, and you don't have that interaction with the individual judges with the same frequency that you used to,
so that having large numbers invariably impacts upon that. On the other
hand, I think it is wishful thinking to believe that we are going back to the

days of Learned Hand and have all of this excess time, small courts, and the rest of those things. Time has passed that by, and the public demands much more. So although the decision-making process would be much better with just a few opinions, a lot of time to think, all sitting in the same courthouse, and a few members on the court, society does not let us do that anymore. Society is going to say that those quality controls and efficiencies are no longer worth the cost. And we don't want forty or fifty or sixty circuits.

Another judge dismissed the issue of court size: "Collegiality is not a question of numbers, it is a question of motivation and attitude."

Also, like high geographic dispersion, large numerical size carries potential advantages of increased civility and diversity. As one Ninth Circuit judge said,

> I think the advantages of a larger circuit are diversity. When you have a small court, and personality differences emerge, those differences can dominate the court and cripple the court. In a larger circuit, such as the Ninth, although there are personality differences and philosophic differences, those, to a great extent, are minimized because of the rotation, three-judge panels. I think, as one judge said to me, "Well, there are awful weeks, but then you are done with that week and on to the next panel."

Another Ninth Circuit judge explained,

> I actually think that a larger number, say a number in excess of ten, helps with collegiality, because you are not sitting with the same two other judges all the time, you are not so persnickety at each other. I have got a good friend who is on [a state] supreme court that has five people. They sit with the same five people all the time. They conference week in, week out. They can write each other's opinions, they know each other's thinking so well, and there are some divisions on that court and sore feelings. I think . . . if [some judges on this court] had to sit together every month for the next five years, it would start to wear on their friendship. They have got a really remarkable friendship, but I think it might start to wear, as it would on any friendship.

Nevertheless, even judges who expressed the advantages of large numerical size recognized that, at some point, a court can become so large and dispersed that it can no longer function as a collegial body. As one Ninth Circuit judge put it,

> I suppose there is an upward number where you would probably have to have name tags at a court meeting. I can't tell you what that number is—

forty, fifty, I don't know. But right now, with twenty-eight authorized and . . . twenty-two active, I don't see [the number of judges on the court] as a problem at all. That is a small group. That would be a small law firm in most practice areas in the country—certainly no larger than the medium size. And I think if you asked most lawyers what would be an ideal size law firm, which involves some of the same interactions, most people would tell you somewhere between fifteen and thirty-five.

Thus, those judges challenged the traditional idea that a court should have a relatively small number, but at some point, a court can grow so large that it cannot operate adequately. One Ninth Circuit judge said,

There are some givens, and the given at the moment is that there are a maximum of twenty-eight judges. That's what we had when I came on board, and I wouldn't think of changing that at the moment. I do feel that somewhere between twenty-eight and forty-eight there will come some invisible breaking point which will be a very, very serious impediment to reasonable communication, or collegiality, or just functioning as a single level court. People keep asking, "What's the number?" I don't know what the number is. I think twenty-eight works reasonably well.

Just as technology has helped to alleviate some of the difficulties of geographic dispersion, technological advances have allowed judges to maintain cybercollegiality in the face of increasing numerical size. As one Ninth Circuit judge explained,

I think one of the areas over my twenty-five years that has made some of the largest changes in the decision process has been the advance of technology, automation. We can do things now that we could not have done before. There is no way, in my judgment, that we could have effectively functioned—twenty-eight judges—without e-mail. There is no way that we could carry out the extensive calendars we do without simple processes, like word processors. There is this wide variety of technical advances that have helped us be able to achieve things in the decision-making process that we could not otherwise have done.

In part because of increasing technology, a court with many judges can manage. One Ninth Circuit judge even suggested that the court would not be harmed by further increasing its size:

I don't think it makes any difference. It is like when it gets over 120 degrees in Phoenix—who cares if it goes to 140? Once you get over a certain number of judges, until you get to be outrageous like ninety judges or something, I don't think it makes a difference whether we go from twenty-six to thirty-six to forty.

V.   Conclusion: The Role of Interchambers Structure in the Appellate Judicial Process

Three kinds of distance separate judges on U.S. Courts of Appeals: physical distance, social distance, and professional distance. The relationship among these three factors, together with variables that intervene in those relationships, shapes appellate judicial decision making and can have varied consequences for the balance between autonomy and interdependence.

Physical distance includes the circuit's geographic span, the judges' geographic dispersion, the structure of the courthouses in which the judges are stationed, the location of judicial conferences and meetings, and whether the judges of the circuit listen to oral argument at the same time in the same place.

Social distance refers to the personal relationships among the judges and is measured by how personally close the judges are to one another. Civility is a critical dimension of social distance, but it is not alone. Social distance also accounts for judges' familiarity with one another and how often they speak informally both about cases before the court and about other topics. These factors are a function of, among other things, a court's numerical size.

Professional distance refers to the professional relationships among judges and is measured by how and when the judges formally discuss cases either in person, by memorandum, in oral argument, or in conference. What distinguishes a formal in-person discussion of a case that indicates close professional distance from an informal discussion that indicates close social distance is often a matter of how the judge perceives the communication.

As each of these distances increase, there is a tendency to decrease the interaction among judges and thus to shift away from interdependence and collegiality. How the effects of these types of distance interact, though, also affects the balance between autonomy and interdependence. Although there appears to be a relationship between physical and social distance, the nature of that relationship remains somewhat opaque. The relationship between physical distance and social distance can be characterized by the old adage "absence makes the heart grow fonder." Where judges must deal with one another with the frequency of geographically small and intimate courts, small disagreements may grow from minor irritations to hemorrhaging gashes. However, judges who do not get along with one another more often simply avoid contact to the extent possible. Even when their chambers are along the same hall, such judges rarely see one another. Conversely, judges in the same building who already are socially close find it possible to further develop their social relationship. Those judges socialize more and therefore have more frequent and more fruitful informal discussions regarding cases as well as other aspects of judging. Accordingly, close physical distance reduces social distance. Thus, it appears that the correlation between physical distance and social distance is large and positive.

Social distance appears to be weakly but positively correlated with professional distance. Judges reported that they rarely discussed cases in person and that they found that they did not more frequently speak formally to judges with whom they were socially close than to judges with whom they were socially distant. However, the nature of those communications appears to differ somewhat. Judges who are socially close appear to communicate more often and less formally, and the nature of those communications appears to lend some support to the observation that judges who are socially close also tend to be professionally close. Again, though, that correlation appears positive but weak.

The relationship between physical distance and professional distance is easier to understand. The correlation between physical and professional distance is large and positive, a finding that does not appear to have changed since Wasby's 1977 study. The slowness of the mails and the inconvenience and difficulties of communication by telephone combine to make formal communication difficult and time-consuming. As a result, judges separated by large physical distance also are separated by relatively large professional distance. Advances in technology have somewhat undercut this correlation, however. The advent of electronic mail and fax machines has altered the way that judges formally communicate with one another. Electronic communication enables judges to send written memoranda instantaneously and simultaneously to all judges for whom the communications are relevant.

That change, however, has altered the way that communication is accomplished. Judges reported that e-mail communication appears to be more formal than in-person communication but less formal than written memoranda. Because electronic communication is virtually instantaneous, though, judges reported some concern that written communications have become less clear and sometimes more harsh. Moreover, because judges separated by larger physical distance can more easily communicate in formal written memoranda than by relatively informal telephone communication, decreasing professional distance appears to have increased social distance. Thus, technology has not decreased social distance in the same way it has professional distance. In short, the adoption of electronic modes of communication by geographically dispersed courts has created cybercollegiality marked by shorter professional distance but greater social distance. Increasing numerical size also appears to have increased both social and professional distance. Judges on the Ninth Circuit reported that they do not feel as familiar with their brethren as they did when the court was numerically smaller. Judges sit with one another less frequently and do not feel as able to keep up with the large quantity of opinions released.

The one-two punch of increasing geographic and numerical size compounds judges' feelings of isolation and disengagement. These feelings indicate that, at least in large circuits, there has been a shift toward autonomy and away from interdependence. Nonetheless, some judges point out that even in small circuits, most communication is in writing, for reasons entirely independent of court size. Distance therefore can increase civility and collegiality. Large geographic and numerical size, however, isolates judges from their cohort, both physically and socially. Because judges generally communicate in written documents and e-mail, large size can intensify the structural difficulties of information flowing across court boundaries. Accordingly, circuits with a larger geographic and numerical size face an increased threat of an imbalance toward autonomy and away from interdependence.

CHAPTER 6

Organizational Culture in the
Appellate Judicial Process

In addition to the formal controls and structural mechanisms that maintain the balance between judges' autonomy and their interdependence, the court as an organization relies heavily on informal institutionalized cultural norms to constrain and shape the ways that judges decide cases. As Owen Fiss has written, the judicial office is "structured both by ideological and institutional factors that enable and perhaps even force the judge to be objective—not to express his preferences or personal beliefs, or those of the citizenry, as to what is right or just, but constantly to strive for the true meaning of the constitutional value."[1] Those informal institutionalized cultural norms, therefore, play a substantial part in constraining judicial autonomy even as they ensure that judges maintain a level of independence from their brethren's influences. In subtle ways, the court's institutionalized culture works to maintain the critical balance between judicial autonomy and interdependence that sits at the center of the appellate judicial process.

Although informal institutionalized cultural norms play as important a role in maintaining the critical balance as the formal and structural aspects, the informal institutionalized cultural rules are far more elusive. That is in part because the concept of institutionalized culture is itself somewhat slippery and because, unlike the court's formal rules or structure, cultural norms rarely are discussed in written opinions or articles considering judicial administration. Instead, the court's institutional culture exists in the interaction among the court's organizational actors, stealthily setting the social boundaries of acceptable actions and covertly delimiting not only what decisions judges make but also how they are made.

This chapter discusses the court's cultural realm. It delineates the overar-

---

1. Owen Fiss, *The Supreme Court, 1978 Term—Forward: The Forms of Justice*, 93 HARV. L. REV. 1, 12–13 (1979).

ching cultural themes that define and demarcate the limits of judicial action and then presents some of the myriad normative rules and rituals that stem from those broader cultural themes.

I. The Concept of Organizational Culture

In the sense that I mean it, *organizational culture* is both "something that an organization *has*"[2] and something that it *produces*.[3] Collateral to its production of goods and services, the organization creates "cultural artifacts such as rituals, legends, and ceremonies."[4] Those cultural artifacts contribute to the "overall systemic balance and effectiveness of an organization" by serving as "social or normative glue that holds [the] organization together."[5]

Thus, organizational culture is something concrete that shapes the way that organizational participants perceive their world and their behavioral options within that world. In that sense, organizational culture is an institutional phenomenon: that is, the organizational culture limits the actions that a judge may take because it sets the options for action that the judges perceive.[6] Cultural rules influence organizational actors' choices by making them feel that one potentially available option simply is not right. As W. Richard Scott has explained, cultural belief systems within organizations

> define a general mission sustaining commitment to something larger than self; . . . provide guidelines by which participants can choose appropriate activities; . . . create sources of meaning and identification such that participants not only know what they are to do for the good of the organization but want to do it.[7]

In that way, participants experience cultural constraints as the product of intuition. Where participants perceive that given the situation, they can act in any

---

2. W. Richard Scott, Organizations: Rational, Natural, and Open Systems 291 (1987).

3. Linda Smircich, *Concepts of Culture and Organizational Analysis*, 28 Admin. Sci. Q. 339, 344 (1983).

4. *Id.*

5. *Id.; see also* Noel Tichy, *Managing Change Strategically: The Technical, Political, and Cultural Keys*, Organizational Dynamics 59, 59–80 (1982).

6. *See* Ronald Jepperson, *Institutions, Institutional Effects, and Institutionalism* in The New Institutionalism in Organizational Analysis, 143, 146–47 (W. Powell & P. DiMaggio eds., 1991); John Meyer & Brian Rowan, *Institutionalized Organizations: Formal Structure as Myth and Ceremony* in The New Institutionalism in Organizational Analysis, 41, 44–45 (W. Powell & P. DiMaggio eds., 1991).

7. Scott, 1987, *supra* note 2, at 291–92.

of two or more ways and where a cultural rule constrains that behavior, the actors perceive that one of the options is correct—that is, it simply is the way things are to be done.

Breaching cultural rules does not necessarily result in a formal sanction, such as a judge being overturned by a higher court for breaking a formal legal rule. Breaching a cultural rule, however, can result in social sanctions from other participants in the organization who view the action as morally wrong. It also can result in a feeling of discomfort. In that sense, culture becomes embedded within individual actors and causes them to feel compelled to act in accordance with cultural rules.

Organizational culture therefore implies that there are broad cultural themes that translate into relatively steadfast normative rules and rituals of how action is to be taken. Those cultural themes reflect the court's "organizing principles" or "central logic."[8] *Organizational culture* implies that transgressions from those rules and rituals, when possible, result in feelings of discomfort. Accordingly, the first step in identifying how organizational culture affects function is to identify the broad organizational myths and ideals. It then becomes possible to understand how those overarching cultural themes are reified into rituals and normative rules that have the potential to constrain organizational action.

II.   The Cultural Themes of Autonomy and Interdependence

Overarching themes of court culture reflect the tension between the individual judge's autonomy and the need for judicial interdependence. On the one hand, the cultural theme of the judge as a solitary knight errant questing for a grail of justice pervades both the court and the literature surrounding the judicial mission. That vision of the judge-hero helps to shed light on the cultural themes that translate into normative rules. As Terrence Deal and Allan Kennedy have explained, cultural belief systems, which define the organization's general mission and constrain organizational action, often find their expression in the creation of mythical organizational heroes who personify the achievement of the organization's goals.[9] In the courts, that observation proves accurate.

The legal community generally views judges in heroic terms. As David

---

8. Roger Friedland & Robert Alford, *Bringing Society Back In* in THE NEW INSTITUTIONALISM IN ORGANIZATIONAL ANALYSIS 232, 248 (W. Powell & P. DiMaggio eds., 1991).

9. TERRENCE DEAL & ALLAN KENNEDY, CORPORATE CULTURES (1982); *see also* Scott, 1987 *supra* note 2, at 291–92; THOMAS PETERS & ROBERT WATERMAN JR., IN SEARCH OF EXCELLENCE (1982).

Riesman has said, "It is astonishing how strongly the image of the judge stands out as the image of lawyer-hero."[10] One judge described how legal culture portrays judges as heroic figures:

> As a result of the Warren Court, many think of judges as big actors on a stage of civil rights and civil liberties. They become liberal heroes or conservative devils. Law schools present judges as the high priests of the religion of the law, and, therefore, clerks come in with the expectation that these are very important figures in the legal profession. They perceive them not necessarily as heroes but close to a godhead.

Indeed, within the Olympian hierarchy of the judiciary, judges themselves perceive certain judges to transcend mere hero status and to attain an almost godlike stature. Those judges, including Benjamin Cardozo, Learned Hand, and Oliver Wendell Holmes, represent the mythic ideal of what it means to be an appellate judge.[11] According to that ideal, the judge should be at once an isolated, individualized, autonomous decision maker and a modest participant in a collegial process that must produce a unified appearance and thus has little room for individual stars. That is, the heroic individual decision maker must sit as a member of a collegial body that acts not as a collection of individuals but as a single unified entity.

Thus, even as judges I interviewed repeatedly referred to how great judges such as Cardozo and Hand were ideals of individualized decision makers, they referred to the "court" as a single entity. Even as these judges recognized and voiced that they strove to act as individualized stars such as Cardozo or Hand, they referred to the "Warren Court," the "Rehnquist Court," and the "Ninth Circuit" as though those courts did not have shifting memberships, but rather existed as single bodies over time. Moreover, the judges constantly recognized that acting overly individualistically today would be inappropriate and, in fact, might be impossible.

The overarching theme of interdependence is supported by a strong institutional commitment to collegiality. Court culture suggests that a court's abil-

---

10. David Riesman, *Towards an Anthropological Science of Law and the Legal Profession*, 57 Am. J. of Soc. 121, 122 (1951); *cf.* Richard Posner, Overcoming Law 109 (1995) (distinguishing "heroic" judges from "ordinary" judges).

11. That is so even though both Cardozo and Holmes were Supreme Court justices rather than judges on U.S. Courts of Appeals. Judge Posner has argued that what makes a jurist a great Supreme Court justice differs from what makes a great Court of Appeals judge. Richard A. Posner, *The Learned Hand Biography and the Question of Judicial Greatness*, 104 Yale L.J. 511 (1994) (reviewing Gerald Gunther, Learned Hand: The Man and the Judge [1994]). Nevertheless, the frequent reference to how those three jurists worked demonstrates that the distinction that Posner draws has not prevented Supreme Court justices and appellate judges from intermingling on the heights of the judicial Mount Olympus.

ity to act as a unified collegial body serves as the root of the court's moral authority. Court culture teaches that a court that presents a unified face has fewer fragmented opinions, has a higher degree of civility among its judges, speaks with a higher degree of moral authority, and enjoys a higher degree of legitimacy. The court's institutional commitment to collegiality results in a normative rule that decreases judges' propensity to write separate dissenting and concurring opinions and sets a higher expectation that judges will act civilly toward one another. As one judge said, the degree of collegiality and civility on a court depends not so much on structural features, such as court size, or even on the judges' legal or political differences, but rather on "the traditions of the court."

One consequence of the institutional commitment to collegiality is the existence of a normative rule that requires a judge who disagrees with the view put forth by another judge to provide an alternative solution in place of the criticized material. As one Ninth Circuit judge explained,

> We have this rule that if you don't agree with a disposition, you not only have to say why you don't agree, but you have to give substitute language. I just think that is one of the best rules we have got, because somebody cannot say, "Well, I think it is too long here," or "I think it is too general here," something like that. Well, what . . . does that mean?

As one D.C. Circuit judge explained, that rule works in favor of uniformity because it is much easier to criticize and to tear an argument down than it is to build a replacement argument. One Ninth Circuit judge stated that in trying to rewrite an argument, he often becomes more sensitive to the problems that caused the argument to be written as it was. With that increased understanding, he will sometimes find that he is more ready to defer to what he perceives as a slightly flawed argument.[17]

The institutional commitment to collegiality also increases civility among judges. For example, when judges receive communications that lack the expected civil tone, they may suspect that the messages fail to represent what the writers intended:

> Sometimes [communications] will come over in a very sharp way, maybe because a clerk has suggested to a judge, "You ought to send this off on this case." But if you know the judge personally, and that doesn't sound like Judge X, you will phone them instead of getting angry and responding in kind.

---

12. *Cf.* Ruth Bader Ginsburg, *Remarks on Writing Separately,* 65 WASH. L. REV. 133, 142–44, 148–49 (1990) (discussing the conditions under which appellate judges should and do write separately and calling for fewer separate opinions).

Another judge explained,

> The attitude that the [civil] attitude was expected of us . . . is more critical
> [to collegiality]. And . . . the expectation is that you will be decent with each
> other and not competitive or harsh except in the substance—not even
> harsh there. That has been, over the years, I think, the attitude in the Ninth
> Circuit. I think that is very important.

One critical aspect of the institutional commitment to collegiality is that
judges may feel compelled to come to results that differ from what they personally feel are the correct resolutions. One judge described how on some occasions, he will go into conference having decided that a case should come out
one way but will be confronted with two colleagues who strenuously disagree
with his view. Sometimes, after arguing unsuccessfully with them, he will find
that a decision should represent the view of a united panel. As a consequence,
he said, he will sometimes simply defer and vote with the other two judges.

The dueling cultural themes of individualism and collegiality, of individual
judge-heroes and of stable unified courts, resolve themselves into two sets of
sometimes conflicting normative rules: one set that reinforces a judge's autonomy, individualism, and isolation, and one set that reinforces interdependence, interaction, and communication among judges.

Rule 1: A Judge Should Not Discuss a Case with Another Judge Who Is Not on the Panel

Rule 1 prevents judges from being influenced in their decision making by
judges who are on the circuit but are not on the panel assigned the case. One
judge explained:

> I would feel a little uncomfortable [consulting with a judge who was not on
> the panel]. I would be a little worried about the ethics of it. I feel like it is
> my duty to decide the case within my three-judge panel and to make an
> autonomous, individual judgment in consultation with the other two
> judges.

As discussed in chapter 5, it is not entirely clear that communication with
judges outside the panel would often be of significant benefit in any event. As
one judge explained, communicating the specifics of a case to a judge not
familiar with it can take a great deal of time and effort. Because judges are
already extremely busy with their own cases, that invasion on their time could
become burdensome.

Nevertheless, in spite of the informal normative rule against such communication, some judges reported that they do, on occasion, find it valuable to use one of their brethren as a sounding board. Cases arise that present similar issues over time, and, on occasion, judges find themselves confronting issues similar to those already decided by other judges. Under those circumstances, one judge reported, it is sometimes valuable to consult. Another judge reported having a close relationship with another judge on the circuit, and the two will talk frequently and informally about a wide range of subjects. Sometimes during those discussions, one judge will bounce a problem from one of his cases off of the other, and the judge often found those informal discussions extremely helpful. However, such exceptions were relatively rare. By and large, the judges I talked with expressed hesitancy and discomfort with the idea of using their brethren as sounding boards.

Rule 2: A Judge Should Not Discuss the Merits of a Case with the Other Judges on the Panel prior to Oral Argument

As one judge said, "We have an ethic that says you cannot discuss cases with one another on the panel. Not everybody adheres to it. It is a rule, but it's one of those things." This rule prevents any kind of communication, written or oral, prior to the oral argument, thereby preventing one member of the panel from lobbying the other members. As one judge explained,

> I could go down the list of judges and pretty well tell you what their basic philosophical concepts are. I don't have to communicate with them to find out about it. And I do not do it before oral argument because I think each of us is entitled to our own independent decisions. And I resent it when somebody else on the panel particularly calls me and tries to lobby a position because I think it is our own independent judgment that is necessary.

However, it is not obvious that lobbying would be prevalent without that normative rule. One judge explained that prior to his appointment to the federal appellate court, he had sat on a state appellate court in which communication prior to oral argument was common:

> I have sat on [a state court] where we were all on the same floor, in the same suite, and we had a totally different approach. . . . In [that court], the judges exchange drafts of opinions before the oral argument, and they ask for criticism. The day before oral argument, the judges sit down and go over a draft and criticize it if it needs a change. By the time of oral argument, they will have come to a conclusion on twenty-five of the thirty cases all three have agreed to. And it is ready for filing within a few days. If a judge has a question . . . I would steer him to a colleague who was really a

whiz on [that area of law]. . . . And we would have whatever length of discussion we wanted, and there was no cultural concern about that. There was no belief that I was going behind the back of the third judge.

The judges on the courts of appeals do not necessarily believe that the rule of no communication prior to oral argument is the way that the process ought to proceed. However, because the tradition remains, new judges adopt that stance. For example, one judge who had been relatively newly appointed explained that he had no opinion about discussion prior to oral argument: "I personally am very flexible. I mean, if judges really like to chew over things ahead of time, I think that is great. If they prefer not to, that is fine with me too." Yet the judges who had served for long periods of time repeatedly expressed that communication prior to oral argument would threaten the ideal that they enter oral argument with a relatively open mind and, therefore, without having had discussion with the other judges on the panel.[13]

The rule's origins and underlying purpose are not entirely clear to the judges. One judge explained,

> I asked [a judge who had been on the court for a very long time], "Where did the idea come up that the judges should not talk to each other until after the oral argument?" So he said that it came from a conversation with some old lawyers, including [two who were still alive at the time]. . . . So I confronted [those two lawyers], and I said, "[That judge] tells me that you objected to judges communicating with each other before oral argument, because . . . you wanted to get the judges' attention before any writing started and before that judge talked to the other judges." Both of them denied ever having that conversation. So it is all built on a folklore that at least the sources that I went to deny.

Moreover, to keep the judges entirely free of influences prior to oral argument, it would be necessary for them to avoid their law clerks' input. As one judge related,

> [The judges] believe that it was sort of an honorable thing for a judge to keep the mind open completely, to read the briefs and sort of each judge communicate with the lawyers that way. First, reading the briefs and then

---

13. One consequence of this rule is to minimize the chances to trade votes, which would be the ultimate form of influence. As Evan Caminker has pointed out, even though strategic voting may be acceptable and, indeed, unavoidable, there is a strong normative rule that prohibits vote trading. *See* Evan H. Caminker, *Sincere and Strategic Voting Norms on Multimember Courts,* 97 Mich. L. Rev. 2297, 2380 (1999).

listening to the response to the judge's questions before the judge was tainted by talking to the other judges. Now, of course, the problem with that . . . is that the judges had bench memos from kids that are just out of law school before they talked to the lawyers. If they wanted really to keep it pure, they would have no bench memos and they would have law clerks not working on helping the judge prepare for oral argument but only kick in after oral argument.

There are some exceptions to this rule that derive from the need for discussion when specific issues require discussion prior to oral argument. Judges may discuss the merits of a case if one of the judges on the panel has suggested that the case be submitted without oral argument. Judges also may discuss limited aspects of the case if those aspects have not been briefed by the parties but one of the judges has recommended that the panel require the parties to submit additional briefing on that aspect.

At least in the Ninth Circuit, the perceived workload crisis has weakened the normative rule against communicating prior to oral argument, as can be seen particularly when judges exchange bench memoranda prior to argument. As discussed in chapter 5, judges' views often influence bench memoranda. In many chambers, judges work alongside clerks to prepare bench memoranda, which reflect the judge's views. In other chambers, the judge reads over bench memoranda and acknowledges that the views they express are at least supportable. In those instances where the judge exercises some influence on the bench memorandum, the bench memorandum can serve as a means to circumvent the normative rule prohibiting communication prior to the oral argument. In fact, where judges rely heavily on bench memoranda for their preparation, they can undercut the perceived purpose of the rule because a judge can enter the oral argument without ever having looked entirely independently at the case.

The tension between the use of the shared bench memorandum and the normative rule against preargument communication is reflected in the discomfort that some judges feel in participating in the pooling process. Even those judges who participate in the pooling process often do so with some discomfort:

I do [still participate] just because I am a team player. I have tried not to do it. I have suggested, for example, at panels that we have bench memoranda in [more complex cases] but use our own chambers to prepare [easier cases]. That has not been successful. There are just some judges that just want to have that memo in every case. They have become used to it now, and it is hard to change. They have not seen how it might function in another context, so it has not changed.

Several judges indicated that they would prefer not to participate in the shared bench memorandum process but that they do so because they believe that it is expected of them.

Rule 3: A Judge Should Not Discuss a Case with Only One of the Other Judges on the Panel

This normative rule prevents a judge from speaking to one judge on a panel without having the same discussion with the other judge. This rule prevents informal discussion of cases because a judge must arrange to have both other judges involved in the conversation. As one judge explained, "It is not appropriate for one judge to talk to another judge of a three-judge group without all three talking. So to call up someone and say, 'Why don't we whatever?' is not the way a panel works. We don't have a mechanism to do that, as far as I know." Another judge explained that this informal rule inhibited communication: "With the culture we have," a judge might be offended if left out of even an informal discussion between the other two judges on the panel. On the state appellate court on which this judge had sat prior to his appointment to the federal appellate court,

> I felt free to put my feet on the desk as a judge and say, "Let me brainstorm our problem with you." They had no problems with that. They trusted each other. It was not a question of ganging up on someone. It was just a question of my going to someone that I really respected on a particular area.

This rule, therefore, can limit not only the amount of communication but also its informality.

Rules limiting communication effectively prevent judges from having any regular communication outside of their chambers during the preparation phase. Judges, therefore, are limited to their law clerks when they wish to bounce ideas off of another individual. That limitation has two effects. First, judges autonomy is forcibly increased because they must stand alone when preparing to decide a case. Second, the clerk's role as sounding board becomes more important, and as a result, judges become more heavily reliant on law clerks.

Rule 4: Formal Justice Is Favored over Substantive Justice

By favoring formal justice over substantive justice, this rule helps to remove judges from political influence. John Rawls, in his groundbreaking book, *A Theory of Justice,* distinguished the concepts of "formal justice" and "substantive justice." To Rawls, formal justice exists where an institution adheres to its formal rules.[14] In the court, then, formal justice would be achieved when the judges follow the formal doctrinal rules and refuse to depart from those rules to achieve an end in accordance with their ideas of just solutions. In contrast, substantive justice is achieved where an institution reaches a result that accords with objective morality as determined by natural law.[15] A judge may view one answer as substantively correct but feel constrained to reach the formally mandated result.

Rawls carefully notes that merely accomplishing a result that is formally just does not necessarily create a substantively just solution, and treating similar cases similarly is not a sufficient guarantee of substantive justice.[16] That is because formal justice "in the case of legal institutions is simply an aspect of the rule of law which supports and secures legitimate expectations."[17] Consequently, formal justice becomes substantive justice only when the institution's formal rules are themselves substantively just and are capable of changing in response to changes in the environment.[18]

To protect the judge's autonomy from the political system, the court has in place an institutional rule that requires judges to follow the formal doctrinal rules (i.e., stare decisis and standards of review) rather than to have the responsibility to make political decisions in an attempt to achieve substantive justice. That normative rule is exemplified by one judge's statement:

> I don't think I have a [political agenda]. I became a judge at a very early age, and I decided that it was none of my business whether the statute was wise or foolish or whether a case was liberal or conservative. I didn't care. I figured, "Let somebody else worry about it." If we were legislators, I would worry about it. I have spent [many] years on the bench now, and I have been enforcing laws that I would have voted against if I had been in government.

The liberation from weighing the wisdom of legislative judgment constrains judicial behavior by requiring judges sometimes to follow rules that they do not view as wise or substantively just.

Thus, adherence to the formal doctrinal rules plays an odd role in maintaining the balance between autonomy and interdependence. As discussed in

---

14. John Rawls, A Theory of Justice 58 (1971) ("Formal justice is adherence to principle, or . . . obedience to a system").

15. *Id.* at 59.

16. *Id.*

17. *Id.*

18. *Id.*

chapter 3, the requirement that judges follow formal rules sets the boundaries of a judge's autonomy. Yet the cultural requirement that judges follow the formal doctrinal rules liberates judges from the politically charged need to find substantively just solutions where those solutions conflict with the formal doctrinal rules. As a consequence, judges are constrained to follow the formal doctrinal rules by both formal means (the threat of being overturned either by the Supreme Court or by an en banc panel of the circuit court) and by a cultural, institutional force. Moreover, the cultural imperative carries more force than the formal imperative because, as discussed in chapter 3, judges recognize how unlikely it is that they will be reversed. Accordingly, even when a situation arises in which a judge recognizes that at least one other member of a panel has a similar political interest in not following formal rules, the judges are likely to follow the formal rules. That becomes especially critical on larger circuits, where there is a higher probability that two politically aligned maverick judges will be assigned to a panel and there is a lower probability that the court will carefully review any given decision en banc.

III.   The Institutional Conundrum: Institutional Culture and Organizational Change

The court's culture revolves around the publicly defined mission of the court to determine "just" solutions for the conflicts that come before it. Just as the institutional logic of capitalism is accumulation and that of religion is truth,[19] the institutional logic of the courts is the creation of justice. However, what it means for a solution to be "just" is not always clear to the participants in the judicial process. Judges regularly referred to their mission to "do justice" or to deliver "equitable solutions," but many of those judges also expressed some hesitancy to pinpoint precisely what the terms *justice* or *equity* mean. As one judge put it, "There is no such thing as *equity*." Nonetheless, judges are constrained by a strong cultural imperative that requires them to strive to create justice—whatever that may be.

Yet at the same time, the court's age-old normative framework exists within the shadow of an emergent cultural theme that overwork, together with insufficient time and resources, results from the indisputable empirical fact of the increasing appellate caseload.

As discussed in chapter 1, many judges and court observers have argued persuasively that the court faces a caseload crisis. And almost all of the judges with whom I spoke described ways in which they perceive that the increased caseload has affected them. Curiously, though, with few exceptions, all of the

---

19. Friedland & Alford, *supra* note 8, at 248.

judges indicated that they personally had not yet been affected by that work-load crisis, although they knew that other judges on their or other circuits had been seriously and negatively affected.[20] Moreover, the judges who spoke on the matter uniformly indicated that if the caseload continued to increase, they will soon be significantly hampered in their ability to do their jobs.

Whether an overwhelming workload actually has resulted from the increasing caseload, judges undoubtedly perceive that such a crisis exists. Orga-nizations commonly institute changes only when faced with the impetus of cri-sis, whether real or perceived. As Neil Fligstein has explained,

> The major impetus toward [organizational] change can be generated inter-nally or externally. In either case it will rely on a *perceived* crisis. The crisis can be that the company is losing money, or only that the actors in the company want to achieve more growth or profits. Either way, certain actors in key organizations must interpret their organization's problems and propose a solution, which can follow practices of other organizations in their field or be novel.[21]

The courts are no exception to that general rule. Consequently, the belief in the workload crisis, whether well founded or not, has had serious implications for the way that court culture has translated into normative rules, causing a shift both in the culture itself and in the way that the cultural beliefs have translated into normative rules.

The interaction between the normative ideal of justice and the judge's per-ception of an emergent workload crisis has resulted in a tension between the drive to change the court to make it more efficient and the concern that such changes also make the court less able to achieve justice. However, that tension has not resulted in a total stalemate. As the perception of the workload crisis progresses, the judges develop an emergency attitude and are consequently willing to accept changes in court organization that they would not otherwise countenance. To accept those changes, though, the judges must perceive that such innovations increase efficiency and that the cost to justice is minor. That institutional conundrum results in the slow adoption of relatively minor changes to the appellate judicial process and in tremendous difficulty in the adoption of more substantial changes. Two Ninth Circuit accommodations to

---

20. Because judges have a culturally created view that in the face of the caseload crisis, judges still can provide a high quality of justice, judges may have an overly optimistic view of the ability of the court as whole to compensate for the caseload crisis. As discussed in chapter 1, this optimistic view potentially creates an insider bias so that when asked, judges report that the court still is capa-ble of providing justice at a high level.

21. Neil Fligstein, The Transformation of Corporate Culture 9 (1990) (emphasis added).

increasing caseload pressure demonstrate judges' willingness to accept change that may significantly affect the court's institutional culture: the adoption and use of an en banc review process involving panels with fewer than the court's full complement of judges, and the use of visiting judges.

The Mini–En Banc

As a court increases in size by adding additional judges and as the number of cases the court decides increases, the potential for intracircuit conflicts also rises. More panels deciding more cases makes it more difficult for a judge to locate all of the applicable precedents relating to a particular formal legal rule. Moreover, under caseload pressure, judges have less time to devote to any single case. At the same time, an increase in the court's membership makes it increasingly difficult to rehear a case en banc. Problems of coordinating the judges' schedules, together with the problems of deliberating in a larger group, place a significant burden on the ability of a court to hold en banc proceedings. That tension suggests a critical mass where a court becomes so large that it requires numerous en banc proceedings to maintain the clarity of its laws, but is too large to enable it to fruitfully conduct en banc proceedings.

The first court to seriously confront that dilemma has been the Ninth Circuit, which has instituted a system by which the court can rehear cases in panels consisting of less than its full complement of active judges.[22] In that system, the active judges on the court can vote to rehear cases in panels of eleven judges called mini–en banc proceedings. If a majority of the active judges votes to rehear a case, the clerk's office randomly chooses ten judges who, together with the chief judge, rehear a case and have the authority to overturn circuit precedent. If dissatisfied with the outcome of the mini–en banc, a majority of the active judges on the court can vote to have the case heard by a full court en banc. Over the history of the mini–en banc procedure, the judges on the Ninth Circuit have voted on three calls for a full-court en banc, but a majority of the judges has not yet voted to rehear a case decided by an eleven-judge panel.

Given the size of the Ninth Circuit, the judges view the mini–en banc process as a necessary procedure. One judge declared,

> I think we would not be a circuit if we did not have it. I think if we had to
> have twenty-eight judges sit on every en banc case, that would be pretty

---

22. The so-called mini–en banc system, in which a court of appeals may elect to utilize fewer than its full complement of active judges in the en banc review process, was authorized in 1978 for circuits with more than fifteen active judges. *See* 28 U.S.C. § 46(c). Only the Ninth Circuit utilizes the mini–en banc system. *See* 9th Cir. R. 35–3.

bad. We would not be effective. We could not use it often enough to correct the inevitable conflicts that arise. You know, we do a lot of things to avoid them from the beginning of the calendaring. The computer is instructed to put cases having the same issue before the same panel. . . . The panel is advised if the same question has been before another panel within the preceding six months. . . . I think they miss quite frequently. It just does not get done. It does not work out. But in any event, we have to be willing to take a case, cases in which there is a conflict.

Many judges are skeptical that the Ninth Circuit could have an effective en banc process without the mini–en banc procedure:

I do not think we could possibly hold en bancs with all of the judges. The history of the Fifth Circuit is that they found it intolerable with twenty-five, and I think that the eleven has worked extremely well. I think in general in all circuits there is a kind of dissatisfaction about en bancs because . . . you do not have them unless there is a certain amount of strife, so they are not the most pleasant things to go through. But they are a kind of necessary evil.

Another judge stated,

I am [satisfied with the way the en banc process works]. I think that it was an occasion that was required by the growth of the court up in excess of twenty. At the moment, we are perhaps the only circuit that is authorized to hold en bancs on a so-called mini–en banc basis. Our experience has been that the eleven-member en banc is a satisfactory way to dispose of a case that must be heard en banc.

Another judge concurred:

To date, I think that any more than eleven judges on an en banc panel . . . gets a little unwieldy for deliberation purposes. So I think for the most part it has worked pretty well. That is one thing that interested me when I came on the court, because I was just surprised that you would never even have an eleven-judge en banc that could ever include a majority of the court. But it seems to work, and people do give it legitimacy and treat it with appropriate seriousness, and no one seems to be really willing to go to a twenty-two- or twenty-five-judge en banc hearing.

Other judges believe that the mini–en banc is better not only for the judges, but also for the attorneys because it makes for more effective oral argument:

I have talked to counsel who have argued en banc, and . . . people who have argued in front of the eleven-judge en banc court find eleven judges pretty damned intimidating. I think they would find twice that number overwhelming. . . . . There is virtually no argument—all questions from the judges and responses from the counsel. That is what 90 percent of the time is taken up with.

Thus, the Ninth Circuit has accepted the mini–en banc as a necessary process.

That the judges view the mini–en banc as acceptable reflects a change in attitude about the purpose of the en banc and its proper place in the appellate judicial process. Central to the traditional concept of the en banc was that the court sat as a single, collegial body and that its dictates would be the final statement of the court's position. Judges on the Ninth Circuit separate those two aspects of the en banc proceeding and now recognize the finality aspect as primary even to the exclusion of the collegiality aspect. One judge, for example, stated,

[Some] say it is not en banc because the full court is not there. Once more, we are going back to the days of Learned Hand and being arbitrary that the en banc process of all the court's [members] is necessarily the only and the best way of doing it. Once you take a look at the process and what you are being asked to do, it is terribly efficient. That it came out differently than the full court would have had it come out is not significant to me as the court is willing to treat it as final. . . . If they come out that way, fine. They have had a look at it, and let's let it go. We always can ask for full-court en banc. . . . I have felt that this limited en banc process has a lot of virtue, and I think that it should be looked at carefully in the future. My view on it is that any court with fifteen or more judges should use it.

Another judge declared,

I am [satisfied with the mini–en banc process]. It depends on your approach to what you want an en banc to be. If you want everybody's hand on the pencil, then it's a deficit. If you are just wanting another review by a larger number and you are willing to treat [it as final], then this limited en banc court has great merit.

Similarly, still another judge said,

If you get away from the idea that you always need a majority on the court . . . for some purpose of mirroring all of what the judges would look at, then you have a problem with the numbers, and they have got to go up. But if you are looking at reasonable finality, reasonable review, then the number eleven is as good as any. . . . I do not look at the en banc as needing to mirror the entire court because we have the full court to do that. We can vote as a full court if we choose to do so. So to me, it is getting a reasonable number that the judges feel comfortable that they have had a good review, a good number of judges have looked at it.

One judge explained that although the mini–en banc allows only a limited number of judges to sit on the panel, it still allows the whole court to participate in the vote to determine whether an en banc rehearing is necessary:

Somewhere you have got to draw the line on the system functioning. I suppose you could design a system where everybody had a voice in everything all the time to the ultimate degree, and we would never make a decision. So everybody gets a shot at reading the petitions for rehearing. Everybody gets a shot at calling it. Everybody gets a shot at the vote.

Some judges, however, have held fast to the fact that, at least in important new issues, the en banc process must entail the court speaking as a single collegial body. As one judge said,

I am no longer satisfied. I was willing to go along when I came on, and I gave it the full benefit of the doubt, but I am very troubled. [We should hear cases with the full court] if we are making new constitutional law and venturing into an area that the Supreme Court really had not touched before, or . . . where the Supreme Court likely [will not] touch it because it could only affect two states and both states are in our circuit. You know, six to five, that is close. I think even eight to three is reasonably close [when] you are talking about frontier or cutting-edge constitutional decisions.

Other judges view the mini–en banc system as an unfortunate necessity of a large circuit, with potentially significant consequences:

[The mini–en banc] is a disadvantage [of being a large court] in the sense that one never knows whether you are getting a true vote of the circuit. It has worked to date because of the degree of legitimacy that the full court is willing to give an eleven-judge panel. I think the fact that we have never had a full-court en banc illustrates that fact. However, there are cases, as I add up the votes, I wonder whether that would have been the same result had all the judges voted, and to that extent maybe that is not the truest version of what the circuit believes.

That suggestion that a vote of a mini–en banc court may have a different result from what the whole court would have done is the most common and serious criticism leveled at the mini–en banc rule.

In short, there remains a bad taste in judges' mouths, as is reflected in the fact that many judges have a real problem with a minority of the court sitting as an en banc court. As one judge said,

> I do not think that the mini–en banc process is effective. Eleven judges out of twenty-eight is a minority, and it is a small enough minority so that it is statistically likely that a fair number of en bancs will not be representative of the views of the entire court.
>
> Often it does not matter, because often en bancs are not on subjects that engage any of the philosophical differences among members of the court. For example, I sat on an en banc that, in my view, was very important, but it did not engage any philosophical differences at all. It was about letters of credit. Democrats or Republicans do not have differing views on letters of credit, and liberals and conservatives don't have different views. Even your opinion about legislative history does not have any bearing on letters of credit. It is just a traditional, common law kind of subject. So on that one, a mini–en banc is fine. You pretty much just grab the first eleven judges that come out of the computer, and that is fine. But if you take some of the things that do engage judges philosophically, like English-only or something like that, [it is a different story].

Similarly, another judge stated,

> I think probably the number should be increased to fifteen to reflect at least well over half of the people on the court. [There is] the mathematical possibility of [a split] in a court that has about almost a fifty-fifty split of judges that have been appointed by conservatives and judges appointed by whatever Clinton is, [so that the decision does not reflect the view of the court as a whole]. I have concerns that when you have only eleven you may well end up with a distortion in reflecting a cross-section of our backgrounds and our views.
>
> I think I am satisfied with less than twenty-eight. If you ask me a different question, which is, "Is eleven the right number?" my answer is, "No, I think it should be fifteen." I think [the number eleven] does present a problem. . . . It can distort. In other words, it can produce an opinion that would not reflect the views of twenty-five judges.

One judge provided an example of how having a minority of judges on a mini–en banc could lead to problems:

I remember a case where the majority of the court voted to go en banc, and the mini–en banc, which is less than a majority of the court, decided that the en banc had been improvidently granted, and I think on that case we came as close to having a full-court vote on that as we ever have. It is such an arrogant thing for a minority of the court to do. I think the en banc would be better if it at least represented a majority of the court.

Another judge explained that the mini–en banc system was effective but seemed a quick fix because as the number of judges increased, the number of judges on a mini–en banc panel would need to increase to justify the finality of its determination:

I think [eleven] is marginally acceptable on a twenty-eight-judge court. If we got another ten and went to thirty-eight judges, I think an eleven-judge en banc would be an intolerable way to make law of the circuit. But you sure as hell don't want a seventeen-judge en banc or something like that. . . . I think the validity of eleven judges speaking for the whole court would be really suspect.

One response to the problem of a mini–en banc panel is that, once it is agreed that any number less than the full court is acceptable, deciding how large the panel should be is merely a matter of statistics. As one judge said,

The minute that you decide that less than twenty-eight can handle an en banc, you could almost go down as low as four. And you would have achieved an administrative resolution of the need to have the court speak at the en banc level. Now the only thing that gives that legitimacy is that if you still have, as a safety valve, the possibility that the full twenty-eight judges could hear it, which is the only way it seems to me that we can honestly tell the public that we have a court position. . . . The thing that most judges who follow the eleven-judge en bancs will either be generally acquiescing in the majority view or won't feel strongly enough if their view is not represented to do anything about it. And that is part of a sort of general tolerance factor that we have as judges on this kind of a court, but that does not cover all issues. It certainly does cover issues where there are fundamental rights at stake that have very broad implications on how cases in the future are going to be handled, and that sort of thing.

Another judge said,

It is no different than the three-judge panel. Sometimes a small minority of the court sets a [precedent] that for one reason or another does not get called en banc or fails by one vote to go en banc. So it is endemic. It is part of the process that whenever you have a multijudge court that under certain conditions, a decision that binds everybody is going to be made by a very few people. In fact, that is what happens [in three-judge panels]—two judges with a third judge dissenting out of a twenty-six-judge court with ten seniors can make the law of the circuit.

Similarly, a third judge explained,

I don't think I would reduce [the number of judges on a mini–en banc panel], but it has been an arbitrary number, and it was resolved after a vote of the whole court on numbers [including] nine and thirteen and other numbers. It was sort of a compromise number. I would think that it would probably be better if the en banc panel consisted of at least a majority of the court. But on the other hand, the decision of that majority [panel] is one more than half [of the judges on the panel], and we would be talking about six or seven or eight members who are making a decision of the law of the circuit, and that is not a majority at all.

Other judges point to the probability that a mini–en banc panel adequately represents the views of the whole court:

Maybe theoretically it permits a decision that does not totally reflect what the views of the court would be if all active judges voted. But I don't think that happens too often, and if it is wrong, I am content to let it lie, and the Supreme Court can straighten it out, or it will stay wrong. I would not try to hold a twenty-eight-judge hearing. . . . I think there would be some falloff if it got, say, below nine—falloffs in the odds that you are getting a panel that is substantially out of sympathy with the view of most people on the court.

Another judge stated that the court had done a study that concluded that statistics suggest that eleven judges closely represent the views of the whole court and that to increase the probability that a panel with fewer than the full complement would represent the whole, the panel would need to have fifteen judges. That judge suggested that the small marginal benefit of adding more judges would not be worth the added inherent difficulties.

Many judges recognize the problems in having a minority of the judges sit as a mini–en banc court but justify it by referring to the safety valve of having a full-court en banc. As one judge pointed out,

I understand [the argument against mini–en banc proceedings], because with the eleven you could get a six-to-five majority writing a rule of law,

and you could have seventeen other judges who see it the other way. And
to allow a check and balance for that possibility, you need to have some
sort of mechanism sitting on top of it.

That judge explained that the possibility that a minority of the judges on the
circuit represented the entire court did not concern him because there
remained the option of a full-court proceeding. Similarly, another judge stated,
"Since we have been [using the mini–en banc system], we have had three
requests for full-court en banc [review], all of which have failed." That judge
took the failure of the court to vote for full-court proceedings to demonstrate
that the mini–en banc system works. Another judge explained,

> I understand the argument that could be made. There is always the possi-
> bility that it is a six-to-five decision and that you are permitting a distinct
> [minority] in the court to decide the law of the circuit. That is a possibility.
> But that possibility has been accommodated, at least in theory, by the
> opportunity to go to the full court, and we have not yet accepted that invi-
> tation as yet. The fact that we have not accepted the invitation is some evi-
> dence that the present system is really working rather well. I do not think
> that I have to agree with the decisions made by the en banc panel. But I am
> saying that the process, in light of reality with a twenty-six-, twenty-
> seven-, or twenty-eight-member court, I think it is necessary.

Similarly, another judge stated,

> [That we have never had a full-court en banc] to me indicates the check-
> point, because we all have opportunity—that is, all active judges have an
> opportunity—to request that it go to the court totally en banc. . . . I think
> [the mini–en banc] is satisfactory in view of the check that we have that
> every active judge has a right to request a vote on whether it should go
> totally en banc. That seems to me to be a crucial point in our limited en
> banc procedure.

Still another judge stated,

> The fact that enrages people, sometimes to outsiders and [members of]
> Congress who are after the circuit to divide it up for different reasons, is
> that they were afraid that now you could have a big decision made by a
> small minority. You can have six out of twenty-eight judges deciding. The
> majority may disagree with it. Well, there is a full-court en banc process.

Other judges, however, are highly skeptical that the full-court procedure can
remedy the problem.

Some judges suggested that the possibility of a full-court en banc is merely a comfortable fiction. They believe that the court will never hold a full-court en banc and indeed could not hold one:

> What I have found . . . is that the majority of the judges on this court do not subscribe to the idea that there should ever be a full-court en banc. It is a misnomer, and frankly it is almost deceptive to the public to even suggest we have a full-court rehearing because I am satisfied that we will never have a full-court rehearing because a majority of the judges simply do not feel that it is appropriate under any circumstance.

Another judge explained,

> Nobody can see how you would ever get through [a full-court en banc]. You have to beat people over the head when you have got eleven on the en banc to get the thing out. Suppose you had twenty-eight? Now, I look at an en banc as a sort of lost year on the case. I think if you had twenty-eight judges, you would have lost two years on the case. Twenty-eight judges have to read every word, every citation in that opinion, and that is really tough.

One judge stated that he thought the possibility for a full-court en banc did nothing to resolve his concerns about the mini–en banc. He explained:

> We have never had [a full-court en banc]. It is not even 100 percent clear under the rules whether we can have one. And it is not really a solution, anyway, because it would be too big to be deliberative. . . . The fact that we have never voted for a full-court en banc means none of us are very optimistic that a full-court en banc would be a useful device.

In response, some judges have rejected the pessimism regarding the full-court procedure and have instead asserted that there are reasons why a full-court call has not yet been accepted. One judge explained,

> The fact that [there has not been a full-court en banc] primarily is because by that time [of the vote whether to have a full-court en banc], it is not that important to anybody. It has been a year or more that has passed by. People get a better perspective. They understand by that time that you were not really inventing perpetual motion or finding the Holy Grail, you are just dealing with another legal problem. The en banc process as it is [is] acceptable. It makes it practicable.

Those judges recognize that a full-court call is unlikely but believe that one will eventually succeed:

> I think [a full-court en banc] will happen. I have not seen it yet, because most people in their heart of hearts, even though they disagree with the en banc court, don't feel that passionately that they think that all of the resources of the twenty-eight judges should be called together. So over a period of time, we have schooled ourselves to realizing that we do not have to have our own way in every case and that that is sufficient for an en banc or secondary review. The time will come, I am sure, when the majority of the court will feel passionately that we should do it, but the case has not come up yet.

Still another judge reflected on the discussions regarding the calls for full-court proceedings and suggested that the seriousness with which the judges discussed the calls reveals that the full-court en banc is a real probability.

> I think if you looked at the [memoranda] traffic in [one recent case], you would be hard-pressed to make the argument that there is some sort of institutional feeling that we should never go full-court en banc. I think the vast majority of the court during that memo exchange made clear that that is a live real possibility.

Ultimately, however, a number of judges throw up their hands and rely on the Supreme Court to handle any grievous mistakes of a mini–en banc panel. Those judges state that it is really irrelevant whether the court would ever hold a full-court session because, as one judge put it, "If there really was the kind of case [that required a full-court en banc], the Supreme Court would take it." Another judge explained, "If we do something on an en banc case that is that bad or that outrageous, the Supreme Court is watching us." That judge further explained that, with the mini–en banc, even cases that the Supreme Court does not take up still "get a lot of introspection." For cases taken up by the Supreme Court, many benefits of a full-court en banc would be significantly diminished or even nonexistent.

Visiting Judges

A second consequence of the increasing caseload is that some courts, such as the Ninth Circuit, have become increasingly reliant on the use of visiting judges to supplement their complement of regular judges. The court uses judges from other circuits and district judges who sit by designation on Ninth Circuit panels. As table 7 demonstrates, the Ninth Circuit uses a large number of visiting judges relative to the other circuits, although its use of visiting judges has remained relatively stable over the past decade. Indeed, since 1990, no circuit has used a greater number of visiting judges.[23]

Visiting judges sit on courts of appeals for various reasons. Some do so because they find the experience inherently rewarding, others sit because of the opportunity to travel. The fact that visiting judges sit on the courts of appeals for different reasons creates some problems, as their reasons are often reflected in their diligence. For example, one Ninth Circuit judge stated,

> Many judges are district judges who don't involve themselves intentionally in the work of the circuit. They just sit because they are asked to sit, and they expect the work will be done by the sitting circuit judges. They don't really contribute much. But on the other hand, there are some judges that are of a contrary mind. They do actively participate in the affairs of the court. But I don't see any choice. We must borrow judges in order to dispose of our work.

Because the performance of visiting judges varies tremendously, most Ninth Circuit judges would prefer to limit the use of visitors, although the caseload pressure prohibits that option.

The Ninth Circuit judges perceive that the increasing use of visiting judges creates a corresponding decrease in the level of collegiality. Where one of the three judges on a panel is a visitor, and where the two circuit judges split on how a case ought to come out, the law of the circuit is being made by a judge who is not a member of the court. As one judge explained,

> What [the use of visiting judges] means is that a lot of decisions by the Ninth Circuit are not decisions by the Ninth Circuit. It reduces the predictability of decisions for lawyers, and it reduces the degree to which our court makes decisions collectively. A court really should be making decisions collectively. A district judge is supposed to make them individually, and a court of appeals is supposed to make them collectively. That facilitates stability in the law, moderation, and predictability.

Another judge explained,

> It is a very awkward way to run a railroad. . . . You have the law of the circuit being made by visiting judges, particularly where you get a split deci-

---

23. It is interesting to note that since 1990, the Second Circuit has increased the number of visiting judges it uses from approximately forty-one to sixty-eight in 1998 and seventy-five in 1999 (the most used by any circuit in any year). The Second Circuit has since reduced its usage drastically, using forty-nine visiting judges in 2000.

sion and [the] visiting judge is in the majority. . . . They are not really up on the way that we do business. They are not on our e-mail system. They can't enter their own orders. So it is just more work if there is somebody that is not on the circuit sitting with you.

Similarly, a third judge commented,

You are getting a whole lot of different voices in this decision process, and that makes it kind of incoherent—Ninth Circuit law or lack of it—although I find that the visiting judges are more willing to follow our precedents and to not take bold steps in one direction or the other. They are pretty good on this score. But if you, say, get a very liberal judge who is a visitor and two judges from our circuit, one who is conservative, they are skewing the case, or vice versa.

Consequently, where the circuit's law is not being made by the circuit's judges, the collegial, unified nature of the court is threatened.

Moreover, visiting judges generally have an unhealthy tendency to defer to the circuit judges on a panel. As one Ninth Circuit judge said, "There is no question that if a visiting judge comes in, it is as an unequal partner." Another Ninth Circuit judge stated,

When that judge comes in to argue, and we exchange views, there is a slightly different orientation because the district judge visiting [is sensitive] to the hierarchy. . . . A visiting district judge sometimes feels, "Well, I'm only a district judge, and these guys are circuit judges." . . . I remember when I was a district judge and I would sit with the circuit judges, I was a little bit deferent because they were appointed by the president to sit on the court of appeals. I had just been invited by the circuit executives to sit on the court of appeals. So there is that kind of hierarchy and a little bit of a barrier there. Whereas a visiting judge from the Eighth Circuit was an old-timer that we all had known for years and had seen at a lot of conferences and so forth. He comes in and slides into the spot, and it is just like somebody coming off the bench from your own baseball team. You don't have to do a lot of trying to find out where they are coming from. We know where they are coming from. They do this every day. It is just a three-judge combination.

Another judge concurred with this view that the negative effects of visiting district court judges were greater than those of visiting circuit court judges because the federal appellate judges are "pretty well acquainted with one another" and because the institutional and doctrinal rules of appellate courts generally resemble one another. Even judges visiting from other circuit courts, though, may have a tendency to defer. As one judge described,

TABLE 7. Number of Judges Providing Services as Visiting Judges by Circuit

Year	D.C. Circuit Circuit Judges	D.C. Circuit District Judges	1st Circuit Circuit Judges	1st Circuit District Judges	2nd Circuit Circuit Judges	2nd Circuit District Judges	3rd Circuit Circuit Judges	3rd Circuit District Judges	4th Circuit Circuit Judges	4th Circuit District Judges	5th Circuit Circuit Judges	5th Circuit District Judges	6th Circuit Circuit Judges	6th Circuit District Judges
2000	5	0	4	10	12	37	13	26	4	30	6	21	5	47
1999	0	0	9	11	17	58	16	30	3	29	1	14	9	45
1998	2	0	5	18	18	50	12	26	3	43	2	15	11	24
1997	0	0	3	16	12	43	9	28	2	42	3	15	7	43
1996	0	1	4	15	5	29	10	21	3	30	5	25	5	53
1995	0	1	1	17	8	29	6	23	5	36	6	34	7	48
1994	4	3	2	12	12	43	4	28	5	40	6	39	4	44
1993	3	0	9	14	10	41	3	14	3	39	5	34	6	42
1992	7	0	8	19	5	34	3	14	4	47	6	28	4	44
1991	5	0	6	16	6	32	8	24	3	38	3	14	1	51
1990	4	7	10	12	11	30	6	27	1	43	3	8	2	51

TABLE 7—Continued

Year	7th Circuit Circuit Judges	7th Circuit District Judges	8th Circuit Circuit Judges	8th Circuit District Judges	9th Circuit Circuit Judges	9th Circuit District Judges	10th Circuit Circuit Judges	10th Circuit District Judges	11th Circuit Circuit Judges	11th Circuit District Judges	All Circuits Circuit Judges	All Circuits District Judges
2000	2	3	4	28	11	54	3	13	16	29	85	295
1999	3	3	3	35	12	55	1	7	15	32	90	319
1998	2	4	6	33	10	42	5	9	15	29	91	303
1997	5	12	4	27	12	58	9	13	18	26	84	323
1996	8	14	6	18	11	60	10	24	18	25	85	315
1995	19	25	9	25	13	47	11	35	10	27	95	347
1994	12	29	7	26	14	49	10	35	9	28	89	375
1993	8	24	4	22	13	50	9	35	14	18	87	333
1992	6	17	6	27	3	63	7	36	13	13	72	342
1991	2	9	11	27	3	58	6	34	20	15	74	318
1990	2	10	6	19	7	61	7	32	19	29	78	329

Note: Data for 1992 through 2000 are from Tables V-2 to the Administrative Office of the United States Courts report "Judicial Business of the United States Courts," and data for 1990 through 1991 are from Tables V-2 of the *Statistical Tables for the Federal Judiciary*. Information regarding the Federal Circuit is unavailable.

> If I sit with judges that I have been on this court with for eleven years, I
> come into it with certain feelings about our past experiences and how we
> are going to get along. And I get along with the judges—that is not a prob-
> lem. But it is a knowledge of how people work together. And a new judge,
> especially for district judges that come in off the streets sometimes, are—it
> is not their circuit. I mean, everybody tries to work hard and all, but there
> is a whole different infrastructure. [They tend to say,] "I don't know any-
> thing about your circuit law, and I don't want to tamper with your circuit
> law, so maybe you ought to write the decision." There is deference. . . .
> Some visiting judges try to keep away from messing in our circuit law and
> don't know why we have gone en banc three times around a problem. And
> they probably don't care.

According to this judge, visiting circuit judges sometimes attempt to throw
their weight around, trying to show that the way their court does things is superior. This behavior sometimes annoys local judges, who wish to figure the
problem out for themselves:

> We say, "We don't care what you are doing in your circuit. We are going to
> try to figure this out on our own, and even though we don't want to make
> a conflict, this is the way we are going to think about it." We have judges
> from out of circuit who like to come in and throw their weight around and
> try to change our circuit law.

Another problem presented by the use of visiting judges is that it skews the
work on a panel onto the active judges, for three reasons. First, the judges on a
circuit prefer to retain the important cases because they perceive that it would
weaken the authority of an important rule if it were written by a visiting judge.
As one judge described,

> [With visiting district court judges], you have to have in mind [that] he is
> a district judge . . . so some of the decisions are ones that probably he or she
> would not want to write. . . . Some decisions ought to be written by a cir-
> cuit judge, and you have that in mind. The result of all of this is that a dis-
> trict judge, as invaluable as they are to us to keep going, provides a differ-
> ent type of mix in your decision-making process that you would not have
> if you had three members of the court.

A court's collegiality can be affected by increasing the burden on the circuit
judges, and additional deference on the part of the visitor can also result. As
one judge said, "The judge who comes does not have the knowledge, back-

ground, and experience of how we function and, therefore, comes in as an unequal partner."

Second, a visiting judge may be unfamiliar with the circuit's procedures and norms and therefore may require assistance from local judges. As one judge explained,

> Some of the visitors, because they are not acquainted with the responsibility, need a little more discussion about the way we usually do [things]. You get calls from a district judge, . . . and they will say, "Do you mind if my clerks talk to your clerks about how to do a bench memo?" or "How [do you] get over this hurdle or that?" And I tell them, "Absolutely." I will say, "If you want copies of old bench memos that I think are well done, we will ship that to you too." So I do that sort of thing.

Third, the visiting judges—especially visiting district court judges—are extremely busy with their own work and therefore can create delays and difficulties. One judge explained,

> If we bring district judges in, they come as volunteers, and of course, we appreciate all they have done for us. We could not have functioned without them. But their work goes on in their absence. They are on a wheel, and they get the same number of cases, and no one takes them off the wheel for one or two rounds in order to come visit with us. Maybe that would be nice if they did, but they don't. So you have to be mindful in assigning decisions. . . . We are not asked to do any more, where[as] a district judge is asked to write opinions plus do all the work which he does. So invariably, the presiding judge is going to have that in mind in assigning opinions and not assign opinions that are very time-consuming.

Another judge related,

> We get some visiting judges who are absolutely first-class troops, and they pull their weight and it is no problem. If you pull off a sitting district judge, an active district judge with a busy calendar, and put them on a panel with us, they get no credit for sitting with us. So this kind of thing is really kind of a distraction to them. They have a helluva time getting their share of the work done, so that slows us down some. I never feel that we are really first on their plate.

Because of the potential for delay, several judges indicated that the court should to try to use fewer visiting judges and to institute procedures to screen potential visitors. As one judge said,

I think it is dishonorable to have visiting judges except when we need them. And when we need them, only to have those who have proven track records because some of us have sat with visiting judges who have not carried their fair share of the load, and even when they do, they do it in an untimely manner.

Perhaps the most significant problem associated with the use of visiting judges, though, is the those judges' more general effect on the court's culture. Visiting judges affect the court's culture in two related ways. First, visiting judges are socialized in the cultures of their own courts, and the two cultures may conflict. As one judge explained,

[The use of visiting judges] is part of the problem. . . . Nobody has enough help, so you use these methods. I don't like visiting judges because . . . no matter how large [a court], if you have a consistency of the people doing the same job all the time, you have a consistency in the way you think in the sense of resolution on an appellate level. You bring a district court judge in, and they have a different meter, they are coming out of a different pace. They have got a different point of view because they are district judges. And, sure, they help us over the hump, but a lot of them defer to the circuit judges. You have to have circuit judges working with circuit judges with the same power and the same power structure. We are making decisions, that is what we are doing. . . . There is a feeling on my part . . . that district judges have a different pace to them. They look at cases differently because they are always being reviewed. So some of them come in with more of that attitude than others.

Another judge stated,

[Visiting judges don't] affect collegiality if your people are used to working in a collegial way with other people. In other words, if you are used to group decision making, and you accept that as a modus operandi, which we do—if we did not, we should get into another line of work—then it does not affect collegiality very much. You are either collegial or you are not. If you have people who come out of the same culture, like a visiting judge from another circuit is probably easier to work with than a visiting judge from the district court, because a visiting judge from the district court is not accustomed to group decision making as a general day-to-day thing. A visiting judge from the district court is accustomed to making up his or her own mind after consultation with the lawyers and the judge's law clerks. Then, the judge makes up his or her mind, and that's it. That's the judgment. That's the decision.

In short, judges find that it is simply easier to deal with a judge with whom they have regularly worked. One judge explained,

> You have a judge you don't know, you are not familiar with his habits. If it is a district judge, you don't know what kind of load the judge has back home, so you tend not to assign. Those judges tend to get a lighter assignment so that the circuit judges have heavier loads when they sit with a district judge or visiting judge. . . . I think it is easier to work with two people whom you know well than with one that you do and one that you don't.

According to another judge,

> There are some things that are different with visiting judges, just the mechanics of it. You have less of a database to turn to in terms of what to expect their reactions to be on something. It is kind of the way you always relate to a stranger or to somebody that you are not extremely familiar with.

Second, the use of visiting judges disrupts the circuit's cultural development. As one judge explained, each court and each panel has a cultural life that derives from the intellectual intimacy between judges. When a visiting judge is introduced into that mix, it can disrupt a court's balance. One effect of using visiting judges as well as senior judges to fill up panels is that those judges do not ordinarily hear a full calendar load of cases. In the Ninth Circuit, where the use of senior and visiting judges is exceptionally high, the judges sit in panels for one week out of each month. Consequently, individual panels develop their own individual interactional norms. When one of the three slots on the panel is taken up by visiting and/or senior judges, that set of interactional norms shifts and may never form in the sense that it does when the panel contains a consistent membership. As one judge explained,

> On this court, there may be six hundred or seven hundred possible combinations of people that you work with, so life with the panel—that is, the socialization of the panel—varies. And what is really aggravating is where you have a panel that starts out on Monday with two judges from this court and a third judge from somewhere else. Tuesday, you have still another judge, and the third judge sits somewhere else. Wednesday, still another third judge. And in five days, you have had five different third judges, and each time this happens, the whole society of the panel changes. It may be in acceptable ways, and it may not affect the outcome of the cases or anything, but it affects the way you get your work done.

Of course, the use of visiting judges is not without benefits.[24] Visiting judges introduce new cultural influences that can be healthy for a court, and interacting with judges on other courts can provide judges a valuable opportunity to learn new ways of doing their judicial business. As one judge stated, "I have learned tremendously from some of the very hard-working visiting judges." Moreover, interacting with judges from other courts can increase the collegiality and civility among the appellate courts. According to one judge,

> I think that it's an opportunity for me to meet a lot of district judges and circuit judges from other circuits and to meet with them on a professional level and a frequency level, too, because I see them every day during the period that we are sitting. We exchange memoranda during the months and weeks in advance of calendar. So it gives me an opportunity to increase my level of collegiality, at least outside of the circuit, and I don't think that I am giving up much within the circuit either.

In addition, the presence of visiting judges can have a positive impact on the civility within a circuit. Because judges feel that they have to be on their best behavior in front of visiting judges, their presence can help to achieve a heightened level of civility. One judge explained,

> I think [the use of visiting judges] may enhance [civility] because I think all of us want to put our best foot forward when we have a guest like we do in our homes. So that if there are any tensions between a couple of the Ninth Circuit judges that may have hung around from some past experiences, a visitor kind of puts everything right because we are trying our best to be gracious at least to the visitor. And that may well heal an old wound along the way.

Another judge said,

> I think you have got to be more polite [with visiting judges]. I definitely do. They are not used to the rough-and-tumble of life on the Ninth Circuit. Most circuits are not like this. Most people are not at each other's throats as much as we are. People are not as vigorous in their arguments. Or you find most courts are [not] split politically as we are—some are far left, some are far right. Not all of these courts have this kind of problem. I think that a lot of courts are much more polite and civil with each other. We make a real effort in this circuit.

---

24. Indeed, one law professor recently suggested requiring all circuits to use visiting judges on all en banc panels. *See* Michael Abramowicz, *En Banc Revisited*, 100 COLUM. L. REV. 1600, 1618 (2000).

Similarly, the presence of visiting judges may encourage circuit judges to be better prepared for argument because they wish to avoid embarrassing themselves and their circuit before an outsider. One judge said that sitting with a visiting judge "certainly affects me. . . . Maybe it makes me do my job better, . . . maybe I am on my toes more." But that judge also stated, "It seems to me that it would be better for the circuit not to have visiting judges."

IV. The Ritual of Oral Argument

The oral argument phase of the appellate process is the only part of the process that the public can witness, and it carries a cultural structure that is among the last of the spectacle-like holdovers from the ancient legal systems that Michel Foucault and Émile Durkheim have shown to be on the decline in modern legal and penal systems.[25] In addition to having significant practical value as an opportunity for the judges to engage in discussion with the attorneys and with one another, the oral argument has a ritual-like quality that serves an important role in the appellate court's cultural life.

I have argued that the court's culture revolves around a critical institutional logic of achieving justice. I have argued that this institutional logic is achieved through a commitment to two cultural dimensions that are in tension with one another: an ideal of autonomy and an ideal of interdependence. Both ideals resolve themselves into hardened, steadfast normative rules that limit individual judges' behavior and facilitate the court's structural dimensions of autonomy and interdependence. I also have argued that there is a myth of an emergent workload crisis and that this myth has had some effects on the way that the ideals of autonomy and interdependence operate. Thus, the court has been able to overcome cultural friction against structural and procedural change and has, in response, made some significant changes, including the shared bench memorandum system, the mini–en banc, and the use of visiting judges.

This section discusses how the oral argument serves as a cultural expression of the tension between the ideals of autonomy and of interdependence. Organizations, like societies more generally, have rituals that serve both as expressions of the society's culture and as institutional builders of new cultural rules. In the appellate courts, the most critical ritual shared by all the participants in the appellate process is the oral argument.

In neoinstitutional theory, the role of ritualized behavior goes far beyond the more commonly discussed rational, maximizing functions of the organiza-

---

25. *See* Michel Foucault, Discipline and Punish: The Birth of the Prison 32–69 (1979); Émile Durkheim, The Division of Labor in Society 101–25 (1984).

tion. Instead, ritual behavior within organizational action enables the individual actors within the organization to make sense of their behavior in relation to the symbolic institutional logic inherent to the organization. Consequently, ritualized behavior within an organization expresses the organization's social cosmology. Thus, Roger Friedland and Robert Alford have explained that

> through the quotidian and most institutionalized ritual behaviors, individuals reproduce the symbolic order of the institution and the social relationships that connect this world to a transrational order. Individual participation in various social relations should be analyzed not only in terms of the material interests that operation of the institutions serves, but in terms of the symbolic meaningfulness of that participation. Just as differentiated religions have their cosmological systems which account for the origin of the world and the words by which they understand it, so too do the most important institutions.[26]

The ritual nature of oral argument acts as a dramaturgic expression of the overarching organizational myths of individualism and of collegiality, of the ideals of autonomy and interdependence.

In that way, the oral argument acts in a manner similar to the rituals described in anthropological literature. For example, just as Clifford Geertz described how a Balinese cockfight acts as a dramaturgic expression of the nature of status and power in Balinese society,[27] the oral argument serves as a cultural expression of the process by which appellate judges deliberate to create "justice." Geertz explains that the Balinese cockfights not only express social status in Balinese culture but also provide a vehicle for creating and changing Balinese social structure. The oral argument serves a similar function, not only expressing the cultural themes of autonomy and interdependence but also creating and reinforcing structural aspects of the appellate process.

What does it mean for social action to be "ritualized"? In the words of Victor Turner, a ritual consists of "prescribed formal behavior for occasions not given over to technological routine, having reference in mystical beings or powers."[28] That is not the only definition of *ritual*, however. Geertz, for example, has relied on Durkheim's theme of the separation of the sacred and the profane to define ritual simply as "consecrated behavior."[29] In contrast, Claude Lévi-Strauss has argued that ritual is the acting out of a cultural myth using the structural, action-oriented elements of the ritual to correspond to the struc-

---

26. Friedland & Alford, *supra* note 8, at 250.
27. CLIFFORD GEERTZ, THE INTERPRETATION OF CULTURES 87–125 (1973).
28. VICTOR TURNER, THE FOREST OF SYMBOLS 19 (1967).
29. Geertz, *supra* note 27, at 112.

tural elements that are components of the myth.[30] E. E. Evans-Pritchard has presented a more general definition of ritual as behavior that "is accounted for by mystical notions."[31] However, while there is a broad range of action that can be considered ritual, Turner's definition seems to identify the basic components of what it means to be a ritual: prescribed formal behavior rooted in mystical beliefs and utilizing symbols that represent those beliefs. The oral argument has those components.

When Turner includes prescribed formal behavior as an essential component of his definition of ritual, he means simply that a ritual must contain some system of formal or informal rules that dictate the ordering of events, what is proper behavior for the individual actor to perform at certain times, how those behaviors must be acted out, and who does the particular behaviors. Durkheim refers to that last element when he defines a *rite* as an action that provides rules of conduct to prescribe how actors behave in relation to the sacred.[32] Turner speaks of the ritual in terms of a successive series of episodes where the steps must be repeated each time the ritual is accomplished. It is that regular series of behaviors that characterizes the ritual and allows the ritual to provide a structured and predictable atmosphere in which the participants can act out the cultural drama necessary to fulfill the ritual's cultural function.[33]

Like the rituals described by Turner and Geertz, the oral argument has a distinct rule system that dictates which actions are to be taken, who is to take those actions, and when those actions must occur. For example, the oral argument session is marked by a ritualized beginning and end. The session begins when the judges enter the courtroom to sit on the bench, a raised podium at the front of the courtroom. The judges generally enter the courtroom from a door that leads directly to the bench. As the judges enter, the bailiff of the court announces their entrance by rising and proclaiming, "Oyez, Oyez, Oyez. All rise for the [judges of the court in question]. God bless the United States of America and this honorable court." With that announcement, all persons in the court rise as the judges take their seats behind the bench. The presiding judge sits at the center, with the most senior judge not presiding at his right and the junior judge to his left. The judges wear the black robes of their position over the suits of their profession.

Only when the judges are seated do the remaining participants and audience members sit. The presiding judge then announces the first case to be argued. Similarly, when the session ends, all persons in the courtroom again

---

30. Claude Lévi-Strauss, Structural Anthropology 232–41 (1963).

31. E. E. Evans-Pritchard, Witchcraft, Oracles, and Magic among the Azande 229 (1985).

32. *See* Émile Durkheim, The Elementary Forms of the Religious Life 52, 121 (1915).

33. Turner, *supra* note 28, at 151–280.

rise as the judges depart the courtroom. The act of arising is reminiscent of religious ceremonies in which the members of the congregation must rise when certain actions are taken or prayers uttered. For example, in the traditional Jewish service, whenever the ark in which the Torah is kept is opened, the congregation must stand to acknowledge its sacredness.

Within the argument of a particular case, there is an invariable ordering of the presentations. Appellants present their cases prior to appellees. Appellants also speak last, rebutting appellees' arguments. In addition, there is a firm rule regulating whose speech has priority. When a judge interrupts a lawyer with a question or comment, the lawyer is expected to defer even if in the middle of a thought or a sentence. The lawyer must respond to the judge's question before continuing his prior line of thought. That rule is rarely broken, and when it is, there may be severe repercussions for the attorney. For example, I observed one instance where a lawyer violated that rule. While the lawyer was presenting his argument, one of the judges on the panel interrupted him with a series of questions. The lawyer answered each in turn, and each answer was followed by another question. After several minutes of this continuing questioning, the lawyer became visibly upset, shifting from leg to leg and rushing his answers. The lawyer finally interrupted the judge's questioning with an attempt to respond to the entire line of questioning. The lawyer spoke over the judge in a harsh tone reflecting irritation. The judge reacted angrily. He stopped the lawyer's response by again speaking over the lawyer in an angry but quiet tone. When the lawyer finally stopped speaking, he discovered that the judge was issuing a severe reprimand. The judge stated that it was "quite inappropriate" to interrupt a judge in this manner and that any further misconduct would result in sanctions.

The informal rules that dictate how and when participants in the oral argument act are grounded in the mystical belief that the appellate process creates justice. In addition to simply having a prescribed set of rules that formalizes behavior, however, Turner specifies that those rules cannot be the implicit structure of technological routine. The prescribed social rules must require action that has either latent or manifest meaning to the participants. That intertwining of action and thought, of rite and belief, separates ritual from mundane, rule-oriented action. Accordingly, it would be incorrect to conclude that, for example, a simple assembly line consists of ritual action only because there are strict and formal rules that dictate precisely how and when a participant must act. Whereas an assembly line typically does not contain the complex intertwining of action and belief, behavior associated with the Balinese cockfight or the Ndembu circumcision ritual does have such an intertwining. Thus, many anthropologists have concluded that without reference to beliefs in some mystic power, a rule-bound situation simply is not a ritual.

The oral argument stage has only passing reference to a "god" or mystic power in the bailiff's pronouncement "God save the United States and this honorable court." That pronouncement, though, does not seem to carry the significance of a religious benediction, although it may well have at one time. However, that does not mean that the ritualized aspect of the oral argument ceremony has lost any mystic significance it might once have had.

The oral argument is imbued with a strong, although contested, faith in the mystic power of the law as an institution and in justice as its will. The concept of justice is invoked as legitimation of and as justification for the court's actions. The law, therefore, exists as its own self-contained symbolic system that is religious in nature. It is represented totemically in the form of statues such as Blind Justice, and it is invoked in both the letter of the law and in legal institutions.

Metaphorically, then, the judges serve as the priesthood of the religion of the law.[34] That should come as no surprise given the references to the judges as the "godhead" of the legal profession discussed earlier. That priestlike quality is reinforced by oral argument's ritualized aspects. The judges are placed in the front of the room on a raised dais. The judges wear robes that reinforce the separation between the judges and the other participants.[35] The court may be addressed only by an attorney who, in addition to being admitted to the bar in a state jurisdiction, has been specially admitted to the bar of the specific federal appellate court. Admission to the bar consists of requirements that one law clerk referred to as "purely trivial." Applicant attorneys must be sponsored by an attorney already admitted to the court's bar. The application requires provision of little more than name, address, and the state bar to which the applicant already has been admitted, as well as a nominal fee. Finally, applicant attorneys must swear an oath that they will uphold the circuit's laws.

The ritual-like qualities of the oral argument develop and reinforce the central ideals of autonomy and interdependence. It has been observed that the ritual-like quality of the oral argument is legitimizing for the public.[36] Because the judiciary is a public, democratic organization, it has been suggested that at least some of the appellate process ought to be public. The oral argument serves that function. As one judge said,

---

34. Riesman, *supra* note 10, at 125 (quoting E. S. ROBINSON, LAW AND THE LAWYERS 28 [1935]).

35. *See* JEROME FRANK, COURTS ON TRIAL: MYTH AND REALITY IN AMERICAN JUSTICE 254–61 (1950) (judicial robes present an undemocratic image of the judiciary as a "priestly tribe"); *see also* Charles Yablon, *Judicial Drag: An Essay on Wigs, Robes, and Legal Change,* 1995 WISC. L. REV. 1129, 1145–46 (1995) (arguing that English jurists retain their wigs and robes because it is rooted in history); Milner Ball, *The Play's the Thing: An Unscientific Reflection on Courts under the Rubric of Theater,* 28 STAN. L. REV. 61 (1975) (claiming that the robes have a significance in indicating the transformation of the courtroom into a dramatic setting).

36. *See, e.g.,* Robert Martineau, *The Value of Appellate Oral Argument: A Challenge to the Conventional Wisdom,* 72 IOWA L. REV. 1, 11–12 (1986).

Without oral argument, we could no longer be a judicial body worthy of credence. Because if we were behind closed doors and all they received is these little written messages that came out every once in a while, [the court] would be no more valuable to them than the paper that came through the door. And they have to know what we think about, they have to know what we look like, and they have to be able to dialogue with us to understand that. And it gives the public the confidence that they need to obey our decisions, to have respect for our decisions.

What has not been observed, though, is that the oral argument also serves a similar legitimizing role for the judges themselves. As one judge explained,

I find each oral argument is very valuable to me. Now, the value of having an oral argument on a case that you are 99 percent sure under the law and facts are going to go one way is only the fact that you can convince yourself that you are the judge sitting on the bench.

Even judges who are not strongly affected by the oral argument's cultural qualities can be reassured by its ritualized aspects.

I think some of those ceremonial, cultural—I am trying to find the right word—manifestations, I guess, of traditions and so on. They do have a legitimizing effect on the process. I think some of the liturgical sort of phrases and so . . . are probably obsolete now and irrelevant. For instance, "God save these United States and this Honorable Court" is a liturgical phrase that has probably lost whatever meaning it had in pioneer times. But it sort of has meaning—sort of a clock in a steeple striking the hour. It is reassuring. You are not necessarily sure that that is the exact time, but it is a generally familiar connection. It is a connection with the past. I have not thought much about it lately, but as a young lawyer preparing to argue a case before the appellate court, . . . I though those contributed to the aura of the court as an important place whose function was solemn. I suppose a certain amount of the ceremony is necessary. In fact, I would not want to do away with it, because then it is just another bureaucracy. The court has enough bureaucratic negatives, just because it is bureaucratic. To make it less solemn, or less magisterial, would put us on the level of driver's licenses and under county tax assessors or something. We do have kind of a hierarchy government structure and that obviously has some reinforcing function, some majesty. . . . I have been a judge so long. . . . It is like somebody who has been a vicar in a small parish for forty years. He may wonder a little bit about whether there really is somebody up there that knows what is going on all over the place. After a long time, you have gotten used to the idea of doing what you are doing, you don't think much about it.

That institutional legitimacy forces the judges to prepare and to respect the autonomy ideal. As one judge said,

> I think that if it became less formal, it would become less controllable. There is some benefit of directing counsel to specific issues when you are on a hot court and everybody has read the briefs. I am inclined to think that an informal proceeding would provide some advantages of communications, but there would be some disadvantages. I remember before we [moved to our new courthouse], we had to hold one argument in a conference room. I felt that the lawyers were not pushing themselves the way they should. One of them did not prepare the way he should. He thought he was coming into a conference to confer about a case instead of arguing his case to us. I think there is something about coming to court, something about three judges being on the bench, that causes lawyers to gear up and get ready that may be missed if we did not have that. I think [oral argument has that same effect on the judges]. I think each judge feels that he or she has to be prepared and ready to go and feels uncomfortable when they are not fully prepared.

That the oral argument helps to reinforce the ideal of autonomy is demonstrated by the judges' resistance to conducting discussions with the attorneys in a less formal atmosphere. One judge related,

> I have participated in some [oral arguments or conferences] by telephone. I think that that holds some hope because it is very expensive these days to have lawyers come to court, and I have found that in some cases where the issue is clear—at least the identification of the issue is clear—there are no surprises, but you do want to have help from counsel. There have been times when I encourage the telephonic oral argument, and I have been satisfied with that process in selected cases.

At the same time, however, oral argument's ritual-like quality reinforces the ideal of interdependence by presenting the court as a single collegial body, depersonalizing the judges. For example, the judges' robes reinforce the "pretense that judicial reactions are uniform."[37] Moreover, the robes designate the judges as interchangeable by hiding their individuality. That the judges sit on an elevated dais and are referred to collectively as "the court" further reinforces the uniformity of the court.

---

37. Frank, *supra* note 35, at 254.

V.   Conclusion: Court Culture and the Meaning of Balance

The court's institutional culture has the most subtle and perhaps most critical role in maintaining the balance between autonomy and interdependence. Because the court's institutional culture defines the ways that judges view their work and their environment, it guides them in their view of how the balance between autonomy and interdependence ought to be struck. At the same time, because the court's cultural myths are transformed into normative rules that limit and define the ways that judges interact, the court's institutional culture creates and maintains that balance.

At its most fundamental level, the court's culture defines for the judges what they perceive as the proper balance. By shaping the judges' perception of what it means to be a judge and how ideal judges should do their work, the court's culture informs the ways that judges do their work and defines how successful judges believe they are. Thus, the institutional culture shapes the way that judges act through identifiable cultural rules. For example, cultural rules define when and how often judges should communicate with their brethren as well as the degree of independence judges should maintain from their colleagues. Cultural rules mediate the interaction between judges and their staffs by defining the way that justice is best produced.

At the same time, judges have an institutional belief that the emergence of a significant workload crisis threatens to undermine their ability to create justice. Consequently, even as the institutional culture defines how the balance must be struck and mandates specific procedures as the most efficacious means to accomplishing the overarching organizational goal of creating justice, another aspect of the institutional culture requires that the judges change the decision-making process to accommodate the perceived caseload crisis. Even as all judges believe that they currently are able to produce high-quality justice, most judges believe that there is an imminent workload crisis that threatens to undermine their ability to continue to do so, and many judges believe that the crisis already has caused other judges to sacrifice justice for efficiency. The dissonance between these culturally defined beliefs creates an institutional conundrum in which judges believe that some changes in the judicial process and the structure of the courts are necessary to increase efficiency but that such changes themselves can threaten the court's ability to produce justice.

As a result of this institutional conundrum, judges already have begun to adopt potentially significant changes in the decision-making process that have caused the judicial process to evolve farther from the ideal of the judge as a solitary decision maker. As a result of the institutional conundrum, courts have adopted changes, such as the Ninth Circuit's adoption of shared bench memoranda, use of mini–en banc proceedings, and increased use of visiting judges.

These changes have increased the court's efficiency but also have shifted the balance of autonomy and interdependence. For example, the growing number of visiting judges decreases the influence of each circuit judge on that circuit's law and thus decreases interdependence. At the same time, the use of visiting judges waters down the collegiality of a court because an increasing number of decisions represent a smaller number of a court's active judges. Similarly, the use of the mini–en banc limits judges' ability to influence a circuit's law and thus shifts the balance away from interdependence.

The institutional conundrum also makes judges hesitant to adopt changes that they believe could increase efficiency at too great a cost to the quality of justice. For example, even in the face of the perceived workload crisis, judges hesitate to adopt such changes as the shared bench memorandum. Even in the Ninth Circuit, where the workload already has provoked the adoption of the shared bench memorandum, many judges remain uneasy about using work from other chambers and thus require their clerks to supplement shared bench memoranda with internal chambers memoranda.

As chapter 7 will show, because the institutional conundrum enables courts to adopt evolutionary changes but makes judges hesitate to adopt revolutionary changes, it will prove to be both the greatest hope for and the most perilous hindrance to creating significant organizational change to accommodate the caseload crisis.

CHAPTER 7

Tilting the Balance: Organizational Behavior and Organizational Change in the U.S. Courts of Appeals

T his study began as a response to the view that, as a result of a perceived crisis of volume, the courts of appeals have become bureaucratized and now are unable to continue to produce a consistently high quality of justice. This study has provided an organizational behavior analysis of how the U.S. Courts of Appeals function within the context of this emergent caseload crisis. The promise of this work was that by understanding the court's organizational nature and its inherent tensions, students of the court would be better positioned to understand how external pressures and internal changes can affect the ways that judges do their work. Furthermore, by confronting the "bureaucratic spectre" with the empirical tools of social science, students of the court would be better able to assess the courts' future and proposals for changing it. This chapter fulfills those promises by providing concrete conclusions about the way that the federal appellate courts' organizational nature shapes the judicial process.

I. The Organizational Analysis of the Courts of Appeals

In chapter 2, I showed that the organizational morphology of the federal courts of appeals suggests that they must overcome a central tension between the autonomy of individual judges and their chambers and the task interdependence that merges the court into a single collegial body. That organizational tension, I intimated, is reminiscent of the organizational tensions central to the functioning of private-sector corporations organized in the multidivisional form. Yet I underscored that the courts of appeals differ fundamentally from

211

multidivisional private-sector corporations because the courts lack a central office that coordinates the behavior of the disparate organizational subdivisions. That critical difference suggests that the problem of balancing autonomy and interdependence is overcome in the courts by other, more subtle solutions.

The court's organizational nature contains three sets of inherent features that work to maintain that pivotal balance: formal features, structural features, and institutional/cultural features. From the empirical discussions throughout this book, it is apparent that each of those features covers a broad range of organizational attributes that can vary substantially from court to court. For example, the size of a court is a structural attribute, but it varies among courts—whereas the Ninth Circuit covers an enormous geographic span, has a high degree of geographic dispersion, and has a large numerical size, the D.C. Circuit covers a tiny geographic span, has a relatively minuscule degree of geographic dispersion, and has a medium numerical size. Because the court's features consist of numerous highly variable attributes, the features themselves are highly variable. Yet each set of features serves a critical role in establishing the nature of a court's balance between autonomy and interdependence.

Formal Features

The formal features of the courts of appeals set the limits of an individual judge's autonomy by providing formal doctrinal and procedural rules that require the judge to act in certain, specified ways. It is true that judges have the ability to circumvent these restrictions because judges are free to interpret ill-defined rules, and the range of permissible interpretation is sometimes remarkably broad. However, formal constraints provide mechanisms to circumvent dubious interpretations. Key among those constraints is the formal structure that requires appellate judges to act only in groups. Those formal procedural rules require the judges to interact in specified ways and at specified times. Much as the formal features of the court set the limits of autonomy, those rules set the base level of interaction that mandates a certain level of interdependence. That is, without interaction, judges are formally prohibited from taking any official action in any case, thereby establishing the base level of interdependence.

Changes in the formal rules that dictate how judges must work, as well as changes in the formal doctrinal rules that judges interpret, can significantly affect the balance between autonomy and interdependence. For example, replacing one formal doctrinal rule with a rule that is more indefinite can shift the balance in favor of autonomy because individual judges become freer to interpret the rule as they see fit. Similarly, limiting the amount of interaction by reducing the amount of oral argument or the amount of formally prescribed discussion in the review a case receives from the panel (such as the decreased conference time for each case given during the review of screened cases) can decrease the judges' influence on one another and thus can increase autonomy. At the same time, though, judges still can act on their interpretations only if they can convince at least one other judge on the three-judge panel that the interpretation is correct.

Structural Features

The court's structure has two important dimensions, intrachambers and interchambers. Each dimension has significance in the balance between autonomy and interdependence. Intrachambers structure refers to the way that judges structure the interaction with their staffs, particularly law clerks. Intrachambers structure affects judges' autonomy by determining, among other things, how well prepared judges are to discuss cases with their brethren and to defend their views. That, in turn, can affect the quality of the interaction among the judges and their ability to influence each others' views.

Interchambers structure refers to the way that judges interact with one another in deciding cases. Interchambers structure affects how judges interact by establishing the physical, social, and formal distances between the chambers. The relationship among those three categories of distance significantly affects how strongly interdependent judges are by influencing the way that they interact. Built into the courts are numerous means for judges to span the boundaries that separate them, including such often examined methods as written and in-person communication as well as such less frequently discussed methods such as the directed and undirected use of the clerk network. In addition, because of the advent of advanced communication technology such as electronic mail and faxes, judges now are able to communicate instantaneously in writing over long distances, thereby creating a cybercollegiality in which judges in circuits with a large geographic dispersion are separated by a relatively small formal distance but a relatively large social distance.

The failure of either of the two dimensions of the court's structure can create a serious organizational problem. Where the internal structure of the judicial chambers shifts from a structure wherein judges act as the primary decision makers to one in which judges delegate their responsibility to clerks and retain only an administrative role, the balance may be seriously upset. When judges overdelegate to their clerks, judges limit their autonomy by hindering their ability to independently review a case in the detail necessary to act intelligently in the three judge panel. Consequently, overdelegation to law clerks can isolate judges because they cannot contribute to interchanges. That may not mean that such judges do not interact with other judges as often as do those who do not overdelegate. Indeed, judges who overdelegate may need to rely more on other judges because of inadequate preparation.

As discussed in chapter 1, the problem of overdelegation to judicial staff has often been discussed in the literature on bureaucratization. The organizational approach discussed in this book reinforces the view that overdelegation to judicial staff presents a potentially significant structural dilemma for the court. However, the organizational approach also suggests that the problem may be overestimated as a current source of trouble. Judges on all of the courts of appeals have in place checks on the influence of the law clerks, including such formal and structural elements as reliance on the judges' own legal and personal expertise to evaluate and critique clerks' arguments and suggestions; judges' use of briefs, legal research, and personal review of the record to check and reinforce clerks' opinions and arguments; and other chambers' input into judges' decision-making processes. Some courts have in place additional checks, such as the shared bench memorandum process used in the Ninth Circuit, that provide the judge with additional perspectives. Moreover, with some exceptions, judges who delegate opinion-writing responsibility to their clerks felt that the ultimate product represented work that at least represents the judge's view, and some judges felt that opinions derived from clerk-written drafts constituted superior product because of the clerks' initial familiarity with the case and consequent ability to structure the opinion. Accordingly, the quality of justice does not appear to be substantially threatened by the overdelegation of judicial responsibility to law clerks.

However, the organizational approach taken in this study does reveal another danger to the quality of appellate justice: the overdelegation of responsibility across chamber boundaries to other judges on a panel. Overdelegation across subdivisional boundaries has been ignored in the literature on bureaucratization.[1] Overdelegation to other judges occurs when individual judges do not prepare adequately independently of their brethren and consequently must rely on research and arguments presented by others. That problem is virtually nonexistent in courts in which judges prepare for cases in relative isolation from their peers. It becomes potentially more problematic, though, where judges divide their work among the three chambers by using shared bench memoranda, as in the Ninth Circuit, or by dividing the work in complex cases, as in the D.C. Circuit. In the Ninth Circuit, for example, numerous judges reported that they rely on the bench memoranda prepared by other chambers and virtually never use their own clerks to research or comment on issues in cases for which they do not have bench memorandum writing responsibility.

---

1. That is no doubt because many of the most comprehensive organizational studies of judicial decision making have revolved around narrow aspects of the appellate process (*see, e.g.,* Thomas Davies, *Gresham's Law Revisited: Expedited Processing Techniques and the Allocation of Appellate Resources*, 6 JUST. SYS. J. 372, 372 [1981]) or around the trial courts, in which interaction among the judges is virtually a nonissue (*see, e.g.,* WOLF HEYDEBRAND & CARROLL SERON, RATIONALIZING JUSTICE: THE POLITICAL ECONOMY OF FEDERAL DISTRICT COURTS [1990]).

Those judges, therefore, enter conference prepared only with the view of the clerk of another chambers, a view often representative of the thinking of that clerk's judge. In such cases, the judge responsible for writing the bench memorandum also usually retains responsibility for writing the opinion or memorandum disposition. Consequently, judges who rely only on bench memoranda from other chambers have no opportunity to delve into the case to the degree required to write an opinion. The result of that all-too-common judicial process is that a judge's only check on the work of another chambers is personal expertise, which can be limited and outdated. In that situation, there is a real danger that judges have surrendered autonomy to other judges and become dependent on them rather than interdependent with them.

Institutional/Cultural Features

The court's institutional culture plays the most subtle role in maintaining the balance between autonomy and interdependence. The court's culture contains two themes that translate into identifiable normative rules. One of those cultural themes corresponds to the concepts of judicial autonomy and independence. Corresponding normative rules regulate the timing of and limit the quantity of interchambers communication. For example, normative rules militate against interchambers communication prior to oral argument. At the same time, other normative rules correspond to the concepts of interdependence and collegiality. Those interdependence-oriented normative rules require that judges work within the collective parameters of the panel as a whole and consequently proscribe judges from isolating any judge on the panel. For example, normative rules require that a judge include both other judges on a panel in any communication. The interaction and mixture of those sets of normative rules establish the critical balance between autonomy and interdependence.

At the heart of the court's institutional culture is the presence of a powerful normative ideal that a judge should work alone to come to a well-reasoned, well-researched decision but should then function within a tightly woven collegial court to decide the case in close conversation with the other judges on the panel. That ideal reinforces the notion that the idealized judge is best capable of creating a just result and that the creation of "justice" (in whatever sense it may be meant) is the ultimate goal of the appellate judicial process.

That concept of the ideal judge is offset by a myth of an emergent workload crisis. This myth says that the caseload crisis confronting the court is—or soon will be—causing judges to be incapable of providing the degree of attention necessary to give each case before the court adequate review and a just result. The perception of an emergent workload crisis slowly overcomes the institutional myth of the ideal appellate judicial process so that judges can justify accepting minor changes in that process that move the court away from the "ideal" judicial process. Consequently, as the crisis myth gains prominence over the ideal-judge myth, the court slowly—and sometimes reluctantly—accepts such fundamental changes in the way that the judges do their work as the mini–en banc and the shared bench memorandum process. Those changes not only disturb judges by threatening the myth of the ideal judge, but also comfort judges who perceive the changes as necessary to overcome the perceived workload crisis. However, the changes that result from that process can shift the balance between autonomy and interdependence in ways that in time may create further imbalance between the two myths. The consequent tension begins the process anew and can result in further institutional pressure and, accordingly, further organizational change. However, the two institutional myths serve as bookends to prevent the court from adopting radical or extreme changes because they would disturb one or both of the myths. The resulting difficulty in creating organizational change makes up what I have termed the court's "institutional conundrum," an institutional aspect of the appellate courts that can have significant consequences for the court's ability to adopt major changes in the appellate judicial process but that make a slow evolution of the courts possible and preferable.

Interaction of the Features

In addition to the relative organizational resiliency derived from the independent functioning of each of the organizational features, the organization derives a further degree of resiliency from the interaction of the court's formal, structural, and cultural features. In addition to the capacity to maintain the critical balance between autonomy and interdependence, the organizational features also work in conjunction with one another, and that interaction enables the court to sustain its balance even where enormous external pressure is brought to bear.

The interaction among the organizational features exists because the potential causes of organizational trauma run through each of the organization's three features, and each of those features provides an independent solution to those problems. For example, in chapter 6 I discussed the Ninth Circuit's reaction to the combined impact of increasing caseloads and increasing numerical size. I demonstrated how that combination of problems created a dilemma for the court because it magnified the potential for maverick panels to ignore or manipulate precedent and minimized the court's ability to regulate itself through the traditional en banc process. The Ninth Circuit answers that problem, which itself derives from a combination of structural and formal changes, with solutions deriving from each of the court's organizational features. Formally, the court adopts changes that make it easier to vote to hold en banc proceedings, including altering the court's internal formal rules so that the court can hold en banc proceedings with eleven active judges rather than the full complement of twenty-eight judges. That formal change is paralleled by structural changes, such as allowing for voting over the electronic mail system, which lowers the boundaries for interchambers communication. Thus, the judges are able to communicate more often regarding each case, and the judges can vote instantaneously to determine whether an en banc proceeding should go forward. At the same time, the court's culture slowly evolves so that the judges view the role of the en banc as more of a regulatory institution and less as an opportunity to speak as a whole collegial court. Simultaneously, the court's culture prevents the problem by applying normative pressure for judges to follow precedent and frames that normative rule as a procedural means of establishing justice.

A similar multipolar response occurred when the Ninth Circuit was confronted by increasing formal distance as a result of increasing caseload pressure. The court implemented and enforced formal internal rules that require parties to provide detailed arguments and references to legal sources as well as to update the court with supplemental missives that instruct the judges of recent authority of which the judges may be unaware. Structurally, the court implemented a system in which judges share clerk resources by sharing bench memoranda. Again, the court's culture slowly shifted so that the judges view the shared bench memoranda as efficient but deemphasize the potential of the bench memoranda to serve as what one judge called a "cheat"—a mechanism where judges do not accomplish their own work. In response to that potential, however, the court's culture maintains a normative emphasis on judges' individualism and autonomous preparation.

The interaction of the court's three organizational features generates organizational resiliency against changes in the organization's environment because, where an environmental change has an impact on one of the organizational dimensions, the other two can compensate. Consequently, changes in the court's environment that appear detrimental may be harmless because other facets of the court's organizational nature may offset the change's negative reverberations. For example, where increasing caseload creates a strain on the consistency of formal rules, structural changes, such as the shared bench memorandum, enable the court to have greater efficiency in interchambers communication so that intrachambers research is supplemented by research from other chambers. Or where caseload pressure makes it inefficient to have a strict application of the cultural rule that constrains interaction among the judges prior to oral argument, shared bench memoranda and increased interchambers e-mail communication enable some release from the need to abandon that important cultural rule.

However, even as resiliency can allow the court to function in the face of changes that may appear detrimental, it also can lead to substantial obstacles to successfully introducing changes intended to lessen the impact of the caseload crisis. Because the organization's resiliency can allow the court to function normally even when one aspect of the court is facing substantial environmental pressure, it is possible for that resiliency to hide weaknesses in the court's ability to function properly.

Two potentially troublesome consequences can result. First, a change to the court can have unforeseen secondary effects on function because a change in the court can weaken an aspect of the court that had itself served as a crutch for another weakened aspect. Second, changes that cut across all three organizational aspects, such as the use of the mini–en banc or the shared bench memorandum, can have disproportionately significant effects because such changes attack the organization without leaving other avenues to balance against those changes. Because of those two consequences, the organization's natural resiliency may be damaged, which can have the kinds of negative repercussions traditionally attributed to increased bureaucratization, including increased delegation and loss of collegiality.

II. The Prospects for Organizational Change

The organizational model developed in this book suggests that the federal courts' slow evolution has enabled them to continue to produce a similar quality of justice without sacrificing the ideals that have characterized the appellate process throughout the courts' long history.

This observation comes amid numerous alarmist calls that the judiciary is faltering and that revolutionary changes are the only hope for revitalization. For example, Martha Dragich recommends that the court system be overhauled almost entirely by merging the courts of appeals into a single, national appellate court with discretionary jurisdiction and adding an appellate division to the district courts.[2] Most recently, a commission made up largely of federal judges has recommended significant structural changes to the Ninth Circuit, including administering the circuit through regional subdivisions.[3] These and other radical changes could result in unforeseen disaster.

The organizational model suggests pessimism for the efficacy of revolutionary changes for two reasons. First, organizational resiliency makes consequences unpredictable. As discussed earlier, as a result of the interaction

---

2. *See* Martha Dragich, *Once a Century: Time for a Structural Overhaul of the Federal Courts,* 1996 WISC. L. REV. 11 (1996).

3. *See* COMMISSION ON STRUCTURAL ALTERNATIVES FOR THE FEDERAL COURTS OF APPEALS, FINAL REPORT 47 (December 18, 1998).

among the three sets of features, a change to one feature may not appear significant because other features may compensate. A second change in the court's organizational construction not only may weaken one feature but in so doing may undermine the ability of that feature to compensate for the earlier blow. Accordingly, organizational changes can have hidden and unpredictable consequences for the court's ability to function.

Because revolutionary changes create the potential for unforeseen negative consequences, a conservative evolutionary approach is appropriate. Slow evolutionary options constitute relatively small and discrete changes in courts' internal functioning. Evolutionary changes can include such things as changing the way that cases are screened from the oral argument calendar, increasing the use and amount of sanctions and waiver, adopting shared bench memoranda or the mini–en banc, and adding small numbers of new judges. The conclusion favoring an evolutionary rather than revolutionary approach is particularly warranted because, as this book demonstrates, the courts appear to be functioning reasonably well, even in the face of the severe time constraints resulting from an increased caseload. That is not to say that today's judges are producing the same quality of work as in the past.[4] However, that judges are not functioning at the same level as in the past does not necessarily justify radical changes in the court system. Indeed, the courts I observed and in which I interviewed, particularly the Ninth Circuit, have adopted sometimes significant stopgap measures that have enabled them to continue their work unhindered. And aside from general observations about the relative quality of their work, there have been no substantiated empirical claims that even the Ninth Circuit is no longer providing just resolutions as frequently as it did in the past.

But that does not mean that there is no danger. Judges have begun to change the way that they decide cases, and those changes have moved the currently applied appellate judicial process farther from the ideal of judges working individually yet collegially to produce just results. There has been a marked decrease in the frequency of oral argument, which has subtle and far-reaching significance. There has been an increased reliance on visiting judges, which temporarily relieves the caseload problem but offers the potential long-term cost of deteriorating a court's culture and collegiality. There have been significant changes in the use of law clerks, bench memoranda, and the en banc process. Nevertheless, even assuming that the idealized appellate judicial process is the best way to achieve just results in any given case, the courts do

---

4. Judge Stephen Reinhardt may not have overstated the point when he said, "Those who believe we are doing the same quality work that we did in the past are simply fooling themselves." Stephen Reinhardt, *A Plea to Save the Federal Courts—Too Few Judges, Too Many Cases*, 79 A.B.A. J. 52, 52 (1993).

not appear to have moved so far from that ideal that they currently are unable to consistently achieve just results or to achieve results that differ significantly from the results achieved if the courts more closely approximated the ideal. It would seem, therefore, that major revolutionary changes are a risky resolution to a problem that has not yet reached a state of emergency or crisis.

The organizational approach suggests an additional reason to doubt the efficacy of revolutionary change: the influence of the institutional conundrum. As I discussed in chapter 6, the institutional conundrum, by its nature, works against the adoption of major changes because the dueling myths of the ideal judicial process and of the emergent caseload crisis act to limit significantly the range of changes acceptable to the judicial community. On the one hand, judges are so concerned with the perceived workload crisis that they will not accept changes that advance justice but do not reduce the caseload. On the other hand, judges also hesitate to accept changes that increase efficiency because they often move away from the idealized concept of the appellate judicial process. Some minor changes can work between those mythically created walls, but major changes endanger the balance of power between the dueling myths and result in much hesitancy to accept major changes. As Judge Stephen Reinhardt of the Ninth Circuit has written, "Article III judges . . . are all aware that we have gone too far in our attempts to preserve the traditional structure of the appellate courts. Yet, we shy away from any significant action that might alleviate the problem."[5] Thus, unless Congress is willing to adopt revolutionary changes to the judicial system over the strenuous objections of at least a large portion of the judicial community, systemic changes are doomed never to find their way out of the pages of law reviews or legislative committee chambers.

This book's organizational approach gives far more reason for optimism about the efficacy of slow change through the adoption of relatively minor evolutionary changes. Evolutionary change has three advantages that contribute to its potential efficacy. First, as discussed previously, relatively minor evolutionary changes have greater potential for adoption because they have a greater probability of fitting within the constraints of the institutional conundrum. Second, because minor changes can be easily made in one court without being made in all of the appellate courts, individual courts can act as laboratories to test innovations. Changes that work well in one court can be tried in other courts, and changes that do not work well can be rejected. Third, minor changes can set the ground for the slow evolution of the courts into organizational bodies capable of efficiently handling a greater caseload by initiating self-sustaining reactions. As minor changes are implemented, they can act back on

---

5. Stephen Reinhardt, *Surveys without Solutions: Another Study of the United States Courts of Appeals*, 73 TEX. L. REV. 1505, 1520 (1995) (reviewing THOMAS BAKER, RATIONING JUSTICE ON APPEAL: THE PROBLEMS OF THE UNITED STATES COURTS OF APPEALS [1994]).

the court's institutional culture and alter the way that the judges perceive how decision making should be done. That, in turn, can create a new breach in the institutional conundrum that itself can enable the court to adopt additional minor changes that can then act back on the institutional culture, starting the process anew. As the organization retains changes that the judges find effective and that do not disable their ability to dispense justice (a goal protected by the effects on judges of the institutional myth that they must create justice), and the organization rejects ineffective changes, the organization slowly will evolve. The dynamic relationship among the court's three organizational features means that when changes to one feature are adopted, there will be repercussions on the court's institutional culture that can enable the court to adopt further changes. Consequently, relatively minor changes to the court's form and structure can serve as an engine for further organizational change.

III. Tilting the Balance: Organizational Change and the Future of the Courts of Appeals

Even in the face of the urgent and alarmist calls for immediate and significant change, the courts of appeals must be allowed to work to produce changes with the support and assistance of the other branches of government. The president and U.S. Congress must continue to increase the resources available to the courts and must work together to maintain the full number of judges on each circuit. However, this study strongly suggests that the courts can best be served by slowly adopting relatively small changes. That process of slow evolution is preferable to a risky revolution, which could have dire and unforeseen consequences. As Chief Judge James Browning of the Ninth Circuit has emphasized, the stakes are far too high to risk the stability of the American judiciary by adopting revolutionary changes:

> The Ninth Circuit is the only remaining laboratory in which to test whether the values of a large circuit can be preserved. If we fail, there is no alternative to fragmentation of the circuits, centralization of administrative authority in Washington, increased conflict in circuit decisions, a growing burden on the Supreme Court, and creation of a fourth tier of appellate review in the federal system. If we succeed, no further division of circuits will be necessary. Indeed, combining the circuits into four or five might well be feasible—creating stronger and more effective appellate courts, lightening the burden on the Supreme Court, and resulting in a decentralized and more efficient administrative system for the federal judicial system.[6]

---

6. Unpublished speech delivered to the Alaska State Bar, quoted in Mary Schroeder, *Jim Browning as a Leader of Judges: A View from a Follower*, 21 Ariz. St. L.J. 3, 7 (1989).

That is not to say that the courts are not facing serious threats from the drastically increasing caseload, or that the increasing caseload is not significantly and negatively affecting the court's ability to dispense justice. Instead, the point is merely that further research may be necessary to establish exactly what those problems are and the potential secondary effects of any proposed revolutionary change. This future research must take to task the assumptions that the ideal model of the appellate judicial process actually is ideally suited for efficiently achieving just results and that an organizationally sophisticated court cannot consistently achieve just results.

Although the situation facing the courts ultimately might be remedied only by significantly restructuring some aspects of the courts or by retreating from the view that only an ideal court of highly individualized, sagelike, and autonomous judges can effectively perform the appellate judicial function, the evidence indicates that such changes may be best achieved by allowing the courts of appeals to continue the slow structural evolution that has enabled judges to decide cases fairly and efficiently in the face of their burgeoning dockets. Accordingly, although the federal courts of appeals continue to face significant challenges from their increasing size and complexity, the "bureaucratic spectre" may turn out to be nothing more than an organizational will-o'-the-wisp.

Index